'ishof has the same relationship with music as Bar-
Bailey had with the circus: He loves it! He's always
assionate about getting ordinary people involved in
g it. From his early support of VH1 Save the Music, an
ization dedicated to keeping music in schools, to Rock
ll Fantasy Camp, he's always thinking about bringing it
ome to the people who want to make it. *Rock Your Busi-*
has the answers to becoming the entrepreneurial rock
you were meant to be."

—Roger Daltrey, CBE; The Who

l of case studies and examples that are valuable and also
rtaining, *Rock Your Business* is a book you not only should
but one that you will want to read."

—David Eilenberg, SVP, Development & Current
Programming, One Three Media, a Hearst/
Mark Burnett company

"David Fishof has produced some of the largest music tours,
represented some of the most famous acts and athletes in the
world, and created the well-known Rock 'n' Roll Fantasy
Camp. In *Rock Your Business*, he shows you how you can use
the tools that make rock stars household names to launch
your own vision."

—Bob Pittman, CEO, Clear Channel
Communications

"David Fishof is a pure example of the spirit of the entrepreneur. After almost becoming my first manager, I knew that I wanted David as a friend for life. I have been amazed at how he has allowed each chapter in his life to inspire the next. Where he is now is a great American success story that he so generously shares with all of us in this book. As a beginner drummer, I had the pleasure of realizing one of my all-time fantasies when I played a gig at the Whiskey. Who said it? It's a long way to the top if you want to rock and roll! David Fishof can guide you there."

—Scott Hamilton, Olympic Gold Medalist

"I've said it before, and I'll continue to say it, when it comes to business and the Rock 'n' Roll Fantasy Camp, David Fishof is a genius! He took his vision and created a way to make dreams come true for so many. This book really digs deep into his mind and besides a great entertainment read, he shares many helpful tips on how you can develop your ideas and turn them into profit-making business deals. A must read for anyone wanting to be involved in not only the music business but a positive, self-improved life as well!"

—Billy Amendola, Associate Editor, *Modern Drummer* magazine

"Passion, inspiration, street smarts, cultural savvy, and raw unfettered guts have always been the main drivers of rock-and-roll success stories. David Fishof has all of those qualities, as well as an almost magical ability to make things happen. So you can take the safe path and fall in step with the bazillions of other suits who are reading the same business treatises as everyone else, or you can embrace some cagey rock and roll attitude and MAKE YOUR BONES like a superstar."

—Michael Molenda, Editor-in-Chief, *Guitar Player* magazine

PRAISE FOR
ROCK 'N' ROLL FANTASY CAMP

"Live your dreams at Rock 'n' Roll Fantasy Camp."
—Slash, Guns N' Roses

"David Fishof has been able to bring giants of the music world together and help make people's dreams of creativity come true for that moment in time—a life-changing experience and what a rush! A brilliant move on David Fishof's behalf."
—Lita Ford, former member of The Runaways

"I would recommend this training experience to any industrial or service industry executive as a way to promote team building within your organization."
—Lorenzo Simonelli, President & CEO,
GE Transportation

"I am still spinning from the experience of the Rock 'n' Roll Fantasy Camp from the past few days. The guys in my now-defunct band won't talk to me, and I don't care because I have lived the dream."
—Don Weintraub, Director of Sales &
Marketing, Rancho de los Caballeros

"Sometimes when you have a fantastic experience with an individual, you just can't wait to tell others. Such is the case with David Fishof of the Rock 'n' Roll Fantasy Camp. . . . David's professionalism and attention to detail—not to mention his amazing talent—made the Rock 'n' Roll Fantasy Camp something none of us will soon forget . . ."
—Paul J. Caine, EVP & Chief Revenue Officer, Time Inc.

"Rock 'n' Roll Fantasy Camp offers a great time and inspires people with a vibe."
—Jack Bruce, Rock and Roll Hall of Fame Inductee, Cream

"We're gonna rock your world."
—Simon Kirke, Bad Company

"Rock 'n' Roll Fantasy Camp is a way for me to get in touch with and thank a lot of people who have bestowed this huge honor on me."
—Paul Stanley, KISS

"David Fishof is perfect for his job because he has indisputable respect in the industry, plus a booming personality that makes him a natural camp counselor."
—Gerry Gittelson, Syndicated Columnist, SledgeMetal.com

ROCK YOUR BUSINESS

ROCK YOUR BUSINESS

WHAT YOU AND YOUR COMPANY CAN LEARN FROM THE BUSINESS OF ROCK AND ROLL

DAVID FISHOF
WITH MICHAEL LEVIN

BenBella Books, Inc.
Dallas, Texas

BenBella Books, Inc.
10300 N. Central Expressway
Suite #400
Dallas, TX 75231
www.benbellabooks.com
Send feedback to feedback@benbellabooks.com

Printed in the United States of America
10 9 8 7 6 5 4 3 2 1

Library of Congress Cataloging-in-Publication Data is available for this title.

978-1-936661-45-9

Editing by Debbie Harmsen
Copyediting by Eric Wechter
Photo editing by Thuy Vo
Proofreading by Amy Zarkos and Chris Gage
Indexing by Kathy Bennett
Front cover sculpture by Liz Lomax
Cover design by Kit Sweeney
Text design and composition by Cape Cod Compositors, Inc.
Printed by Berryville Graphics

Distributed by Perseus Distribution
perseusdistribution.com

To place orders through Perseus Distribution:
Tel: 800-343-4499
Fax: 800-351-5073
E-mail: orderentry@perseusbooks.com

Significant discounts for bulk sales are available. Please contact Glenn Yeffeth at glenn@benbellabooks.com or 214-750-3628.

To the best wife of them all, Karen, for her love and support.

My late parents, Cantor Mark & Edith Fishof,
who gave me tools for life with much love.

My children, who bring me such joy as I watch them grow:
Shira & Shlomo Einhorn
Ilana & Noah Mulhstein
Joshua
Mordechai
Talia

My grandchildren:
Yisrael, Estee, Ariella, Eliyahu

My brother, Rabbi Joe Fishof

In loving memory:
Rabbi Menachem Brayer
Davy Jones
Levon Helm

FOREWORD
by Hank Gilman

I attended my first, and only, Rock 'n' Roll Fantasy Camp back in 2003 as part of a promotion with my employer, *Fortune* magazine. There were a lot of great moments. You don't get to back up Roger Daltrey of The Who on "Summertime Blues" very often; nor rehearse the classic hit "All Right Now" with Simon Kirke (drummer for Free and Bad Company). Playing on the stage of the legendary, but now defunct, The Bottom Line nightclub in New York City wasn't too shabby either. The house was packed. And the stars in the audience—like the late Levon Helm of The Band and Marky Ramone of the Ramones—weren't cringing or laughing as you lumbered your way through chord changes a five-year-old could pull off.

But to tell you the truth, none of that was surprising. What did surprise me was how much I enjoyed rehearsing and spending time with the ordinary Joes in my band. When the rock stars wandered in during our rehearsals, it was nice. But we were all anxious to get back to work to prepare for our show. I'm not much for sappy, off-site, team-building experiences. But this, I thought, was just about the best. We hardly knew one another—well, actually, we *didn't* know one another—but we had to work together quickly. If one us messed up, the whole band messed up. After a few days of rehearsing, it was like you had been working together for years. You knew one other's strengths and weaknesses. You learned how to work efficiently with your band mates, even if you didn't like one or two of them all that much. You learned how to do your part and not become disruptive because you didn't get much of a solo on "Wild Thing." (Was there even a solo on "Wild Thing?" I can't remember.)

So, keep that all in mind when reading the David Fishof's book. To be sure, there's a lot about rock and roll and the experience of playing in a band—he is the grand master of the fantasy camp after all. But at its core, David's book shows you how to build great teams: conjuring up ideas, overcoming obstacles, and pulling together to produce the best possible product in the end. In that way, David's camps, and book, is a lot more about doing business than you might think. Fantasy? Only when Roger Daltrey walks on stage with you.

—Hank Gilman
Deputy Managing Editor
Fortune magazine

FOREWORD
by Edward Oates

David Fishof and his Rock 'n' Roll Fantasy Camps have hit upon a fantastic way to use music to teach and inform business people and others about elevating their skills to the next level. The camps inspire participants, teach about teamwork, and provide an avenue for attendees to perform with some of the best in the business. And they're a lot of fun.

Music and business share some similar traits. Among them is that neither has an equivalent in the animal kingdom. Some animals make pretty sounds, but those are used for attracting attention or mates by demonstrating the health and mental acuity of individuals, communicating as a substitute for language (birds and whales sing, for example), and for similar survival necessities.

Only in humans is music used to entertain and inspire. Only in humans does this activity become a purely abstract art form. Music has been used to symbolize nature ("Rites of Spring" by Stravinsky for example) or other abstract ideas ("Carnival of the Animals" by Camille Saint-Saëns), but in only rare cases would a listener think that the music is trying to recreate natural sounds as if it were a recording. Even the most highly structured music ("The Well Tempered Clavier" by Bach for example) is enjoyed for the beauty of the music as well as its structural purity.

The interpretation of music by the listener and artist alike is emotional and personal. How often are we taken away to a dream-like place when listening to a musical piece in a dark room? "God Only Knows" by Brian Wilson can bring one to tears with its beauty; "Magic Carpet Ride" by Steppenwolf makes you feel the wind blowing through your hair on a motorcycle ride; "Do You Believe in Magic" by the Lovin' Spoonful makes you happy with the promise of young love. Nothing else can move us like music, and it is shared by all cultures worldwide from time immemorial.

Music seems to be hard wired into human brains differently than other human activities that are consciously experienced. *Musicophelia* by Oliver Sacks (Vintage, revised & enlarged edition, 2008) describes how music is processed in the brain in various ways. Music prodigies are apparently born with a gift of music: the ability to expertly play an instrument or sing songs with a single hearing of a performance; to spontaneously compose complex pieces without any training whatsoever. Some have experienced induced musical abilities not present before some catastrophic event: lightning strikes, strokes, traumatic life events. The surprising presence of musical memory and ability in patients suffering even advanced dementia or other mental incapacities: Alzheimer's patients respond to music, even dancing, singing, and playing it when their faculties have sadly been severely compromised by the disease. Brain scans show music being processed in varied areas of the brain not related to other activities, and that the brain's ability to process music persists even when basic functions such as speech and self-identity have faded.

And then there's business. Business seems to be the modern human's equivalent of competing with others for resources, status, mating rights, and self-fulfillment. We don't go out and bring back the largest beast to feed the group to show our prowess and value; instead we sport symbols of success: jewelry, fancy cars, big houses. No other animal uses such symbology. Ants are highly organized and cooperative, and some species, such as chimpanzees, cooperate and even elevate a member of the troupe to leadership status based on fighting ability, even going to war with other troupes over territorial rights and access to mating partners, but these appear to be instinctive behaviors that are not consciously performed.

Humans are innately competitive, and almost all cultures involve competition for profit—beyond the needs of the successful individual. Primitive barter systems are documented to have involved negotiations to reach agreed-upon mutual benefit (both parties succeed). Even in highly structured socialist systems, capitalism breaks out, even if illegally. One of the most strictly socialist societies the Earth has ever known, the People's Republic of China, has become a freewheeling capitalist state. It has many state controls and restrictions, but even so, the profit motive dominates.

Both of these uniquely human activities—making music and doing business—require cooperation. They cannot be done except in quite limited ways by oneself. Both involve teams of people to achieve commonly agreed-upon goals in order to be successful. Even those artists or business people who believe they are acting alone require support from many others: writers, publishers, back-up musicians, lawyers, government services, accountants, and more.

Rock 'n' Roll Fantasy Camps show how in music, like business, you cannot successfully perform solo. You need others to make your music (and ideas) happen. When a collection of people who don't know one another at the outset come together with the goal of creating music as a group, the lessons of collective creativity, task allocations, skill assessment, and more are explored in a novel and fun way. And using the nearly universal rock and roll musical idiom allows almost everyone to participate. Even if all you can do at camp is whistle and bang on a tambourine, you are part of the group and its success. The realization of the goal of creating music by playing it for your peers—other participants, family, and friends, or in the case of RRFC Corporate camps, your fellow employees—pushes you to display skills and achieve results you would not have thought possible when you started.

The skill of determining what a group can do based on the talents of its members is intrinsic to business where, like at any RRFC event, you are not in control of who you must work with. I have seen RRFC groups where everyone was very experienced and the challenge was to keep egos in check (try that with three guitar players who want to play solo all the time) and other groups where there was a mixture of skilled and beginner players, and the challenge was to make sure that everyone contributed to the final result. I witnessed Steven Tyler teaching a beginner how to play the harmonica introduction to an Aerosmith song. She of course was thrilled with the interaction with Mr. Tyler, but even more so when we performed that song on stage at the Whisky A Go Go in Hollywood two days later. The band was proud of her and her accomplishment, we were proud of the performance we all did, and we all were rewarded by thunderous applause by our peers. And most importantly, we learned about ourselves and how much we could accomplish—more than we thought at first meeting one another just a few days prior.

All of those skills learned at a Rock 'n' Roll Fantasy Camp have parallels in the business world: organizing, proposing projects, deciding how to accomplish the project goals, listening to experts (in RRFC's case, our Rock Star Counselors), and finally delivering the product. There is no other "camp" of which I am aware that can provide so many skills and experiences that translate to the business world, and is so inclusive of all individuals. Even those who choose not to be in a band participate by experiencing the final product delivery in a gala concert by their peers, and subsequently by the sharing of that experience back at the office. The "water cooler" chatter was never this cool before those inner rock stars were unleashed.

I have personally been to a dozen or so Rock 'n' Roll Fantasy Camps, and can attest to their power. I use the skills learned there in my own rock and roll band that grew from a weekly jam session with no goal in particular, to a cohesive unit that recorded and released a CD of original songs on iTunes and elsewhere (search for CHOC'D, the band's name, on iTunes). I also apply the lessons learned at camp to my professional world of fundraising and community service for a major university and the San Francisco Zoological Society. Stretching to achieve goals, knowing that people can do more than they think they can, organizing a group to use the skills of its members: all these are products of Rock 'n' Roll Fantasy Camp experiences.

Rock and roll lives on.

—Edward Oates (Eddie O)
Oracle Corporation Cofounder

ROCK YOUR BUSINESS

CONTENTS

INTRODUCTION

As I flew home to Los Angeles from Erie, Pennsylvania, I reflected on the amazing training program I had just completed for General Electric.

Instead of General Electric hiring me to book a rock band to entertain their employees, the giant conglomerate asked me to create a "corporate rock-and-roll camp" for 250 of its employees, including higher-ups, engineers, and executives. Nearly a dozen rock stars arrived into Erie for the one-day camp. I separated the employees into groups of 25, with each group matched with a different rock star. The stars included Mark Farner (lead singer/guitarist of Grand Funk Railroad), Lita Ford, and members of KISS, Boston, Whitesnake, etc.

The task for each group was simple—rewrite the lyrics to a song that was originally performed by the rock star and his/her band so that it was about the theme of the meeting or about the company, its clients, its competitors, etc. That's what I call "imagination at work." After toiling through rehearsals and practice in GE's conference rooms, the employees were rewarded with a nice dinner with the rock star, followed by each group performing their revised song in front of their fellow employees.

Now, what happens at GE stays at GE, but what I can say is that this team-building exercise really transformed the company. Teams were in charge of writing powerful, funny, creative, and insightful lyrics, all of which reflected their thoughts of the company, its processes, and all that encompassed their company, GE in this case. Shortly after the camp with GE, I received a letter from President and CEO Lorenzo Simonelli. It was short and sweet, but his words had *me* feeling like the rock star! "While I was skeptical at first, the planning, execution, and final product made me a firm believer in [David Fishof's team's] process for delivering a high-quality, interactive, and exciting team-building program . . . I would recommend this training experience to any industrial or service industry executive as a way to promote team building within your organization."

This is what corporate America loves—to be a rock star. Now, while the employees of GE may not ever have the desire to tour America on a bus and throw guitar picks to screaming fans, they did experience something when they stood up on stage in front of all the other employees. They realized that opening themselves up to their team and the executives was thrilling and riveting. It transformed them! And while they didn't generate millions of dollars like a Bon Jovi concert would, they still discovered their own form of success. That was the boost of confidence, the close bond they developed with other workers, and the feeling that they, no matter their title or salary, were part of the GE "rock star" team.

Of course, it also helped that I brought almost a dozen famous rock stars to perform with the regular Joe Schmoes. But that was the point. The company wanted to reward its employees for their loyalty and commitment while at the same time building an even stronger bond between the company and executives, creating continued loyalty and commitment. The reward was done through rock and roll.

It wasn't always like this though. Before I started my "corporate rock camps," companies went out and booked an expensive performer who was put in charge of entertaining hundreds of employees. Of course, for the entertainer these events can be lucrative gigs. There are no tickets to sell, yet they are paid handsomely. The show is not advertised to the public, so it doesn't cut into the market for an advertised show. The only drawback is the audience (the employees in this case)—since they didn't pay for their tickets, they're not always paying attention to the show. They might be in the back flirting, getting drunk, or dancing at the side of the stage as if the highly paid rock star were an anonymous wedding singer.

I remember I once attended a huge charity event and fund-raiser in New York. It was for the Robin Hood Foundation, which raises money to feed poor students in New York City and is supported by the top hedge funds. Halfway through the dinner, the surprise performer was announced—Beyoncé! But half the audience went home or sat in the back, paying little attention to anything but the drinks in their hands. I couldn't believe it. All too often, corporate audiences stand with their arms crossed, daring the performers to entertain them. Of course, in their heart of hearts, these executives would love to cut loose and rock out. They just haven't been given the opportunity.

I truly believe that inside most, if not all, of us beats the heart of a rock and roller. And so at these functions, the employees really wish they could be up on stage, instead of being Bill from Accounting or Sue from HR. Enter my corporate rock and roll camps.

I once brought Roger Daltrey of The Who to perform with corporate bands of *People* magazine. At the time, only

60 out of 400 employees opted to attend the rock and roll camp; the rest picked the spa day or tennis/golf package offered by the company. When it came time for the 60 employees to perform with Roger Daltrey, the other 340 sat mouths agape and faces green—they were so jealous and wished they, too, had picked the rock camp package as opposed to a day at the spa. Even though there were employees who didn't participate in the rock camp, the president told me he noticed two things about them—they paid attention to the whole performance, and they went wild for their fellow employees performing with Roger! There was 100 percent total attendance and audience participation, as opposed to the year before when *People* had booked a huge-name performer and there was only about 50 percent attendance, with half of the employees sitting in the back of the room paying little attention to the show.

We have to face the facts—times have changed. In today's economy, the practice of hiring top-dollar entertainers has slowed because of budget constraints and because fewer and fewer companies are going offsite to a venue large enough for a major act. But corporate America still loves rock and roll. Executives have fond memories of their favorite musicians from their teenage and college years.

Through the corporate gigs, like those done with GE and *People*, I was able to bring rock and roll to these executives and their employees. Rather than demand entertainment on the spot, the employees got to be *part* of the entertainment process, making them feel like a million bucks!

Accomplishing this had long been a dream of mine. But I also had another dream—to give fans (all fans, not just corporate America) the opportunity to jam with their musical heroes for several days (versus several hours at a corporate gig) in a life-changing experience that will rock their socks off—pun intended. That's why I created Rock 'n' Roll Fantasy Camp, for the general public, not just exclusive to the corporate world.

Unlike the GE corporate camp, where I only brought a dozen or fewer rock stars, these general camps allow the people attending to meet and interact with many rock and roll big shots! At these public camps, which last from three to five days, "camp counselors" are the world-famous musicians who the campers grew up idolizing, and the "campgrounds" consist of a rehearsal studio where the campers form bands with their rock-star camp counselors leading the way. Campers get to perform with their new bands in amazing venues like the House of Blues, Whisky a Go Go, The Cavern Club, and the Playboy Mansion.

I offer people an occasion not only to enjoy a private concert with a rock legend but also to have the opportunity to become part of that legend. Instead of watching the show, the executive can *be* the show.

The Lessons of Rock and Roll

While they're having fun jamming with the musicians, these executives-turned-rock stars also learn that rock and roll is more than power chords and fancy fingering. The rock and roll industry offers some invaluable business lessons to those in other industries—such as working collaboratively, promoting, creating a buzz or sense of excitement, and selling. That was one of my goals in writing this book: to help executives realize just how much they can learn from the music industry.

That was one of my goals in writing this book: to help executives realize just how much they can learn from the music industry.

Let me show you what I mean. Here are a few fundamental laws of the entertainment industry that cross over to the business world:

1. Band leaders need their bands and vice versa;
2. Bands must run in sync for them to work efficiently; and, perhaps most important of all,
3. The most successful bands are ones that listen to one another.

The Rolling Stones would not have been as successful without Charlie Watts and Bill Wyman. Or can you imagine The Who without John Entwistle? You always hear about the stars—people like Paul McCartney, Mick Jagger, Keith Richards, Roger Daltrey, and Pete Townshend—but if not for their entire bands, they could never have reached that level of success. In a rock band, you have different musicians playing different notes. It can become the most beautiful and exciting kind of music—or it can be just embarrassing noise. To play in a band, you have to be cohesive with your bandmates, and you have to listen to each member's ideas, thoughts, suggestions, etc., whether you all end up in agreement or not. The lead singer needs the drummer, who needs the bass player, who needs the man on the keyboard, etc. It's the same for a company. You can play off the same sheet of music and create harmony, or you can ignore one another and create fiefdoms and dissonance, which inevitably leads to failure. CNN published an article that quoted one of my past campers who said, "When you're thrust into a band situation with an oil baron and a software CEO . . . you all have to figure out quickly how to work well together, so your 'presentation' goes smoothly. . . . Let's just say I've newfound interactive skills . . . still paying off in how I run things in my business life."[1]

Like bands, businesses, too, must have employees in sync. Often all it takes is one negative executive to poison a whole department. When I walk into an office, if the receptionist isn't courteous, it affects the way I think about the company. Or you can have a Web site that looks beautiful but actually talks down to the customers, as if the company were operating on some lofty perch and the customer was unimportant. These things inevitably hurt the business climate— and they negatively impact profits, too.

But these three principles are just the tip of the iceberg in terms of what rock has to offer corporate America. I've been learning from rock and roll my whole life, and it's enabled me to have an entrepreneurial career that has exceeded my wildest dreams.

Many of the parents and families of my generation didn't look up to rock stars, nor did they associate any type of value to that career path. I remember my brother tried to become part of a rock band and make it his career, but he was quickly shot down by my parents. But today, nearly everybody sees the rock-star life differently. The moms and dads of today's generation pour hundreds of thousands (sometimes even millions!) of dollars into their children's "rock-star" fund; they want their children to learn to sing, dance, play instruments, or play sports just like the stars they all watch on television. So what has changed?

---

[1]"One time, at CEO fantasy band camp." April 3, 2012. <http://management .fortune.cnn.com/2012/04/03/one-time-at-ceo-fantasy-band-camp/?iid= HP_River>

Well, for starters, it has become very clear to us now that the life of a rock star can be a very prosperous one. Musicians, bands, and professional athletes can earn millions of dollars for outstanding performances and unbeatable talent. We have also learned that when it comes to earning money, the business end is as important as the talent. But how did artists like Bob Seger, Bruce Springsteen, U2, KISS, and The Who become so business savvy? What did they learn about the rock and roll business that helps them gross millions of dollars still to this day?

Taylor Swift, Kenny Chesney, and Dave Matthews continue to bring in money even while they are on tour (and I am not talking about just their ticket sales). Through music publishing, syncing licenses, advertisements, and selling new merchandise, they have figured out how to become entrepreneurs of music. It's my belief that by reading this book, you, too, will become an expert on the business of rock and roll. You will absorb the many lessons I have learned while working in the music industry for the past thirty-five years, and it is my hope that you will be able to apply the lessons to your own successes and growth. I'll show you how to rock your ideas, your business, and the lives of everyone around you—and have fun while doing it. *Rock Your Business* is about what you and your business can learn from my experience in rock.

The same CNN article I mentioned previously notes what a past camper said. Frank Pawlak attended my camp twice, and he stands by my rock camp: ". . . not sure what's more impressive about the rock getaways . . . whether it's the way it makes you a better musician, or how it sharpens your skills so you can become a more intuitive manager."[2]

---

[2]"One time, at CEO fantasy band camp." April 3, 2012. <http://management .fortune.cnn.com/2012/04/03/one-time-at-ceo-fantasy-band-camp/?iid= HP_River>

In the world of rock and roll, things work a little differently, and I think these differences will be very powerful in your business. In the world of rock and roll, we

> ... dream bigger
> ... attract an audience
> ... overcome enormous obstacles
> ... take it to the next level

I've done all four of these things, as have my many friends in the biz. I've organized this book around these four ideas, and I'm going to show you how to do the same for your business.

So, are you ready to rock?

Read on.

SECTION

1

DREAM
BIGGER

Take It to the Limit:
FINDING THE BIG IDEA

There's no shortage of ideas being generated in today's world. Some people come up with new ideas every day, while others have been sitting on the same one for ten years (or a lifetime). But very few of those ideas ever see the light of day. Many people are fearful of taking an idea from the beginning all the way to the end and actually making it happen. They fear their idea will not become a success. They fear that it will get lost in the sea of ideas floating around in the world. They fear that after putting in all the effort, they won't end up making a cent. And they have good reason to be fearful: Not every idea is a winner; some work and some don't. But how will you ever know if you don't try?

In this chapter, I'd like to help you determine whether your idea has the potential to bring you the success you desire, to understand what makes a good idea a great idea, and to learn how to develop your idea into one worth pursuing.

In my decades in the music industry and as a sports agent, it's always been my job to come up with "big" ideas. I've developed countless music concerts, tours, and performances that have attracted millions of people—from reuniting The Monkees to launching my Rock 'n' Roll Fantasy Camp. But before any of these events happened, they were ideas. Ambitious, yes, because it takes a lot of chutzpah to believe you can fill concert halls and arenas across the country—or across the globe—but ideas nonetheless. Everything starts with an idea, even a rock and roll show. The Ringo Starr and His All-Starr band tour wasn't born out of thin air. It started with an idea.

Pepsi and Ringo

Back in the late '80s, I had lunch with a top executive at Pepsi-Co, Alan Potash, who had created the "Pepsi Generation" ad campaign. He had contacted me and said, "I want you to produce a tour for Pepsi celebrating its twenty-fifth anniversary of the 'Pepsi Generation' ad campaign. What do you want from me in return?"

I said, "I want a million to help kick start the tour and the first million dollars of profits." He agreed on the condition that he receive the next million dollars of profit, even though I had made the faux pas of ordering a Diet Coke during our meal! We then negotiated a fifty-fifty split of the balance of revenue from the tour. I had just one problem—I desperately needed to come up with a million-dollar tour! I sat down and thought, "Who are some of the greatest musicians of all time?" Of course, the Beatles came to mind. But who could currently headline a million-dollar tour? Ringo Starr had not been on tour since the band's break up. Now there was an idea—bring the great Ringo Starr back on tour and surround him with some of the greatest classic rock musicians of all time, following the theme of the famous Beatle song "With a Little Help

I announce to the media that I'm doing a tour with Ringo Starr and His All-Starr Band.

from My Friends." But it would certainly take some effort to make this idea come to life.

Sometimes that effort is as minimal as picking up a receiver, punching in some numbers, and then following up with written correspondence. By simply having the audacity to pick up the phone and write a letter, I was able to bring to life one of the most exciting creations of my career—Ringo Starr and His All-Starr Band.

I always had the idea to contact Ringo Starr but knew I couldn't afford him until a corporate sponsor would get behind my idea. This was a great situation because it was amazing to have Pepsi come to me for ideas and offer to pay me the money to back the ideas. It's a formula they use in Hollywood when the studios pay writers to come up with ideas for TV pilots and movies to develop.

After calling Capitol Records and getting transferred fourteen times, I was able to locate the name and contact of Ringo's longtime lawyer, Bruce Grakal. I wrote to Bruce to ask for a meeting. It was that simple. When David Letterman interviewed Ringo and asked him how the tour got started, Ringo answered, "This guy, David Fishof, wrote me a letter and offered me a tour. I was thinking about the same thing at the time, so I said yes." That was it. I just wrote him a letter.

I didn't realize the impact that contacting Ringo would have on my life. I had never gone on any of my tours before because I didn't want to be away from my family. But I had to go on this tour because I had so much on the line. Ringo had even asked me if I was planning to come along with him; I told him yes because I thought that would ease his decision to tour. Additionally, the tour was so exciting that I didn't want to miss a single moment.

The private jet rides during that year on tour were so much fun, with all the banter and chitchat about the show and the stories the rock stars shared—not to mention the fact that Clarence Clemons, the saxophonist from Bruce Springsteen's E Street band, taught me how to play poker, which I ended up becoming quite good at, beating him at it every night.

There were plenty of times in the fifteen years I led Ringo's tour that I wished I'd had a tape recorder hidden on me because the questions that Peter Frampton, Todd Rundgren, or Randy Bachman would ask Ringo about the Beatles years, and Ringo's honest answers, were mesmerizing. Ringo discussed everything from meeting Elvis to recording at Abbey Road (the famous studio where the Beatles recorded many of their greatest songs) to the Beatles' breakup and so much more. All of this only happened because I wasn't afraid to put myself out there, to overcome my fear and self-doubt and just ask.

Good Idea or Great Idea?

Before Ringo's All-Starr band tour was a reality, I had to consider if this good idea had the characteristics of a great idea, which would let me know whether it was worth pursuing. I thought through several questions:

- Would a tour with Ringo Starr produce a strong gut reaction in those who heard about it? I could only imagine yes—he's a Beatle, after all, and the idea of bringing him back on tour would surely be met with great excitement.
- Was this idea new and innovative, distinguishable from what anybody else was offering? Ringo's long absence from the touring scene meant that his return to the arena would put something unique on the market.
- Would people be willing to trade services with me to help fund, promote, and produce this event? With an idea as exciting as this, I was sure others would want a part of it and would be willing to barter their resources in return for a piece of the action.
- Lastly, would the idea generate significant excitement, enough to achieve my goal—the million-dollar tour? Again, I had to say, "Of course!" Anything to do with the Beatles practically has its own built-in hype. A perfect example of this is the Cirque du Soleil show *LOVE*, which celebrates the musical legacy of the Beatles. The show has been running at The Mirage Hotel in Las Vegas since 2006 and continues to be one of the top-selling shows in town. With Ringo as a headliner, I couldn't foresee any problems drumming up ecstatic anticipation for the event.

It certainly seemed that I had come up with an idea that would produce the million-dollar tour needed for the Pepsi-Co deal to move forward. So I began the work of bringing this idea to life.

A month after sending my letter to Ringo via Bruce, I got a call to come to London. The lawyer couldn't tell me when Ringo would see me but assured me it would be sometime that week. I flew in Monday and spent the better part of the week stuck in a hotel room, reading every Beatles book I could find. I was fearful to step out of the room in case I missed the call—this was before cell phones, after all. Finally, on Thursday I got the call, and on Friday I met with Ringo. I pitched my ideas for the tour to him, played him my sample radio promotion that would promote his tour, and then I offered him the million that Pepsi had given me. The rest, as they say, is history.

Ringo Starr and His All-Starr Band is currently on its eleventh tour since 1989. Ringo got his million, and Pepsi and I split a few million each because I was able to sell the show to promoters for $150,000 to $175,000 a performance. It was a win for all involved—Ringo, Pepsi, and me.

The Four Qualities of a Great Idea

Through my experiences developing concerts, tours, and Rock 'n' Roll Fantasy Camp, I've discovered that great ideas all share four common characteristics:

1. A great idea will produce a strong "gut" reaction in people when they hear about it. I like to call that idea a "sock it to me" concept. It's one of those

flashes of inspiration that when you hear of it you know it's going to be a hit.

2. A great idea will be new and innovative and/or clearly distinguishable from what is already on the market—there has to be a reason for people to want to invest in your product over someone else's, and therefore it must be unique.

3. A great idea will be "barterable." It's something that other people are going to want so much that they'll be willing to work with you to make a trade or barter—an idea so fantastic, they're willing to give up something in order to get it.

4. A great idea will generate hype.

You don't have to have an international rock star headlining your idea in order to know if it's worth pursuing, nor do you need a million dollars to make it a success. When I first put together concerts and tours (pre-Ringo) I didn't start off with the connections I have now or with that kind of funding, but making sure your idea has the four characteristics above will ensure that it stands out from the crowd. At first it might feel like your idea lacks one or more of these fundamental attributes. Don't worry. If you look a little harder, and get a little creative, you'll find that there's usually a way to develop your idea so that it meets every one of the four criteria.

From Baseball to Rock and Roll

In this book I am going to share some of my own experiences to show you how developing an idea from good to the "million dollar" great idea can be done. Although my stories are about my work in the sports and entertainment industries, these characteristics apply to all ideas, in all fields.

I was always a dreamer, the kind of kid who generated ideas and then acted on them. I had always known that I wanted to make it big-time—I never wanted to be anywhere but on top; if I saw something I liked, then I went for it. I had launched half a dozen entrepreneurial schemes by the time I graduated from high school, some more successful than others. A few years after graduation, I was working as a sports agent and I had an idea to put together a baseball camp. I approached my client, Lou Piniella, one of the New York Yankees, with the idea, and he loved it. I bought a post office box for $25 and put an ad in the local New Jersey newspaper, *The Bergen Record*, that said: "Send a $50 deposit to sign up for Lou Piniella Baseball Camp." Next thing I knew, there were 215 checks in the P.O. Box for fifty bucks each. I charged $250 for the week, and Lou and I made more than $10,000 in profits. I never did finish college. I was twenty years old and had a successful business. Isn't that why most people went to college in the first place?

I wanted to learn to be a sports agent in school, but now that I had met Lou Piniella, I already had the opportunity I needed to start my dream. I figured that if I went back to school, my window of opportunity would close for good.

From the baseball camp experience, I learned a fundamental lesson—you gotta grab people's attention. In my case, I was able to do that with the help of celebrities. Get the celebrities, and the people will come. You put a celebrity's name on a product, and people's ears will perk up. In other words, they will have that strong "grand slam" gut reaction, which is the first characteristic of a great idea. I didn't start big—I started with someone I could establish a connection with, an ad in a newspaper, and a P.O. Box. My big idea not only brought me an impressive profit but also insight into what makes an idea worth pursuing.

I learned that having a celebrity would produce a strong gut reaction, and that alone could help make an idea successful. Building off this, I expanded the baseball camps, and the following year we brought on Lou's Yankee teammates Reggie Jackson, Bucky Dent, and Ron Guidry, along with Lou. Unfortunately, my great success was not met with delight from all quarters; George Steinbrenner and the Yankees didn't like that the players were making appearances during baseball season, so they capitalized on my idea and created their own "Yankee All-Star Baseball Day Camp" the following year.

This was not the only experience of this kind I had. A similar thing happened when I proposed creating the Quarterback Club with players who were clients of mine, such as Phil Simms of the New York Giants and Vince Ferragamo of the former Los Angeles Rams, at the helm. My idea and thought process was that everyone adores the quarterback, from the high school team to the pros. Imagine a line of clothing or collectables for all kinds of quarterbacks, from retired ones like Joe Namath and Bart Starr to current stars such as Peyton Manning and Drew Brees. I imagined a logo with the quarterback of the New York Giants throwing the football to the quarterback of the Miami Dolphins. For a while, the Quarterback Club turned out to be the number-one bestseller for the National Football League licensing division.

Originally though, the NFL didn't want to help me get this off the ground because they never wanted to promote individual players. It was all about the teams. Years later, however, the NFL wanted to react to the NFL Players Association strike, and they sent their marketing people to approach me about my idea. Their thought was that if we could sign the quarterback of every top team to an exclusive licensing agreement, then the Players Association group licensing program would fail. Corporations, which were licensing a minimum of six players from the association, wouldn't want the license if they couldn't get the big names, like Dan Marino of the Dolphins or John Elway of the Broncos. So when it was in their favor three years later, they came to me and pursued my idea, and I created the very successful Quarterback Club. It took some negotiations, but in the end they paid me for my idea.

It wasn't long before I'd had enough of these kinds of roadblocks. I decided that if I wanted to get creative, I'd do better in a business that is built on creativity— the entertainment business. In the sports world, I was always going up against some league or team that got upset when I wanted to promote certain players or be creative in some way. A sports agent can make a ton of money, but he has only one focus for his clients: the size of the contract he gets from the team. It's like Cuba Good-

---

ROCK OUT IN THE REAL WORLD

The Business of KISS: Gene Simmons

Gene "The Demon" Simmons made his mark as the bassist/vocalist in KISS, the legendary rock band he cofounded in the early '70s. But what a lot of people don't know is that his acumen as a businessman got the kiss of approval in June 2011, when Simmons received the Lifetime Achievement award from *Forbes* at the magazine's thirteenth annual Celebrity 100 list. He was honored for his passion and drive for success during The Entrepreneur Behind the Icon event.

Most people associate Simmons with the flash and fire of his persona. Back then, the band took a risk by wearing theatrical stage makeup, but the risk paid off. Since then, the former rock star has taken successful risks offstage, too. His recent honor was for his place in the creative business community, not for his music. When asked by a reporter if he thought of himself as a rocker or a businessman, he replied, "It's really a business . . . it was never called 'show.' It's called 'show business.'"

Continues

ing Jr.'s character in the movie *Jerry Maguire* says, "Show me the money!" But in the entertainment world, there were so many more opportunities for me to pursue. I'd be able to exercise my creativity freely as well as own the sponsorship, merchandise, and ticket revenues. If my ideas worked, I could make a nice profit (and the more creative I was, the bigger the profit).

Some people said I was crazy . . . [b]ut if you want to move from idea to reality, you have to invest in yourself and your idea and be willing to take big risks.

So, after twenty years as a sports agent, I moved into the entertainment business full time. Some people said I was crazy to move away from my incredibly successful career. I had everything, they thought, and now I

Continued

The cofounder of KISS is also a proven and accomplished entrepreneur, not to mention a reality TV star. Simmons appeared on the television show *The Family Jewels*. He leveraged his rock-star status, transforming KISS into a marketing brand and licensing merchandising machine with more than 2,500 licenses and some 3,000 products, including his own line of condoms.

But it doesn't stop there. This rock star/-cum-entrepreneur is also the life behind Simmons Records, Simmons Abramson Marketing, and the Moneybag apparel line, among other ventures. Simmons cofounded a real-time language translation Web site, Ortsbo.com, and Cool-SpringsLife.com, a unique estate-planning company for high net worth individuals, and his new venture "Rock and Brews," a restaurant chain, with sites in California, Japan, and Hawaii.

When it comes to knowing how to rock his business, Simmons is a bona fide star. Through savvy planning, he's amassed a personal empire with a net worth estimated at $300 million. His partner Paul Stanley is equally successful producing records and selling his oil paintings for hundreds of thousands of dollars.

was about to move into uncharted territory—for what? An idea? But if you want to move from idea to reality, you have to invest in yourself and your idea and be willing to take big risks.

Rock 'n' Roll Fantasy Camp

At the same time that I was working in sports, I was also working in the music business. I started my career in the music industry in 1983, and for the next eight to ten years, I continued to work in both industries.

So now I began putting together music tours, including Ringo Starr and His All-Starr Band. I was doing what I loved, having great success, and making great profits. But what really struck me, as I met and mingled with some of the world's great entertainers, was how amazing the musicians were when they were just having fun. It was when they got to let loose and be creative that things were the most exciting. During these years touring with stars, every day I'd get another phone call: "What's Ringo like? What's Joe Walsh like? What's Billy Preston like?" Everybody wanted to know what it was like to hang out with rock stars. I was feeling like rock stars weren't getting the positive attention they deserved. Everyone only read about their drug issues or how they were ripped off. I wanted people to see how extraordinary many of them were. I started to think—*What if I could give that rock and roll opportunity to others? How incredible would it be to give people a once-in-a-lifetime opportunity to jam with their idols and live like a rock star! Imagine jamming with Bono or Slash!* And that is where the idea for the Rock 'n' Roll Fantasy Camp was born.

I was on tour with Ringo Starr and His All-Starr Band when I first broached this idea with Ringo. "What if we let a president of a company come onto the plane and fly around with us?" He wasn't too keen on the idea since he wanted to keep the plane reserved for the band only. His rule was no managers, agents, or wives. But I wasn't deterred from the overall concept. It was the genesis of a big idea, and I knew it.

More Testing and Refining of the Idea

It wasn't until a few years after sharing my idea with Ringo on the plane, and spending lots of time with the rock stars, that the first version of the Rock 'n' Roll Fantasy Camp came into being. First the idea had to go through a honing process.

After the fourth show of the first Ringo tour, I had a meeting backstage at the Garden State Arts Center (called the PNC Bank Arts Center today) with Eddie Micone, the former president of Radio City Music Hall, to persuade him to bring the show to that legendary venue. Still in my early thirties, I was like a kid hanging around all these world-class rock stars. On top of that, I'd mortgaged my townhouse in Manhattan to make this tour a success. (I gave Ringo the seed money from Pepsi and then I had to have money to foot the bills, to be reimbursed later from ticket sales.)

Suddenly, Clarence Clemons came over to tell me that Levon Helm, from The Band, and Joe Walsh, from The Eagles—both members of the All-Starr Band—were backstage fighting over songs. "Ringo's the band leader," I told Clarence. "Let Ringo figure it out." I went back to my conversation with Eddie. Then Nils Lofgren came to the table to tell me he was quitting the band. He said that there was bloodshed backstage, and he didn't want any part of it.

That did it. I excused myself from the conversation. I could see my tour—and my house—vanishing. I ran backstage to the band dressing room to find Joe Walsh and Levon Helm circling each other, Helm with a smashed bottle in his hand, and Walsh, holding a knife, dripping blood. Everybody could see the terror in my eyes. I didn't know what to do, so I, the "kid" of the group, started screaming at them, "Are you a bunch of babies?"

Suddenly, they all turned around and start laughing uproariously.

What the hell was going on?

It turned out that the guys had decided to play a practical joke on me. Joe and Levon came up with the idea for a fake fight, and everyone pitched in. Joe and Levon had sent the tour manager out to buy all the props—a rubber knife, fake blood, and a breakable bottle. I nearly fainted; they laughed their heads off. When I finally pulled myself together, I had a realization: Hey . . . this is kind of like summer camp—only with rock stars. Everybody was relaxed, playing, and just having fun. And it struck me anew—wouldn't music fans love to hang out and joke around with these guys and see what they are like offstage? My Rock 'n' Roll Fantasy Camp idea took more focus.

There were more trials and tribulations to follow as I worked to turn this fantasy camp into a successful reality. But I knew the idea was worth the effort. It was a perfect example of the second characteristic of a great idea: an idea that is new and innovative, clearly distinguishable from what is already on the market. Sure, there are various times and places where people can meet rock stars. However, the camp would offer something completely different than anything else on the market—an opportunity for people to spend real time with their rock idols, learning from them and interacting with them in their natural environment, jamming with them, and ultimately performing with them on stage. It was unlike any experience someone could have elsewhere, an entirely new product to be sold. In the end, it would be a unique experience for the rock stars as well because meeting these amazing wannabe musicians or executives would remind them of what it was like when they started.

Finding Investors and Partners

I reached a point where I needed to find investors so that it wasn't just my own money on the line. After putting up my home to pay for the tour's expenses and working with what I called "scared money," I found myself at the Palm Aire Spa in Florida. There I met a gentleman who took me to the Orange Bowl, and we were seated next to his buddy Sam Walton—legendary founder of Walmart and Sam's Club. I started talking about my unique idea to create a kind of rock and roll fantasy camp where ordinary people got to jam with rock stars. Sam's friend (whose name I won't mention; he doesn't like publicity) was interested.

"I'll put the money up," he told me. "Let's do this."

So we did. I created the first Rock 'n' Roll Fantasy Camp in 1997, which took place at the Doral Hotel in Miami Beach, Florida. (Why Florida? Don't ask.) Financially, the camp was a failure. We only had fourteen paid campers, and we cut bad deals on the hotels and playing venue. But even though the business lost money, we made big strides with the media, including *People, Newsweek, New York Daily News,* and VH1. In fact, the big music writers showed up. It was terrifying. On the second day, as I was walking through the lobby of the Doral Hotel, they called me over. *Oh no!* I thought. *They're going to skewer me!*

To my utter surprise, they didn't. "We were going to pan you," they said. "We thought it was a crazy idea. But now that we're here, we think it's awesome. We're having so much fun!" Rock 'n' Roll Fantasy Camp earned itself four pages in *People*, from writer Peter Carlin, and a *Newsweek* article the next week. Rock writer Bob Spitz did a great story in Delta's in-flight magazine. Even David Hinckley of the *Daily News*, who had panned me a few years earlier on my Dirty Dancing tour, was impressed and wrote a favorable review. We were on our way.

Over the next few years, there were highs and lows, as is the case with many entrepreneurial adventures. I lost my original investors after their interest in the venture waned. Overcoming these kinds of setbacks and persevering in the face of

Mike Love (right) of the Beach Boys was one of the first rockers to star at Rock 'n' Roll Fantasy Camp.

difficult challenges is something I'll discuss more later on. In addition, Ringo decided in 1997 that he wanted to tour for the next four consecutive years, so I had to put the camp on the back burner.

The next step in making the camp a reality was to find a media partner to back it. I called up Eric Sherman, the former VP of programming at VH1 Classic, the VH1 network that specializes in music and videos from the '60s, '70s, '80s, and '90s. I used an approach that had worked dozens of times before: I bartered. Eric said, "Give us spots at your camp, and we'll promote it with TV commercials." I agreed, and it worked. At the next camp there were sixty-five campers. I still didn't make any money, but I broke even. Slowly but surely, I was making progress.

I was learning that bartering was the key to the process—without it I never would have been able to get the backing I needed to move forward. That third characteristic of an idea, that it be "barterable," is crucial in turning so many ideas into reality. I'll explain this concept in more detail in chapter 6, but here is another quick example of this concept. A few years ago, I phoned an old acquaintance, Paul Caine, who had recently become the president of *People* magazine at that time. He said, "David, come to my office and let's get reacquainted."

At our meeting, he told me he was just getting ready to take his team of four hundred down to the Bahamas for a working sales retreat at Atlantis Resort. I suggested that I produce a Rock 'n' Roll Fantasy Camp for the retreat, and it would feature Roger Daltrey of The Who as well as ten additional rock stars. I told him I would put his employees in a rock band whether they knew how to play an instrument or not and have them mentored by my rock-star counselors. In exchange, he offered to barter several full-page ads in *People* and *Entertainment Weekly*. Naturally, I said, YES! At the event, I felt the level of excitement and energy comparable to that of the final four NCAA basketball tournament. In fact, the team-building event ended up being so successful that it is *still* talked about at *People* magazine.

Because of the event's success, Paul asked me to provide the entertainment for the Screen Actors Guild award ceremony after-party, hosted by *People*, in exchange for more exposure in the magazine. I said yes to that, too! It turned out to be a brilliant move. *Entourage*'s Jeremy Piven went onstage and played drums with the Rock 'n' Roll Fantasy Camp All-Star band; I now had forty million readers seeing my brand. The photo helped me get national exposure to millions of *People* readers, hundreds of whom bought spots to future camps . . . and I was able to rekindle a friendship at the same time.

Generating Hype

Now, it's easy to see how an idea like Rock 'n' Roll Fantasy Camp fits the fourth characteristic: generating hype. Rocking out with rock stars? It's hard for anyone not to get excited by that. But what if you have an idea that's a little harder to sell—or what if it's an idea that is not yet fully formed? This is where you can really get creative. Let me step away from Rock 'n' Roll Fantasy Camp to give you an example.

In 1987, *Dirty Dancing* was one of the hottest movies in the country. I had a hunch that it could be turned into a tour.

I had an idea to take the dancers from the movie and the music stars from the successful record, produced by Jimmy Ienner, and combine them to create a live show. I wanted to integrate the songs, singers, and dancers together on one stage. Originally, I approached Patrick Swayze to headline the tour; he was so desired then that I knew if I got him on stage with Jennifer Grey, I would have a sold-out show at Madison Square Garden. Patrick, unfortunately, turned me down, but I still had a feeling my idea would be a success.

Before creating a show, I placed a full-page ad in the Sunday *New York Times Arts & Leisure* section. I had no dancers, no set—no nothing—just an ad. So how did we go from having nothing at all to selling out eight shows at Radio City Music Hall in eight hours? Let me explain.

I asked a lot of press agents how to create some buzz for a currently nonexistent show, and I kept hearing, "You gotta be different!" Okay, but how do you make your show stand out? Press agent Bobby Zarem, the legendary showbiz publicist in New York, gave me a peculiar piece of advice—create a fake rehearsal for the press. Just get a bunch of dancers together in a rehearsal hall and show off some moves. It sounded crazy, but I decided to try it. I contacted Kenny Ortega, who choreographed *Dirty Dancing* and worked with Michael Jackson. In fact, Kenny was one of the producers of the 2010 Michael Jackson movie, *This Is It*. Kenny recommended that his assistant Dorian Sanchez fly to New York to rehearse with twenty local dancers. We had a top choreographer and a lot of people dancing dirty in the Radio City rehearsal hall, and we invited the press to come watch a private rehearsal. The press didn't know that we had no show! They loved what they saw, and we got wonderful stories written about this "hot new show."

My agent and friend, Dennis Arfa, then suggested we sell the tickets only at the Radio City box office from 9 a.m. to noon, the day before the tickets went on sale, and then open it up to Ticketmaster. This created even more hype because news reports showed people lined up around the block from Radio City at 8 a.m. to buy tickets for the show. As a result, by the time we actually allowed tickets to be sold via Ticketmaster, we had already sold out three shows, and then we proceeded to sell out another five. Unfortunately, Radio City didn't have any more dates available that summer; otherwise we would have sold more. As it was, we sold a million dollars' worth of tickets in just eight hours. We went from having no show to having eight sold-out shows, and soon thereafter, we had a world tour that performed in twenty countries. All we needed to get from point A to point B was the hype—and we created that from scratch through a little ingenuity.

Assessing Your Idea

Does your idea have what it takes to become the next national or international phenomenon? Or, if not a phenomenon, an idea that will bring you success and make you a profit? Is it worth pursuing, taking the big risks, jumping in headfirst? If it has the four common characteristics I've described, then you've probably found your big idea. If you don't think your dream quite has all these attributes covered, all is not lost—keep developing it until you've found a way to cover these bases, and you'll have a potential winner on your hands.

Now that you've got your big idea—are you ready to make it a reality?

Chapter One's Greatest Hits

- Everything starts with an idea.
- There are four questions you have to ask yourself before you begin to bring your project to life:
  - Will it produce a gut reaction?
  - Is it distinguishable?
  - Is it barterable?
  - Can it generate hype?
- Risk-taking is the cornerstone of success.

2

More Than a Feeling:
MAKING IT REAL

O nce you've got a handle on your idea, it's time to devise how you're going to present it to the world. But how do you turn your idea into "more than a feeling"? The first key is creativity. Even a simple idea can bring you success if it's creative. Let me give you an example.

In 1989, I was producing the American Gladiators Live tour. I had a vision for the tour, but it wasn't going as well as I had hoped. I was going through a divorce at the time, and things were really looking down. I knew I had to get out of this rut. I called Ken Feld, who owns Ringling Bros. and Bar- num & Bailey Circus, as well as Disney on Ice, among other franchises. I didn't know him, but my gut felt that he could help me, so I just called him up and introduced myself. I said, "By the way, my show American Gladiators is coming through Baltimore. Since you live in Washington, would you be inter- ested in going to see it?"

Ken saw the show and called me the next day. Without a single compliment, he listed all the ways he could make my show better. It boiled down to the fact that I had overbuilt the show and that it could be produced more efficiently. Albert Einstein, with all of his genius, realized that each of life's greatest projects needed to be distilled to its most basic manifestation. Keep things simple. I was traveling with six semis' worth of equipment, and Ken said I should be traveling with two trucks and two semis of tour merchandise. This affected the price of the union stagehands and labor costs in the arenas, which in turn affected the ticket prices. When you hear that a rock show is loading into an arena with twelve semis, you can expect the ticket to be priced accordingly.

At that point I knew he had interest in taking the show. I said to him, "I'd love you to be a partner on this show. Can we work out a deal?" After some negotiating back and forth, we made a deal. We completed the twenty-five dates I had already booked and then stopped the show so Ken and his crew could rebuild it to fit it in two semis. Ken's company constructed the sets and got all the merchandising going. The latter was especially great because merchandising is Ken's specialty—he sells more merchandise than anybody else in show business.

We decided to relaunch the show in January of 1993 at the Superdome in New Orleans; it would coincide with the well-known National Association of Television Program Executives (NATPE) Conference. The reasoning was, if we could get some of the general managers of the local TV stations to see the show and get behind it, they would promote it in their local markets.

At the opening night of the show in New Orleans, there were 25,000 people in the stands. I was utterly astonished. I had been doing the same tour two months earlier, and I had only 6,000 people in the audience—Ken had mustered up 25,000!

But then something strange happened. I started sweating. The gladiators were sweating, and I could see the people looking around—it was the middle of winter, and the place was getting very, very warm. I made my way over to the head of merchandising, and he said to me, "Fishof, are you hot?" "Yeah, I am. I'm sweating!" I said. "The gladiators are sweating! What's going on?" He said, "I gave the electrician $100 to shut off the air conditioning so we could sell snow cones." That night we sold $50,000 in snow cones, which averaged $2/head.

I was truly amazed. There he was selling ice and water and a little food coloring for $2 a cone—this was ingenuity at its finest. The idea to turn off the air conditioning to sell snow cones was so brilliant and creative, yet so simple. It taught me the power of simple manipulation. It's the same premise as the stories you hear about Las Vegas casinos—how they pump up the oxygen so people stay awake to gamble longer, how they don't have clocks so you don't know how long you've been there, and how you can't walk to your hotel room until you go through the casino. At the Ringling Bros. and Barnum & Bailey Circus shows, you can't walk to your seats unless you walk with your

ROCK OUT IN THE REAL WORLD
Stripped-Down Creativity

Back in the mid-'70s, the great rock and roll manager Shep Gordon booked Alice Cooper to play four shows in London at the Royal Albert Hall. Ticket sales were creeping along very slowly, so Shep decided to get creative. He hired the legendary photographer Richard Avedon to take a photo of a naked Alice Cooper with a snake wrapped strategically around his body. Then he rented the biggest truck he could find and plastered the photograph on the side. The caption read: "Alice Cooper: America's Greatest Rock 'n' Roll Star."

The master touch? Shep hired a truck driver to drive it and "break down" in the middle of rush-hour traffic in Piccadilly Circus. The press came out to cover the story, and over the next day and night, the four shows sold out completely.

kids through all the memorabilia booths, the popcorn, and the candy. As Ken's head of merchandising said to me once, "We lose $200 million a year on the circus, but we make $500 million on the merchandise."

I know what you're probably thinking—this is manipulation. There's no denying it; this is manipulation at its finest, but there is a greater principle at work. This experience taught me one of the most important lessons in the music industry: To have a great idea and make it work, you have to be creative. But a great idea doesn't have to be $E = mc^2$—it can be as simple as turning up the heat and selling ice and water for $2 a pop.

Getting Advice with Experts

Working with Ken Feld also taught me another important lesson, one that is essential to turning a dream into reality: Work with industry leaders to make your idea the best it can be. Without Ken's expertise, the American Gladiators tour would have continued to struggle. With his experience on my side, we were playing to sold-out arenas—crowds of 15,000 to 25,000.

Using industry leaders as a sounding board for your idea is the absolute best way to gauge your idea's potential in the real world. For much of my career, I made an appointment every year with the head of the Creative Artists Agency (CAA) music department, Tom Ross. I would come in and make a pitch to all his agents about my ideas for the year, explaining what I wanted to tour. We would discuss my ideas, I would get their reactions, and I would see whether they thought they could sell it. If they liked it, CAA would book my tour. This was how I determined whether my ideas were sellable.

Meanwhile, Rob Light, the head of CAA's music department, taught me that there are no bad tours; there are only bad deals. In other words, if an idea doesn't make money, it's not a great idea.

Creating Your Sounding Board

Who should be on your informal board of advisors? Choose people in the same industry as your product. If you're in consumer goods, find people who are even more successful than yourself and get their opinions. Same thing with software or graphic design or any field. It's the same idea as if you wanted to improve your tennis game—find people to play with who are better than you are. You should take your idea to people who can benefit from that idea because they will give you the best advice. Just showing your idea to somebody with experience and asking for a response can save you a lot of time. For starters, if you talk to a person in the industry for whom you're creating a product or service, you can find out whether there's a need for your product or if there's someone else already doing it. Second, when you show your idea to someone you respect and understand, you receive constructive criticism, like "Hey, that's a good idea, but I think you've got to go back to the drawing board and add this or that to it, then bring it to marketplace and try to sell it." If you go to five different industry leaders and they each give you five different pieces of advice, go to another five! You can't have too much advice. Some you'll take, and some you'll leave, but it's all worth hearing. There are many retired executives who are just looking to help young people, so you can start with them. If you're seeking advice in the music industry, for example, it would be beneficial to attend the Pollstar Convention. There you can enroll in mentor programs that are taught by experts in the music business.

It's also very important not to be so in love with your idea that you don't listen to advice. With that kind of thinking, you'll never win. You need the insight others can provide, because with every product you're developing and launching, there's much more involved than just the product. There's advertising, marketing, public relations—so many different aspects to business, and you need all of them to be successful.

You need the insight others can provide, because with every product you're developing and launching, there's much more involved than just the product. There's advertising, marketing, public relations—so many different aspects to business, and you need all of them to be successful.

Facing Your Fears

In order to talk with industry leaders, you'll have to go after them. Finding them is not as difficult as you may think. With Facebook and LinkedIn as well as e-mail, it's easy to connect with people—so there's no excuse not to!

Of course, fear is a factor. For one, it can seem daunting to call a big-shot executive out of the blue. I'll talk more in the next chapter about how to do it, but here's a secret to keep in mind: *Everybody likes to give advice.* Everybody wants to be a teacher. That's one of the reasons Rock 'n' Roll Fantasy Camp is so successful. I'm not asking these rock stars to get up and perform in front of 18,000 people every night; I'm asking them to walk into a room and say, "I've become successful; now I'll share it with you." You'll find that most people who are successful are secure about themselves, and they are often willing to share their secrets. Look at Oprah's Master Class, a special series devoted to the lives of "modern masters" in American society. It became an instant hit precisely because celebrities and innovators love sharing information and helping others. The TED conference, an international forum for high-level speakers, has also become a huge success because it relies on the fact that successful people love sharing the tools of their success.

Another fear people often have is that if they show their idea around, someone is going to try to steal it. Unfortunately, this happens sometimes. But if you don't get out there, your idea will never become a reality. There are ways to protect yourself. I recommend signing a non-disclosure agreement—I sign them every day. You can find one I recommend at www.davidfishof.com.

Presenting Your Ideas

Let's say you've set up your meeting with the industry leaders. What do you bring? I'll tell you my tactic: I always draw my idea up—literally. I create the final product: the newspaper ad for the tour or the script for a radio or TV commercial. If you take the time to draw up a finished product, it will not only solidify the idea in your own mind, but it will also show others that you are serious and thinking this idea through to the end.

You don't have to be artistically bent yourself to create the prototype of your product. Via Google, you can find an artist, and for a hundred dollars, or maybe a couple hundred dollars, you can have him or her create an ad, a brochure, or a

flyer for your product. There's a wonderful Web site called
Guru.com that will allow you to hire any type of talented person to do this art for you, at an assortment of prices that are
totally negotiable. All you do is ask for bids on the work you
want done, and the artists get back to you. There is also a
plethora of companies that specialize in designing and building new products. With a little research and effort, you can
create something from scratch.

When people see something they can touch, all of a sudden, it's no longer an idea—it's happening. You've got to show
people that it's happening now, not far off in the speculative
future. Once you visualize your idea and put it down on
paper, then you can move behind it to write the business plan
and put together the numbers. But to get people excited, the
first thing you have to do is show them what the idea is. Too
many people say, "Oh, I have this idea," and they do nothing
with it. For a hundred bucks you can work with someone to
draw up your idea and bring it that much closer to reality. If
you show your idea to people like it's a done deal, like you've
drawn it out, you'll be far ahead of the curve.

*When people see something they can touch, all of a sudden,
it's no longer an idea—it's happening. You've got to show
people that it's happening now, not far off in the speculative future.*

Check Out Your Target Market

You can also use your drawn-up idea to conduct market
research, another essential step in the process. For example,
take the action-movie producer moguls Menahem Golan and
Yoram Globus. These guys start out by creating a poster for a

movie they are thinking of producing. A movie that doesn't yet exist. They will approach a movie star and ask him if he's interested in doing a film. The star says, "I'll consider it; let me take a look at the script." Then they create a piece of art with the star's photo in it—say, Chuck Norris, and the title, say, *The Delta Force*. Then they take the poster to the Cannes film festival, where foreign rights to movies are bought and sold. They showcase the poster and sell the rights to all the different territories that want the film. Only after they have raised enough money do they make the film. If they don't raise enough money on the poster, they don't make the film.

Producer and former CEO of United Artists, Jerry Weintraub, did the same thing. Before becoming a movie producer, Weintraub was a major concert promoter for music acts, including Elvis Presley and Frank Sinatra. Back in the '60s and '70s, he would place a big concert ad in the local newspaper in Seattle, saying "Chicago, Beach Boys Live Concert Coming June 15" or "Three Dog Night, The Beach Boys." If tickets sold for that concert, he would produce a nationwide tour. But if the tickets to that "test concert" didn't sell, he wouldn't do the tour.

That's a really creative way to do market research. By showing their posters around, both Golan and Globus, and Jerry Weintraub, could determine whether there was a good market for their product. It's similar to what we did with the Dirty Dancing tour and the mock rehearsal at Radio City Music Hall. We generated interest and money in advance. In the same vein, you could create a Facebook page for a product that does not yet exist to gauge interest. It might not bring you money, but the market information you gain is solid gold.

You can also conduct informal market research in other ways. You can go to a local college and see if you can present your product to thirty college kids or a college club. This is a great way to do some research on how the younger generation will respond to your idea. Or you can put together an informal meeting of friends and colleagues and have them tell you if they would purchase your product. Most people love to talk, so if you let them they'll give you all your information. The key is to present your product and your wares and gauge the response.

However, you have to be careful that you conduct your research accurately. When I produced the Mortal Kombat live tour in 1995, it seemed like it would be a success. It was the most successful video game in history and a blockbuster movie. But my "market research" was sorely lacking. I asked my son Josh to invite six of his pals to my office after school to ask them to explain the game to me. "Mr. Fishof," they said. "That is the coolest idea ever!" (They said that if I gave out secret video game codes that would help them get to a higher level at the live show, then they would buy a ticket.) That was the entirety of my research. Based on what they said, I moved ahead with the tour, invest-

---

ROCK OUT IN THE REAL WORLD

Passion at Its Peak: The Rolling Stones

"This whole thing runs on passion . . . even though we don't talk about it much ourselves, it's almost a sort of quest or mission."

—Keith Richards as told to Fortune *in 2002*

". . . [T]he Rolling Stones appear supremely alive inside their giant, self-created rock 'n' roll machine. The sheer pleasure of making music that keens and growls like a pack of ravenous alley cats is obviously what keeps them going. Why should they ever stop?"

—Stephen Holden, The New York Times, *April 2008*

The Rolling Stones are proof that passion and persistence pay off. During a rock and roll career spanning more than four decades, the creative machine never sleeps. The band's continued dedication has kept old fans in the fold while simultaneously bringing the music into the cars and living rooms of whole new generations of fans.

Continues

ing to produce two separate shows—one to tour the West Coast and another for the East Coast. I was positive that it would be a hit, despite the fact that I wasn't getting any support from media or corporate sponsors, nor were there any associates onboard. I saw that the Power Rangers were doing business so I felt Mortal Kombat would follow its success. In the end, I lost all of the money invested. If I had conducted the proper market research and other unforeseen circumstances had not happened, I might never have gone through with the tour and lost that money.

There was another important lesson I learned from this experience: The enthusiasm of your son and his friends isn't always enough—you have to believe in the idea yourself. I should have seen early on that the Mortal Kombat tour wasn't going to work out. Why? Because my heart wasn't in it. I wasn't a big fan of martial arts or video games, and I ignored some obvious red flags. I decided to forge ahead anyway—and it ended in disaster. You have to put your whole heart and soul into your project. You have to be ready to break down walls with an ironclad will. That's the most important thing.

Continued

Their musical discography consists of more than a hundred singles, twenty-nine studio albums—ten of which are listed in *Rolling Stone* magazine's The 500 Greatest Albums of All Time—ten live albums, three extended plays, and thirty compilation albums. Talk about a rock and roll legacy!

With passion, persistence, and dedication—not to mention practice, practice, practice—The Rolling Stones continue to make musical history in rock and roll, an industry where the odds of success are stacked against any act lasting months, let alone half a century. Not only are they making history in the music world, but they are also still finding themselves on TV, magazines, etc. In fact, they were featured on an episode of *The Simpsons* along with my business! Mick Jagger and Keith Richards starred in an episode with Homer Simpson, who goes to Rock 'n' Roll Fantasy Camp—talk about a good takeoff for my camp!

If you don't believe in your product, neither will the buyer. You have to give compelling reasons to persuade the buyer to purchase your product rather than someone else's. I had a meeting with the *Elite Meetings* magazine, who were getting ready to put on a big event, and I had to convince them that including a corporate Rock 'n' Roll Fantasy Camp would be the best thing for the event. I went to the meeting and gave them all my reasons, and they said to me, "Your passion, David, is what shows us that we need to do this."

From the Rams to the Rolling Stones

It's this passion that helped me start my career in the music industry. I started out as a sports agent, something I'll talk more about in later chapters. But I always wanted to work in the entertainment business. How did I go about achieving that dream? And once I got into the industry, how did I achieve success? I'd like to share that story with you.

When I was twenty years old, I made an appointment with Larry Fleisher, sports agent and president of the NBA Players Association. I wanted to ask him if I could represent some of his players to book at the Catskill Mountain sports camps. Larry introduced me to NBA greats Earl "The Pearl" Monroe, David Thompson, Celtic great John Havlicek, and Rick Barry, who did a couple camps for me in the Catskills. Earl and I became friends, and when I mentioned that I was looking for office space, Earl recommended that I meet his accountant, who had an office at 1775 Broadway.

I got to the accountant's office, up on the seventh floor, and discovered that he shared it with all of these amazing rock and roll managers: Shep Gordon, who managed Blondie and Alice Cooper, Gary Kurfurst (who represented the Ramones), Talking Heads, and the B-52s—even Madonna's manager was there!

So there I was—this young sports agent in the same office space as these rock and roll managers. Everywhere I looked, there were gold records on the walls. I had always wanted my own gold record, and I had always desired to go into the music business because of the creativity—and because I looked up to my older brother, who was a drummer. Seeing the entertainment business success all around me, I longed to be a part of that world even more.

One day, I got a phone call from a press agent in Hollywood. They'd seen me in the newspapers and on TV, representing LA Rams quarterback Vince Ferragamo. I was in the middle of a long, difficult negotiation over Ferragamo's contract with the Rams. Ferragamo had just appeared in the Super Bowl and had become the darling of the Rams. I had uncovered that Ferragamo's previous lawyer had been offered a $50,000 fee to get Ferragamo to sign a new contract, and the minute I exposed it, Ferragamo asked me to take over negotiations. I started commuting regularly back and forth from New York. I was in the LA newspapers almost every day as the negotiations continued to draw out. I decided to use this to my advantage. Because I wanted so badly to be in show business, I decided that in an interview for the *Los Angeles Times*, I would tell the writer that my main business was the entertainment business. This is another key little secret: When you're doing interviews for media, you can control the interview. Let me explain.

At the same time that I was assembling the American Gladiators Live tour, I was representing New York Giants quarterback Phil Simms. Bill Parcells, the head coach at the time, had chosen Scott Brunner to be the Giant's number-one quarterback. This caused a huge controversy for Giants fans and Phil Simms. Now, in the midst of all this, it was getting to the deadline on the Gladiators tour, and I still hadn't found a corporate sponsor to help fund the project. One day, I got a call asking me to be a guest on CBS-TV at 11:30 p.m. for the *Sunday Night Sports* show with host Rock Rote. In past years, I never did an interview about specific sports questions, never talked about anything my players were involved in unless it was a contract or endorsement. But I was so desperate to get a corporate sponsor for the Gladiators tour that I agreed to do the interview—on one condition: that they ask me a question about my upcoming American Gladiators Live tour, so I could say on television that I was seeking a sponsor. They agreed to these terms. I showed up to the set and saw on the tele-prompter the last question for the host: "If you have time, ask about the American Gladiators Live tour." *If you have time.* That is not what I wanted! I decided to take matters into my own hands.

The interview started, and the host opened with: "So David, tell me about the quarterback controversy with Phil Simms, Scott Brunner, and the Giants." I said, "You know, it really reminds me of the American Gladiators Live tour I'm producing, and by the way, I'm looking for a corporate sponsor for the tour, and you know, these two football greats are two gladiators going head to head, looking for a chance to be the starting quarterback." I was able to get my message in on the very first question. The next day, my phone rang, and it was an executive with the convenience store chain 7-Eleven. He had seen me on the interview and wanted to sponsor the tour. He took me to visit the folks at Coca-Cola, who bought the tour for 7-Eleven. I had my corporate spon-

Radio personality Bob Grant (back row) with NFL greats, from back to front, Phil Simms, Troy Benson, Earl "The Pearl" Monroe, Mark Bavaro, and Phil McConkey, Troy Benson, and former Miss Michigan Diane Arabia, David's son Josh, and David.

sor. All I needed was to take that media opportunity and use it to publicize myself.

In a similar way, when I made a plug about my being in show business in the interview for the *Los Angeles Times*, I ended up getting my first call from a Hollywood agent. The agent had read the article about me in the *Los Angeles Times*, read that I was in the entertainment business (the reporter included that tidbit I'd dropped!), and called me up.

The agent asked whether I'd be interested in representing The Association. I was so young and new that my response was, "Which association would you like me to book entertainment for?" I was so used to my career as a booking agent in the Catskills, booking acts like Sammy Davis Jr. and Bill Cosby for corporations and Jewish organizations, I thought he meant some association wanted a show. I didn't realize The Association was the band! After the press agent explained who The Association was, I jumped at the opportunity and caught a plane the next day to Los Angeles to meet the band. Remember, I was motivated by all of the gold-record walls. I wanted one so desperately back then. I got to the rehearsal studio and met the whole band—all the original members, except Brian Cole, who had passed away. The band started to play me their new music. I didn't quite get it, so I asked them to play me some of their hits. When they launched into "Cherish," "Never My Love," "Along Comes Mary," and "Windy"—their big hits—I got goose bumps all down my spine because they sounded so amazing.

We sat down after rehearsal and they questioned me about my skills and contacts. I told them that I had booked tons of corporate dates. I told them that even though I didn't have any other music clients, I was very connected, and what was more, I wasn't afraid to pick up the phone and introduce myself to anyone. After all, I had something going for me that would get me in many doors—access to the best athletes in the pros. They wouldn't want to reject my calls! The Association was suitably convinced, and it was agreed that I would manage them.

I was incredibly excited. Finally, I had broken into the music-management business! I called my friends at various music agencies to tell them—and each and every one of them reacted like I was nuts. Representing The Association wasn't being in the music business! "Why?" I asked. The agents told me the truth—they couldn't sell the band for more than $2,500 a night, and the band would have to pay their own travel, hotel, and equipment, as well as paying the agency 10 percent and the manager—me—15 percent. There was no way the band could survive on that kind of fee. The agents told me there was no demand. I liked these guys, and they liked me, but they couldn't deliver the dates.

I decided to try another approach. I took a bunch of the agents to individual lunches and told them that I would split my 15 percent management fee with them in return for their working hard to book my band. Lo and behold, the next day, my phone started ringing off the hook with dates from the agents. "Is The Association available for two days at Bogart's in Cincinnati for fifteen grand?" "Can The Association do a gig at Summerfest, the yearly festival in Chicago, for $25,000?" Of course I said yes and yes! I called my buddy Mitchel Etess at the Grossinger's Hotel in the Catskills, and he booked the band on a Thursday night for five grand to help kick off a singles weekend at the hotel. Another agent called and offered me two days starting Friday afternoon at 4 p.m. at the Orange County Fair in Los Angeles.

With offers coming in this thick and fast, scheduling dates and travel was starting to get difficult. I called Terry Kirkman and Jim Yester, the band leaders at the time, to ask, with so many dates, who should give the final okay on which shows to take? Kirkman said, "Our old manager, Pat Colechio, did everything for us. It's your job to accept the dates," then hung up on me. I was on my own.

Even though I had never routed a tour before, I decided that I had enough travel experience to figure it out myself. I figured that the band could do the show at Grossinger's and be offstage by midnight. They would wake up the next morning at 5 a.m., head to one of the New York airports to catch an 8 a.m. flight, sleep on the flight to LA, and do a show at 4 p.m. After all, when I traveled from New York to California, I would leave New York at 9 a.m. and get into LA at 11:30 a.m. I had also seen an ad for an Eastern Airlines special—for $499 you could fly across the country, anywhere in the U.S.A., for thirty days. I figured for the ten guys, $5,000 to fly for a month would really cut travel expenses and let the band make a huge profit.

I probably don't have to tell you what a mistake this all was. First off, I didn't know about gear, sound checks, equipment—all the business of a band traveling. I know now, you need to book a tour from city to city, and that for a tour like this, the band should only travel two hundred and fifty, maybe three hundred miles between gigs—not six thousand!

But the offers were coming in fast. It's amazing when I gave some motivational dollars how the agents miraculously managed to find all of these bookings. We were headlining Atlantic City, Las Vegas, Tahoe, Reno, and tons of festivals. The casinos were great because they would paper the house with free tickets to their gamblers. I'll admit, the majority of the shows were pretty empty, but we got paid. As more and more dates came in, I kept okay'ing them. Some of the dates even made sense: I had a booking from Detroit to Chicago— only 250 miles! But my Eastern Airlines deal ruined it. The band had to fly to Atlanta first and then change planes to Chicago because the rule of the deal was that you could only fly Eastern Airlines, and most of their flights flew from their hub in Atlanta.

I didn't care. I was so proud of the fact that I had booked a million dollars in dates in 1983 for a band that used to average $2,500 a night opening for the Kingston Trio. I loved the feeling—when I saw the crowds in Chicago at the band's performance at Summerfest, I said to myself, "This is far more exciting than sports to me." In sports, the teams and leagues never welcome the agents. I remember going into Yankee Stadium for the first time with Lou Piniella and heading onto the field from the press cafeteria; there was a big sign that said NO AGENTS ALLOWED. But in the entertainment business, the manager was treated with respect, given passes to walk around anywhere—the manager's suite in the Las Vegas hotels was usually even better than the talent's! After all, everyone's thinking, "We're going to need shows in the future, better treat this guy right!"

By the end of the summer, The Association had grossed a million. I made nearly $100,000, and the agents made their money, too. But somehow, the band was left in debt. I couldn't understand how this had happened! I had worked so hard to make them the money, given them these great discount plane tickets, but still they had no money in the bank. I realized that I had pushed these guys too far. Making money wasn't the be-all and end-all—I had to take care of my artists as well.

The following October, The Association was on the same bill as Gary Puckett and the Union Gap, doing an oldies show with Chuck Berry at the Meadowlands Arena in New Jersey. Gary's song "Young Girl" was a favorite of mine growing up. I asked the members of The Association to introduce me to Gary because I wanted to sign him up for management. They told him about me, we had a meeting in my office, and the next thing I knew I was his manager. Again, I was very excited. I thought I was making great strides in the music business—but again, my agent friends told me that I was nuts. "You're representing the biggest athletes in the world—Phil Simms, Lou Piniella—Fishof, you own New York City, and you're spending your time managing these oldies acts!" But I didn't care. I liked these people. They were fun to listen to, and most of them were very nice.

After I signed Gary, I was approached by the Turtles, and I signed them, too. I was gathering all these great acts—now I needed to do something with them. So in 1984 I approached the William Morris Agency, and we came up with the idea of packaging these bands together, along with Spanky McFarland of Spanky and Our Gang, and calling it the Happy Together tour. The tour would feature four bands and a night of only hit songs.

Almost immediately, promoters started buying shows. Jules Belkin, who promoted the Ohio and Detroit markets, bought six shows. Arnie Granit, who promoted in Illinois, bought a bunch. Ron Delsener bought three shows for Jones Beach, the Garden State Art Center, and the Pier in New York City. Ron always asked me to add on acts like Tommy James and the Shondells or Three Dog Night to enhance the package, and that way we could play to a bigger venue and sell more tickets. I have to credit him with some of this advice— some of the best I've received. He said that I have good ideas, but I should spend more money on big-name talent. I might have to pay more, but it would work. I will always feel indebted to him because he always believed in me and my projects.

In November of 1984 something great happened: The movie *The Big Chill* came out. All of a sudden, the whole country started getting nostalgic—and we started selling out shows. We decided to launch a summer tour and booked more than 125 gigs. A year later, I produced another version of the Happy Together tour, adding on Gene Clark's "Byrds," The Grass Roots with Rob Grill, and the Buckinghams ("Kind of a Drag" was the Buckinghams' hit song). This tour did

Concert promoter Ron Delsener (far right) often gave me good advice about the business. Here he is talking with me and Ringo Starr at a 1989 party.

another 125 dates and really helped relaunch some of these musicians' careers.

When "Monkeeing" Around Is a Good Thing

One night in 1986, I was stuck on the top floor of a Holiday Inn in Kansas City, unable to fall asleep at three o'clock in the morning. The hotel manager thought he was doing me a favor by giving me the entire top floor for myself, but it was an eerie feeling. I turned on the TV—and on came *The Monkees*. As I watched, I was overcome with good feelings—this was my favorite TV show as a kid. I used to come home from the yeshiva (religious school), and the only show my parents would let me watch was *The Monkees* (though if I could persuade them, I'd also watch my second favorite, *World Wide Wrestling Federation, WWWF*, which featured wrestler Bruno Sammartino).

In the wee hours at the hotel is when it hit me. I couldn't be the only one who felt this way about The Monkees. So why not reunite them and let people relive this great feeling from their youth, while at the same time introducing The Monkees to a new generation? I immediately started researching, trying to find out who controlled the name and logo of The Monkees. I knew it wasn't the band because it was a TV show first. It turns out Columbia Pictures owned the name, so I called the president, and he told me to call his New York office and make a deal. I called the head of licensing, Lester Borden. Lester said he knew of me and asked me whether I would take him to a Yankees game. So I called Lou Piniella, and Lou said, "Sure, bring him anytime, and if it would help, I'm happy to meet him as well." We went to a game, and all of the players came over and signed autographs and baseball jerseys. I wondered why they were being so nice; I later found out that it was because Lou had asked them to take care of us. I am indebted to him for that because it helped me land a deal to buy The Monkees name and logo. I bought the name for $3,500, no royalty.

It was rough going once I set out to get the band back together. No one was sure that we would be able to sell the shows. Then one day I was sitting in my office and Jim Bessman, a reporter from *Billboard*, came in and said, "Hey, MTV just announced that they're going to air *The Monkees* TV series for more than twenty-four straight hours." I immediately ran upstairs to the seventh floor of my building, where Bob Pittman and Tom Freston, the MTV top executives, happened to have their offices. Bob suggested we help each other out—I would promote his brand if he promoted mine. He promoted The Monkees tour, and I promoted his fledgling network, MTV, in my advertisements.

The show opened in the Concord Hotel in the Catskills in May 1986. This was perfect because we could rehearse there, spending time on creating the show rather than hanging out all over Los Angeles. Plus, I got to eat my kosher meals! It was also during that time that I met up with the late rock promoter Bill Graham. Bill used to be a waiter at the Concord Hotel, and every summer he would return to visit his fellow waiters still working there and Irving Cohen, the maitre d' of the hotel for more than fifty years. It was so cool to break challah rolls and creamed herring with Bill every morning before rehearsals.

When the tour got started, it was amazing. The MTV airing of *The Monkees* TV show helped create that success. People, mostly my younger audience, didn't know that The Monkees was a twenty-year-old group. They thought it was a brand-new band, playing never-before-heard tunes! When we put the tickets on sale, we got all these screaming young girls. They'd come home at ten in the morning, and their mothers would say, "Where have you been all night?" And the daughter would say, "I was waiting in line to buy Monkees tickets!" Then the mothers would say, "Wait a minute, I want to go, too!" In the first twenty rows of the concerts were these young girls, and in the back you would see all these mothers. It was a truly cross-generational concert.

The Monkees ended up being the biggest tour I've ever produced. I heard that Chuck Sullivan, the former owner of the New England Patriots, came looking for me on a Friday night after the concert with a check for a quarter of a million dollars, my share of the proceeds because The Monkees had outsold his Michael Jackson concert. Unfortunately, I wasn't

Hey, hey, it's the Monkees. From left, Peter Tork, Micky Dolenz, Michael Nesmith, Davy Jones, and me.

around to receive the good news, but my accountant brought it to me the next night in Atlantic City. The screams of the crowds on that tour were deafening—probably the loudest heard since the Beatles came to America.

All the executives who were behind The Monkees prospered like crazy. Rhino Records really launched after *The Monkees* TV show—it reissued six of The Monkees' old albums, which landed on the Top 50 Album sales charts. Rhino eventually sold for a hundred million dollars to Warner, and I bet The Monkees contributed to some of that money. Arista Records released a "Greatest Hits," with three new songs, that went on to sell millions. And the executives at Clive Davis's Arista record label went on to become presidents of four labels. It was amazing—this one great concert and band idea kick-started so many careers.

Have Passion, Learn All You Can

There are so many lessons I learned in these first few years in the music-management business. And it's these lessons that are the key to turning your idea from a concept to reality. I first managed to turn my dream of being in the music industry into something that could actually happen just by putting myself out there. Mentioning it in interviews, calling up whomever I needed to talk to in order to get where I wanted to go. I utilized the connections I had in my career thus far, using my relationships with sports stars to help seal deals in the music industry. I even got to meet Jon Bon Jovi, when he was honored by the Nordoff Robbins Charity and requested that Phil Simms give him the award.

Of course, I made mistakes, but I learned from them. I was passionate about my ideas. I always took the time to talk to people with experience, like Ron Delsener, Rob Light, and Ken Feld. I was also prepared for success—able to foster and support growth by having the necessary elements in place when things started moving.

Take your dream, draw it up, and take it to the pros. Put all your passion behind your idea and learn from everything— industry leaders, market research, and your own mistakes. If you can do these things, your idea is already more than just a concept. Now it's time to learn the ins and outs of bringing it fully to life.

Chapter Two's Greatest Hits

■ To make your idea more than a feeling you need creativity.

■ Using industry leaders as your sounding board is the best way to gauge your idea's potential.

■ Put together an informal board of advisors. You can't have too much advice.

■ Don't be so in love with your idea that you won't listen to advice.

■ Draw up a final prototype of your product.

■ The evidence of those around you isn't always an indicator that your idea will succeed.

■ Believe in your product. If you don't, neither will your buyer.

■ When you are doing interviews for the media, you *can* control the interview.

ATTRACT
AN AUDIENCE

3

Money for Nothing:
BRINGING YOUR IDEA TO LIFE

Once you've come up with your idea, learned how to overcome your obstacles, and discovered how to face your fears, it's time to bring your idea into the real world. But how do you do that?

The first step is to do the research. This means researching your exact idea and product, and making sure you have a vast knowledge of the industry you are in, or are trying to break into. Although you may already be an expert in one industry or an established, seasoned businessperson in a field, you need to understand that with every new idea comes new problems, boundaries, and obstacles that need to be overcome. You can have a stellar idea, but if you don't know anything about the industry, your project will end in disaster.

In the '80s, the Sullivan family owned the New England Patriots, along with the team's stadium, then known as Sullivan Stadium. Around the same time that I was doing The Monkees tour in the early '80s, the Sullivans decided that they wanted to produce and promote a concert featuring Michael

Jackson and his brothers. They were sold the Jacksons Victory Tour by legendary promoter Don King and started figuring out the numbers. But this is where the trouble started.

The Sullivans figured they had 60,000 to 80,000 seats to sell in the stadium. They figured they'd charge $100 a ticket, which would gross $6 to $8 million a show. Then they could pay the Jacksons $3 million a show. However, the Sullivans were accustomed to how a stadium is arranged for sporting events, and this was the basis they were using for their calculations. What they didn't realize is that a stadium needs to be completely reconfigured for a concert. For a football game, an 80,000-seat stadium can sit 80,000 people. For a concert, you need to set up a stage, have a backdrop, and hang lights and sound—and after that, you only have about 40,000 seats left to sell.

Not realizing this, the Sullivans went ahead and guaranteed the Jacksons their calculated percentage of the profits, based on the 60,000- to 80,000-seat count. But when they started selling the show, they were only able to sell five-eighths of the stadiums, and it wasn't too long before the family started losing all its money. The Sullivans eventually had to file for bankruptcy, and they lost ownership not only of the New England Patriots but of their own stadium as well.

In my opinion, this happened because, among all their consultants and accountants, they did not have a single person on their team from the music industry. Anybody in the music business could have told them they wouldn't be able to sell all 80,000 seats in the stadium. But they didn't ask, and they didn't budget correctly, and it ended up being their downfall.

Anybody in the music business could have told them they wouldn't be able to sell all 80,000 seats in the stadium. But they didn't ask, and they didn't budget correctly, and it ended up being their downfall.

Get in the Know

The best possible way to learn about an industry is to be a part of it. If your idea isn't in the field that you're already in, then do whatever it takes to be around the business associated with your idea. It doesn't matter whether you're interning, volunteering, working weekends, or working the night shift, as long as you're there. Learn from the inside and then you won't make those huge, easily avoidable mistakes.

I tell people all the time that if they have a passion for something, they should try interning for a company within their interests; if interning is not an option, then pursue volunteering at the company, or working for a less-than-ideal paycheck. Although these are not highly desired positions, they are, in my opinion, the most important things you can do to get a foot in the door in your industry, and to ensure your face and name will be remembered. In this economy, a lot of people think that they should wait it out by staying in school and getting another degree. They figure that when the economy picks back up, they can head back out into the real world and get a job. But let me tell you, it's far better to get out there in the field sooner rather than later. You'll have a greater advantage when the job market picks up than someone who just came out of school and doesn't have any hands-on experience.

When I'm hiring people, I first look for people who have previous experience in the music business as promoters for music-management companies like Live Nation or AEG. Degrees are great, but even more important is the hands-on office knowledge that you can only get from working in the industry. Whether you want to be in the travel business, own a restaurant, or you have a great idea to sell cars—anything you have an idea to do—you should do whatever it takes to get a position in that industry, even if you're doing it for free.

I certainly did my time working for peanuts, just to get that experience and learn how the movie industry ran. When I was nineteen, I worked for a booker in the Catskill Mountains. I sold his shows for him, and at the end of the summer, he gave me a thousand dollars for all my efforts. I was supposed to get $10,000. So I went to see the booker's attorney to try to settle the payment. The attorney said, "What does it cost to go to college?" "Ten thousand dollars," I replied. "Well, then, you got a college education," he said. And he was right. That experience taught me more about the way the business was run—and the kind of people to watch out for—than any college course could have.

Something else I received during my time working that I can forever be grateful for was hands-on experience. I knew that to break into any business, and specifically the movie business at that time, I needed hands-on experience. When I produced the American Gladiators tour, I saw the perfect chance to get that experience. For my tour, I licensed the American Gladiators name from Sam Goldwyn Films. That is when I had my chance to meet Sam Goldwyn Jr. and the president of the company, Meyer Gottlieb. I knew this could be my big break to get into the movie business; I had the passion, I just needed that hands-on experience.

I finally went up to Sam and Meyer and said, "I would really do anything to work on a movie set. Is there any way you can help me out?" Sam agreed, and a few days later he came to me and told me I could go work on the set of a movie he was shooting with Matt Dillon in New York.

Well, the job mostly involved getting coffee and running errands for the director. But being on an actual movie set, and seeing how it worked, was invaluable. Why? Because all it took was one day to see that this was not actually what I wanted to do. It made me realize that where I really wanted to be was on the business side of things. But without actually being on that set, I never would have learned that about myself. Putting in the time, even in the nitty-gritty, also allows you to develop an expertise that sets you apart from the rest. This is the thesis of Malcolm Gladwell in his book *Outliers*. Outliers of society are those who stand apart from the rest because of their experiences. The Beatles primarily became the Beatles because of the thousands of hours that they were able to put into honing their trade.

Even to this day, I like to know about every aspect of the tours I produce. The daily agenda consists of my waking in the tour bus, going to the local radio station, then the local TV station, taking a nap, and then heading to the venue to set up the merchandise booths. It's always important to keep an open mind as you set up each tour, show, or whatever it may be. If you are willing to take on all kinds of roles, not just the role of manager or tour director, you will gain the confidence and experience you need in any position from there on out.

I experimented with taking on other roles. During the Mortal Kombat tour, I donned the uniform of the evil Shang Tsung every night of every performance. The lines were pre-recorded, and I sat on the throne, reigning over the audience, as they watched martial artists perform in front of me. I did this six days a week for six weeks to learn how the stage show worked from the inside. Because I took on the role of the evil Shang Tsung, I became the actor, the tour manager, and the person in charge of all press and merchandising—it just goes to show, the more knowledge you can gain about your industry, the better off you will be. The current TV show *Undercover Boss* operates on the same premise, sending CEOs to work in their own franchises. As described in James B. Stewart's book *DisneyWar*, former Disney CEO Michael Eisner required all high-level Disney executives have to spend a few hours in Disney costumes walking around the theme park. To truly understand Disney, you have to experience interacting with kids from the vantage point of Mickey Mouse.

I am far from the only person who has found success by starting at the bottom and working his way up. Producer extraordinaire David Geffen started in the mail room at the William Morris agency, worked his way up through the ranks, and look where he is today—an ultra-successful record executive, film and theater producer, and noted philanthropist.

When I got into the entertainment and sports businesses, you could go right to an athlete or a music star or a

Goofing around on the set of *Mortal Kombat*, a movie based on the popular video game.

rock band. But it's not like that today. Ever since salaries started becoming well-publicized and people could see how much money there is to be made in the entertainment business, as well as in sports, it's harder to break in. You have to put in your hours at the bottom and learn the basics if you're going to get anywhere. It doesn't matter where you went to school or what kind of degree you have; you have to learn an industry from the inside before you can be successful in it. Even some lawyers from Harvard are becoming interns and working in the mail rooms at talent agencies in the hopes of working their way up.

This insider knowledge is also vital for the process of negotiation, another essential step to bring your idea to life. My first book, *Putting It on the Line*, is about negotiations, and I will tell you that information is a big key to winning almost anything. The one with the most knowledge will usually win. But we'll discuss this in more detail in chapter 12.

Having an internship or a low-level job can also be the best way to get a foot in the door in terms of contacts. Joan Rivers started as a receptionist, working for a booking agency in the Catskills run by Leonard and Lisa Jacobsen. I met the Jacobsens when I worked in the Catskills, and they told me that Joan had said to them, "While I'm working here, I'm going to fill my phone book with all the lead contacts. And if by the time my phone book is full I haven't made it, I'm going to quit show business." But, Lisa told me, Joan always wrote the last four names in pencil. That way, she could erase them and not have to keep her promise to herself of quitting the business. Of course, it paid off. She was able to make contacts and meet people in her industry and launch her show business career.

Contacts within the industry are vital to bringing your idea to life. We've already discussed the importance of using industry leaders as a sounding board to test your idea. An internship or low-level position can be the perfect way to establish contact with those leaders, to whom you can then show your ideas.

If You Build It . . .

What, exactly, are you going to show these industry leaders? The absolute best thing you can do is create a prototype. We discussed drawing up your idea in chapter 2, but now I want to talk about taking it even further. I mean building a full-out prototype of your idea. Whether it's building the actual product, recording a song, shooting a TV pilot, or creating a Web site—you have to actually build it out.

A lot of people don't take this step because they don't know that they should. But a lot of people don't take it because they're afraid of spending the money it takes to create a prototype. And yes, it's scary spending money. But we've learned how to face our fears and take those big risks, and this is a risk that you have to take. You have to spend money to make money.

Now, you don't need to spend a lot of money. You can spend a hundred dollars, or you can spend $50,000. But you have to spend it. You have to rent the studio and record that song. You have to design and build that clothing line. You have to program that Web site. You have to build your prototype.

I spent $50,000 on a TV pilot for my Rock 'n' Roll Fantasy Camp. It was a lot of money, but in my mind, I knew that if I didn't spend the money on the pilot, I wouldn't be able to sell my show. No matter how great my pitch, people wouldn't have the imagination to picture exactly what I wanted my TV show to be. I had to show it to them.

Not only would the pilot explain to them exactly what I was looking to do, but it would put me head and shoulders above everyone else. In Hollywood, everyone pitches. Major media companies have pitch days, where they spend all day listening to people pitch ideas—"I want to do a movie like this." "I want to do a TV show like this." But if a person actually shows them a fully produced fifteen-minute pilot, they've got something different. More than half of TV shows that are sold have a pilot already made—and the sales are made based on that video presentation. I went ahead and invested the money, time, and effort into making a pilot.

If you just verbally pitch your idea, people will look at you and say, "Okay, it's a great idea, but there's no meat to it. You haven't actually put anything into it." But if you walk in with an actual line of clothes, or a real Web site, or a tangible and well-thought-out game plan, you're showing that you're really serious about your product. You're showing that you won't just be pitching this idea today and that idea tomorrow. The more effort you put into your idea, the more you will benefit in the end.

No matter what the project, I find a way to create a prototype. When I created the Quarterback Club for the NFL, I decided I wanted to pick these quarterbacks and create a line of clothing. I went out and had clothing tags made and created sample ads for the newspaper. I also had my friend Nick Summers do radio spots for me with his deep, radio-appropriate voice, which you often hear on a variety of stations. (I actually love his voice so much that I had him create a radio spot for the invitation to my son's bar mitzvah. Imagine getting a cassette back then with a deep radio voice, "You're cordially invited . . .") I'd tell Nick about the product, and he would

ROCK OUT IN THE REAL WORLD

Case Study: Investing from an Investor's Point of View

Barry Rosenbaum is a venture capitalist and technology investor in California. He is the managing director of Blue Note Capital LLC, a family of venture capital funds focused on early-stage and expansion-stage privately held information technology companies. In the interview below, Barry provides valuable insights for entrepreneurs from a venture capitalist's point of view.

Q: What makes a good business idea great?
Barry: Execution. Ideas are cheap and plentiful. There is no such thing as a great idea that makes itself great. There are good ideas and bad ideas, of course, but the difference between a good idea and a great idea is work: hard work, efficient work, intelligent work. As an investor, I invest in people that I know are smart, but more importantly, that I believe will apply the single-minded drive, purpose, and effort to make a good idea into a great idea. Most great ideas are only great in retrospect. Look at Apple. No one believed that the iPod, the iPhone, or the iPad, or especially the Apple retail stores, were

Continues

create a commercial. It wouldn't play on-air anywhere, but when I brought it to a presentation, people's eyes would light up. I signed sponsorships with VO5 thanks to radio spots I created. I signed Ringo by playing him a radio spot. I scored a major sponsorship with 7-Eleven and Coke with a radio and TV presentation. Don't wait to have a customer to create your prototype—it's the prototype that will bring the customer to you.

Don't wait to have a customer to create your prototype—it's the prototype that will bring the customer to you.

Today, creating a prototype is remarkably easy and affordable. You'd be surprised at how cheap it can be to build a prototype—there are so many companies across the world that can build you whatever you need, whether it's clothing or a kitchen product or a Web site design. You just need to be willing to spend that dollar to get it done. It's often not that difficult, either. You can easily find someone to do a radio spot for you for a couple hundred dollars. When you bring your prototype, whatever it is, into a presentation, you'll be amazed at the response you'll get from the other side.

How do you know which of your contacts to bring your idea to, which of them might be interested in investing in your idea? That's where the next step of research comes in: investigating who might be interested in providing promotion and sponsorship for your idea. Who is your idea a good fit for, and who's a good fit for your idea?

A guy came to me once with a prototype for a cup he'd created. The cup and lid were for a coffee cup that was unspillable. You could

Continued

great ideas. It was the brilliance of their execution that made them huge success stories and, in retrospect, great ideas.

Q: *How do you gauge whether or not there is a need for a particular product?*

Barry: You have to talk to a lot of people. It's usually easy to find "professionals" who will concoct market data, and that may help in raising money for your idea, but the best way to find out what the market will buy, and how much of it, is to talk to a lot of people.

Q: *What are the most important first steps a new entrepreneur should take?*

Barry: First, he should determine if he or she has the internal makeup to be an entrepreneur. It takes a special kind of person, one with a mix of aggressiveness and patience, single-mindedness and openness to new ideas, belief in oneself, and the ability to relate to others.

Second, assuming he has already come up with a good idea, he should talk with people he trusts and respects to determine the best way to pursue the idea. During this phase he will most likely be given far more discouraging than encouraging comments, but he will also learn what the obstacles to success are

Continues

likely to be and can then develop strategies to overcome them.

Third, he should get a partner. Very few successful entrepreneurs are one-man shows. Most have partnered with one or more similarly minded but complementary individuals. If the entrepreneur is a techie, he should find a person or people with marketing experience. If he's a sales guy, he might want to pair up with an operations guy. As important as this step is, it's equally important to be sure you know what you're getting into with the partner. Exchange information honestly, have lengthy conversations, and be sure you can work together.

Fourth, figure out the business. Some start-ups can get to success based on building an enormous community by giving something away for free. Most successful companies have a very good idea of what their product or service will cost and are convinced that they can collect enough money to cover that cost and provide a profit. Most investors aren't interested unless they believe that equation.

Finally, keep your hiring standards astronomical. In my experience, A's hire A's and B's hire C's. The first few handfuls of people that you bring onto the team need to all be superstars. After that you can

Continues

knock it over, turn it on its side, and it wouldn't spill. He explained to me that he'd been researching and discovered that the biggest lawsuits Starbucks, McDonald's, and Dunkin' Donuts have faced have all been over spilled coffee. More people sue these companies due to burning themselves with spilled coffee than any other grievance. So he thought, "These other cups, they spill. What would happen if I brought these companies a cup that was impossible to spill, even if it was turned over?" He created a prototype for this cup.

I gave the cup to Bruce Springsteen's tour manager, Wayne Lebaux, to take it to his contacts at Dunkin' Donuts. Unfortunately, we found that they were completely locked into a contract with their current cup supplier. They were very interested; they just couldn't make the change. But I told the guy not to let this stop him. After all, there's more than just Dunkin' Donuts. He could reach out to every store that sells a cup of coffee in the morning. There was definitely a market for his product. I was incredibly busy, so I was unable to stick with the guy to push his idea through to the end, but I told him that he just needed to keep on calling and keep showing his prototype.

The last I heard from him, he was able to sell all his products to mom-and-pop shops across the country. Instead of trying to create some huge franchise out of his cup, which hadn't been working so far, he made it a product that could be carried in smaller stores. This is another way to get your products out there. Just because you can't sign a contract with a huge franchiser doesn't mean your idea should be laid down to rest. Find other markets you can infiltrate and other audiences to reach out to. In this person's case, it was selling to smaller shops.

Continued

scale back to just plain stars. By the time you get to hiring people that are merely above average, it's time to go start another company.

Q: What makes investors want to invest in an unknown product? What makes for a good "pitch"?

Barry: Most good investors are focused primarily on the people they're investing in. Most business plans, no matter how great the idea or market research, evolve rapidly in the early days, and many end up being very different from what was originally envisioned. Investors want to know that the people they invest in are able to manage change in response to new information and to succeed in execution at the same time. Most investors will want to do research on the idea and the market, but they shouldn't be able to find out anything you don't know, and if they reject your idea because they don't believe the market is there, you either haven't done enough research or haven't presented it properly. The best "pitch" is one that's sincere and honest, that's been prepared and well thought through, and which focuses the potential investor's attention very quickly on the benefits of the idea and the entrepreneur's ability to make it happen.

Continues

Continued

One additional piece of advice: If you take money from people you don't respect, you will definitely live to regret it. If your idea and your skills are worth investing in, then you should be able to find an investor who can truly help you.

Making a phone call is one of the easiest things you can do. Do your research and figure out a problem for which your idea is a solution. If your idea is a solution to someone's problem, they're going to take your phone call. I'm not saying you're going to sell it right away, but people will definitely listen to you. If you can show the company that you have done your research on the company and you can give them your predictions of where the company could go and what they could do, then they will listen. You will have that power over them—you have an idea, and by showing you are serious about the company, they will want to listen to your idea.

A Pound of Prevention . . .

When you have all your information and you've created your prototype, you're in a great position to present it to potential buyers. But I'll remind you to take the same precautions that I've mentioned before and ensure that nobody steals your idea; protect your ideas, tell only your most trusted friends, and always sign non-disclosure agreements when talking with major companies, agents, etc. I had a friend who created the musical CDs Kids Pops come to me the other day. The idea is a CD/DVD with young children singing today's hit songs. He told me that he got a call from a major company that was interested in buying his company. He showed them his product and numbers and how he does it. The next thing he knew, six months later the company came out with an almost identical record. He was never made an offer. Luckily for him, the company bombed, but the bottom line is that you always have to be careful.

Another thing to be careful of is cannibalizing the industry. What do I mean by that? I mean creating an idea that ends up destroying the very industry it was intended to benefit. Research can help prevent this.

There have been two great cannibalizations in the recent music industry. The first was the downfall of the amphitheaters. It started with concert promoters. When promoters were selling arena concerts, unless the shows sold 100 percent, the promoter would hardly see any of the money. The promoter would rent the arena, which would sell beer, popcorn, soda, and parking, and the venues would make a profit—none of which came to the promoters. The advertisers got paid as did all the security and production people. The acts, meanwhile, were only letting the promoters take 5 percent of the profit from the show. So unless the promoters sold out the show, they would barely see any money at all.

Eventually, these promoters started thinking: "Why are we making all this money for these acts, why are we making all this money for these venues, but making none for ourselves?" And they had an idea: "Let's build our own buildings! This way we'll own the three Ps—popcorn, pop, and parking." They decided to build their own amphitheaters. This started the mass creation of the amphitheaters, and all these amphitheaters started popping up all over the country. But what they didn't consider was the fact that, because amphitheaters are outdoors, you can really only do shows in June, July, and August in the majority of the country. The rest of the year it's too cold.

This pushed the majority of the rock tours to the summer, and promoters only had three months in which to book all their shows. They would go and offer all these acts all this money to play their amphitheaters in these three months so they could sell the three Ps. But in order to break even, they had to do at least sixty shows—and how many people have the money to see sixty shows in one summer?

One summer I got phone calls from these promoters, saying, "David, we only sold 4,000 seats for Ringo. Do you mind if we paper the house and give away 10,000 seats?" The next day the manager of KISS got the exact same phone call. Now, as a producer, I told them, "Sure, give away all the seats" because the last thing I wanted was for my act to be playing a 15,000- to 20,000-seat amphitheater with only 4,000 people in it. Now that year, the promoters loved giving away seats, because all those people who got the free tickets wouldn't mind paying for the three Ps, and the promoters made their money from the venue. But then something unfortunate happened.

People sitting next to one another at the concert started asking, "How did you get your ticket?" The people who got them for free wanted to brag—"Oh, I got my ticket for free; my brother just went down to the fire department or the local police department or the local union." And the other guy would say, "Oh, I paid fifty or seventy-five dollars for these seats." The next year, when the same bands went on tour, nobody bought tickets, because they were all waiting to get their tickets for free. And that completely killed the amphitheaters, and the promoters were forced to sell.

This led directly to the purchase of all these venues and promoters in major cities by Bob Sillerman, for his company, SFX Entertainment. Sillerman was trying to buy up as many sports agencies, promoters, ticket agencies, and venues as he possibly could, and roll them up into SFX. This roll-up cost him three-quarters of a billion dollars. Then he turned around and sold it to Clear Channel Radio for 4.3 billion dollars, convincing them that they could own every concert in the country. Clear Channel sued Sillerman because they felt they were ripped off and won back 200 million dollars, but they had still lost a minimum of 3 billion dollars. They had to give up 10 percent of their signage business, making billboards and the like, and with the money raised they created their spin-off, Live Nation.

But the whole transaction killed the music touring industry, because it killed the creativity. A great promoter is not one who just sells the tickets—a good hustler; a great promoter is a well of creativity and ideas. A great promoter is someone who can package bands together—like I did—and pay them x amount of dollars each, and then sell them for a profit. In today's music industry, you see all these festivals popping up, Coachella or Bonnaroo for example, which do exactly that—take a ton of well-known and loved bands and put them in one show together. If you can spend three times and make ten times, that's a creative idea. But that creativity, which is the heart and soul of the rock and roll business was lost the minute Sillerman bought out all these promoters. The promoters were forced in the local markets to focus on the "A" tour, like the Billy Joel, Stones, McCartney, and U2 tours, and they let the new acts slip along with the idea of promoting a young band so that when they became big you would see a payoff.

Likewise, there was a great cannibalization of the music recording industry, and that was free music sharing. With the advent of sites like Napster, everyone could get music for free, and fewer people were buying CDs. Record stores closed around the country. The record industry was totally unprepared, because they didn't believe that these ideas were actually going to come to pass. Once they started finally listening to the techies who were telling them about these ideas, it was too late. That's why the record business is only two major companies now. Companies like Disney Records, even with acts like the Jonas Brothers and Miley Cyrus, who sell some CDs, have had to downsize considerably. And it's all because of one idea. If the record industry had been able to catch onto that idea in time, instead of ignoring it, maybe things would have been different. All these changes in the recording industry happened because young techies took over the music business and pursued their ideas while the record companies fell asleep and were fearful of change.

The big music moguls may be afraid of change, but you can overcome that if you are able to embrace the evolution that your idea will go through. The ability to follow what the market is doing and change accordingly is all part of the research you have to do when developing your idea. Creating your prototype will also help you see what changes you might have to make to your original idea—because you will have to make changes as your idea evolves, and that's something we'll discuss in the next chapter.

Creating a prototype has another incredibly important purpose: It will motivate you. That may be the most vital reason you should create a prototype. When you actually see your idea manifested, you will be amazed by how excited you get. When you put that idea on your desk every day, it will drive you to bring it to its full potential. Your prototype isn't just a selling tool to others—it's a selling tool to yourself.

Spend some money and build your prototype. Do all the research; learn all you need to know about your field. Take the time to get your idea exactly the way you want it. For myself, I find that when I formulate my ideas and get them into perfect shape, then I'm ready to roll. Once you're ready to roll, it's time to take the next step: drawing up a business plan.

Chapter Three's Greatest Hits

- Research is the key to bringing your ideas out into the real world.
- Get experience in the field of your interest.
- Insider knowledge is vital for the process of negotiation.
- Starting with an internship or low-level job is a great way to start making contacts.
- You have to spend some money to make money.
- You can't just verbally pitch your idea. Create a prototype!
- Be careful not to cannibalize your industry (destroy the industry you're trying to benefit).

4

Ticket to Ride:
THE BIG SECRET OF A
MINI–BUSINESS PLAN

You've got your great idea, you've got your hands-on experience in the industry and your resulting list of contacts, and you've got your prototype. You're set, right? You're ready to take the world by storm! But wait. Stop and think for a minute about why it is that some people who have created an amazing product can end up with no money, while others go on to make millions with their ideas. What's the missing piece? You need a business plan.

"Why?" you may ask. "I've got this amazing idea. I've done the research and made a prototype. Why do I need an actual business plan—isn't the idea itself enough?" Well, I hate to break it to you, but just having an idea and a prototype is usually not good enough. Your prototype can get people to take you seriously, but it probably won't get you the funding you need to get your idea going. You have to write up a plan for your idea. It helps you focus on who your customer is, what your goals are, and how you will be profitable.

You Gotta Have a Plan

A lot of people say to me, because of the successes I've had, that I'm lucky. But let me tell you a cautionary tale about what happened to me once when I didn't write myself up a business plan. In the late '90s, I came up with the idea for the British Rock Symphony—highly symphonic rock and roll, featuring songs by the Beatles, the Stones, Led Zeppelin, Pink Floyd, and The Who, performed by artists like Alice Cooper, Roger Daltrey, Paul Rodgers, Nancy Wilson, and Gary Brooker. It was a fantastic idea, and the music was absolutely brilliant. But the project failed because I had no game plan. I never took the time to think it through, lay it out, or get it in writing. I tried to just wing it, and it ended in failure.

I knew I wanted to do a tour, a record, and a PBS television special. If I had written out a business plan, I would have thought it through and done a record first, or a television show, then a concert tour. Instead, I started with the concert tour, and that's where all the trouble began.

I thought I had a corporate sponsor for the tour who was going to fund me. Little did I know I was being completely lied to. If I had made a business plan that was completely thought through, I would never have moved ahead until I had the agreement in writing, until I was sure I had the financing. But as I was just winging it, and while I was still waiting for the sponsor to come through, I went ahead and put tickets on sale. I should never have done that because I was totally underfinanced. I finished the *British Rock Symphony* record. Then I toured the show some more, and then I shot a video of it for TV and DVD. But the disaster of the first tour completely killed the project.

Based on the success of the record, I would have sold the tour. But I hadn't thought through the timing when I first had the idea. I didn't have a game plan, and the program never reached the height it should have, where it could be today. This experience proved to me how important it is to follow a game plan, not just go on a whim. I always find that people who are more prepared—who have specific goals and write them down—are more successful. Stephen Covey, in *7 Habits of Highly Effective People*, stresses "beginning with the end in mind." That's exactly what a business plan is. It's taking a snapshot of how your project is going to look in one year, two years, and even ten years from now.

Having a business plan will not only help you have a successful project, it will help you to strategize wisely to get the most out of your project. Billy Joel's agent, and my friend, Dennis Arfa, who also represents artists like Linkin Park, Metallica, and Rod Stewart, has developed the perfect game plan for Billy's tours. Even though Dennis could book five shows for Billy at the Civic Arena in Pittsburgh, he purposefully books only one. The show sells out instantly, and tons of people can't get tickets. So he plays the market, and a week following the concert, Dennis puts up ten more shows for sale—and immediately sells out all ten.

If Dennis hadn't really thought things through, he would have gone ahead and booked those five shows, which would have sold out. But because he had a game plan, because he worked it through to the end, he was able to sell out eleven concerts instead of just five. Dennis figured out his endgame and focused on that, rather than the right now, and made an even greater success out of his concerts. His business plan was not only to strategize on how to gain the most fans and following, but also how to gain the biggest numbers in the end.

Figuring out your endgame is one of the most important parts of creating your business plan. Not only will your endgame lead your project to greater success, but it is the number-one thing that investors will want to know about.

Figuring out your endgame is one of the most important parts of creating your business plan.

Show Me the Money

There is no question that you will need money to launch your idea. To get that money, you'll likely need investors. To get investors, you need a solid business plan. It's one of the best sales tools you have. First of all, having something in writing shows that you have done your research and put careful thought and planning into your project. Second, it will answer the questions investors will have about your product. If people are going to give you money, they will want to know exactly what you are going to do with their money. I found that when I was raising money, people were most concerned with when (how quickly) they were going to get their money back and what the plan was. People want details. The good news here is that the banks aren't giving interest on bank deposits. The stock market is erratic and volatile, which is leading people to invest in more ideas with the hope that they will get greater returns.

The most frequent questions I'm asked when I'm fundraising are, "Where do you want to go? What's the endgame?" If investors are going to invest their money with you, they want to know what you're going to do with it. They want to give their money to smart, creative businesspeople. Every one of my investors has asked me, "What's your endgame? Where do you see things going with the company? Do you see selling it in two years or five years, or are you planning on holding on to it for a while?" They want to know what companies you'd like to be associated with—who would potentially be a good fit to buy your company? Disney? American Express? If you can answer these questions in a way that shows you've done your due diligence, you'll be able to get investors on board.

In the case of RRFC, the idea stemmed from my passion and love for rock and roll and from my vision to create a different aspect of the music business than I had witnessed in all my years on tour. At the camp, I have met many great fans, and seeing how the rock stars connect with their fans is what keeps me motivated in this business. I truly feel that RRFC through the fan's point of view is the purest essence of the rock and roll business. It inspires me to continue to produce a great event that will hopefully change people's lives. My passion about all of this early on fueled my idea that this is an amazing concept and that it would be sellable to a major company in the future, like the Hard Rock brand was sold for billions of dollars. When you are raising money for a business, it is important to make sure that it is something that you love and have a passion for. The goal should be to make something amazing and to market it so it is sellable.

The Nitty-Gritty

I've established how important a business plan is, both for you and for your investors. But now you're probably wondering, what exactly goes into the written document? What are the questions that need to be answered?

Along with your endgame and details on how you're going to use investors' money, you have to discuss details such as who your market is, who you want to market to, what the cost of manufacturing the product or putting up the show is, and who your competition is.

What I'd like to do here is show you parts of one of my actual business plans for a project I'm working on as I write this book, and we'll walk through it together.

BUSINESS PLAN FOR
ROCK 'N' ROLL FANTASY CAMP
RRFC Overview

In its fifteenth year of existence, RRFC Enterprises, Inc. ("RRFC Enterprises" or the "Company") is a profitable and growing, unique live entertainment and media company that was organized as the parent company of Rock 'n' Roll Fantasy Camp ("RRFC" or the "Camp"). The RRFC Enterprises mission is to deliver a powerful, unique interactive music experience where real people play and bond with rock and roll legends and change people's lives in the process.

The company achieves its mission through its two operating divisions: the Live Division and the Content Division. The Live Division currently offers three-, four-, and five-day camps ("full camp"), a one-day "touring camp," and a one-day or two-day corporate camp program for off-sites, corporate development, corporate parties, sales incentives/bonuses, and customer appreciation ("corporate camp"). The camps are the company's high-end, flagship products. Campers of all types get an opportunity to become rock stars during camp by jamming in a rock and roll music environment while playing with famous rock legends. Camp counselors are rock stars who train the campers. Rock stars who participate in RRFC have achieved success in the music industry through hit records, worldwide tours, and hit television series. The camps include guest appearances by rock legends and industry leaders. Each full camp culminates in a recording session and live performance with rock legends in a major concert venue. More than two hundred rock legends have participated in RRFC, including:

Continued

- Dickey Betts of The Allman Brothers Band
- Jack Bruce of Cream
- Roger Daltrey of The Who
- Sammy Hagar of Van Halen
- Warren Haynes of The Allman Brothers Band
- Tommy Lee of Mötley Crüe
- Meatloaf
- Bret Michaels of Poison
- Slash of Guns N' Roses and Velvet Revolver
- Paul Stanley of KISS
- Joe Walsh of the Eagles
- Brian Wilson of The Beach Boys
- Bill Wyman of the Rolling Stones
- Zakk Wylde of Black Label Society

The Content Division includes TV series and specials, online community sites and forums, film, merchandise, digital revenue, training and educational materials, DVDs, CDs, photos, and memorabilia. Among the highlights of this division is *Rock 'n' Roll Fantasy Camp* TV reality series. The hit reality TV series that focuses on the Rock 'n' Roll Fantasy Camp experience debuted on VH1 Classic (reaching 50 million households) in October 2010, and season 2, featuring Sammy Hagar and Paul Stanley, aired in September 2011. *Rock 'n' Roll Fantasy Camp* season 1 was the highest rated original series in VH1 Classic history. The series is produced by the Emmy award–winning television producer Mark Burnett (*Survivor*, *The Celebrity*

Continues

Continued

Apprentice, The Contender, The Voice, Shark Tank, etc.). Season 1 featured Poison's Bret Michaels and other rock stars, including Michael Anthony and Ace Frehley. The show's format places fifteen people in three bands to compete for the best band of the week.

RRFC Origins

RRFC was first introduced in 1997 by David Fishof, an internationally recognized entertainment producer who, among other notable achievements, was responsible for reuniting The Monkees and introducing them to a new generation of MTV fans with a global tour in 1986. Fishof also conceived, created, and produced Ringo Starr's All-Starr Band tours, Dirty Dancing Live Tour, American Gladiator Live Arena Tour, and Dick Clark's American Bandstand Tour, and was a sports agent representing major athletes from the NFL and MLB. Fishof developed RRFC while he was on tour with Ringo Starr and His All-Starr Band and wanted to share this opportunity with other rock music aficionados.

RRFC has received significant media coverage, including multiple features on all three U.S. broadcast network morning shows. The impact of media coverage, reaching millions of people within RRFC's target demographic, has been a large source of business opportunities and marketing alliances, and has helped RRFC establish its brand in the marketplace. RRFC intends to promote its brand promise in all marketing messages: entertainment, education, interactivity, and inspiration.

Continues

Continued

RRFC Growth Strategy—Establishment of Flagship Permanent Location

RRFC has attracted participants from all around the United States, Canada, and the world. In addition to the U.S. market, the series currently airs in Canada and will expand globally to Japan, Germany, Italy, and other countries. As the TV show continues to air in new markets, a permanent Rock 'n' Roll Fantasy Camp, to be located in Las Vegas, can expect to become a worldwide destination.

The draw of RRFC in Las Vegas is the actual fantasy camp where ordinary people learn, jam, record, and perform with rock stars. Having a permanent location for the camp will build on the successful RRFC model launched by David Fishof in 1997. RRFC's proposed flagship property will be located in Las Vegas at a major hotel and casino and become a staple activity in Las Vegas, much like seeing a Cirque du Soleil show or attending CSI: The Experience.

A central driver of RRFC's growth strategy will be a focus on operating one Fantasy Camp per month at the new flagship property. The Las Vegas–based permanent location will increase operating margins by greatly reducing key costs such as catering, hotel accommodations, and venue rental. Additionally, by managing its own facilities RRFC will achieve higher profitability through increased revenues from the expansion of its core business as well as capturing new business opportunities.

Continues

Continued

Based on the success of the RRFC Las Vegas location, we will look to create other permanent RRFC locations in major cities around the world. These permanent locations will make RRFC more accessible to a greater population and provide a facility in which RRFC can host camps, nightly jams, corporate events, and more on a regular basis. RRFC's expansion strategy consists of a plan to open one additional permanent location per year for the next five years across the world (with the targeted cities including New York, Chicago, London, Tokyo, and Orlando).

RRFC Growth Strategy—Sales & Marketing

RRFC currently engages the top public relations companies in the industry and this has garnered extensive coverage for RRFC to date. RRFC regularly invites media to attend and experience the Camp. As a result, many journalists from TV, radio, and print have generated feature stories on the rock stars and individuals who attend camp. RRFC continually receives coverage from major U.S. and international outlets such as:

- BBC-TV
- *Bones*
- *CBS Morning Show*
- CNN
- *Ellen's Comedy Series*
- *Good Morning America*
- *The New York Times*
- *Nightline*
- *Rolling Stone* magazine

Continues

Continued

- *Saturday Night Live*
- *The Simpsons* (Homer goes to RRFC with Mick Jagger and Keith Richards)
- *Sunday Times of London* magazine
- TLC 2-hour RRFC Documentary
- VH1 Classic: RRFC TV Special
- VH1 and VH1 Classic
- *The Wall Street Journal*

RRFC will use the monies raised to complement its proven PR strategy with the addition of critical sales and marketing resources. To continue to drive both brand and revenue growth, RRFC will engage a seasoned marketing/advertising agency and expand its internal sales team.

RRFC Growth Strategy—Core Business Growth

Fantasy Camp Business—Las Vegas Flagship Permanent Location

RRFC's permanent location will be suited to house camps, nightly jams, and corporate events. The property will provide an ideal setting for RRFC's core Camp business due to Las Vegas's reputation as a destination city for individuals and groups of all sorts.

Corporate Fantasy Camp Business—Las Vegas & Traveling

Corporate Program: RRFC provides entertainment for companies and is an excellent team-building program, bringing together employees, VIPs, and clients. The flagship location is ideal for RRFC's Corporate Program to tie in with companies attending Las

Continues

Continued

Vegas conventions. The Corporate Camp business is expected to be a major source of sales growth over the next five years.

RRFC Growth Strategy—New Business Development

The permanent location will allow RRFC to generate significant new revenue through the growth of accessible new lines of business.

RRFC will open the brand to a larger customer base:

- Customers with limited funds
- Customers with limited time
- Customers who are unable to travel
- Experienced youth who need supplemental programming after school

RRFC Nightly Jams

RRFC Nightly Jams will be held on a regular nightly basis. Jam sessions will last approximately two hours. RRFC Nightly Jams give music enthusiasts a chance to hone their skills, gain a mentor, and play with rock stars in a relaxed, loosely structured environment.

Rock Stars at Fantasy Camp

RRFC is the ultimate music experience for adults. It works because our counselors and mentors believe in the program.

Roger Daltrey

- "I feel quite passionate about anything that encourages people in music. Just to see people with enthusiasm, having fun even though they all have different abilities . . . it's fantastic!" Roger Daltrey—The Who

Continues

Continued

- "Rock 'n' Roll Fantasy Camp is about wanting to do something and not caring if you get it wrong. . . . Singing like you do when nobody's looking!"
  Steven Tyler—Aerosmith

Paul Stanley

- "It's a great thing. It's a way for me to say thank you to a lot of people, but, nobody should think that this is just a joy for those people, and that they're getting the thrill. For me to get up and play with people who have that exuberance and energy, it's really a gift to me as much as to anybody else."
  Paul Stanley—KISS

RRFC is also a life-changing experience for most camp attendees.

- RRFC attendee Alan D. said, "Was the Camp worth it? To say 'ABSOLUTELY' would be an understatement. It was the best investment I have ever made."

- After attending RRFC, Bob Fishman, a guitarist who works for CBS Sports, commented, "You have changed my life in a way I could not have imagined."

- Scott Hamilton, former Olympic medal winner and camp drummer, said after attending RRFC, "You have created something amazing! Changing people's lives for the better is something we would all like to do. You have done it in a unique and bigger-than-life way."

The first thing investors want in a business plan is an executive summary. They want to know what the concept is. They want to know the origins—who introduced the concept, as well as some background on you yourself. This executive summary should include a description of the product, what you're looking for, and where you're looking to go.

Also included in this executive summary should be your mission statement. This is an incredibly important part of a business plan—the mission statement for your project/business/company. The official mission statement for Rock 'n' Roll Fantasy Camp is this:

> To deliver an intense, exceptional, and interactive musical experience, bonding with rock and roll legends and changing people's lives in the process; and to capture and deliver this experience in our Content Division, offering entertainment, interactivity, education, and inspiration in our products.

The following mission statement has been abbreviated from a more comprehensive version:

> Music has the power to uplift, heal, and transform. The Camp taps into the power of music in unprecedented ways by bringing together lovers of music from all walks of life and placing them under the tutelage of counselors who are masters of music for the purpose of creating music. Then something magical happens. The music becomes the bond in a transformative discovery of self in the context of a group. People learn to create under the guidance of creative masters. Campers build bridges between one another as they perfect the art of communicating in the world's oldest language: music. The Camp is more than jamming, recording, and playing live with the rock stars; it's an experience that will change your life forever.

One thing you'll notice about this business plan that I want to emphasize is how short it is. For confidentiality reasons, I had to delete some aspects of my business plan, but even full length, it's relatively short. If you look at sample business plans, so many of them are forty, fifty, maybe even a hundred pages long. Writing forty to fifty pages can be incredibly daunting, and I think that scares a lot of people away from creating their business plan.

I know from experience that most people don't have the time to sit and read a forty- to fifty-page business plan. Keep your plan short and to the point. Outline your goals and revenues—specify what you're going to do with the money. And you don't need forty pages to do that. Your business plan shouldn't be redundant. It should be all facts and straight to the point.

Keep your plan short and to the point. . . . Your business plan shouldn't be redundant. It should be all facts and straight to the point.

People who are investing money get hundreds of business plans. If you have a great idea, less is more. If you have a hundred-page business plan, it will be so full of formalities that the idea itself will get buried. It's like filibustering. People aren't stupid today. They can recognize a good idea. If you find yourself writing and writing and writing, trying to convince an investor that your idea is going to work . . . if you've got to spend forty to fifty pages on it . . . it's probably time to rework your idea. After all, as Shakespeare said, "Brevity is the soul of wit!"

So how long exactly should your business plan be? It of course depends on what your project is. If I created a computer program completely unlike any other computer program, my business plan could be pretty short—if there's nothing else like it on the market, it would be pretty easy to sell. But if I'm creating a new soda, like my friend, John Bello, who developed the beverage SoBe, you'll need a much longer business plan. He had to show investors why people would want to drink SoBe over Snapple or Coca-Cola or any of the other hundreds of beverage brands already on the market. Eventually he sold SoBe to Pepsi for $370 million.

If you need some help getting focused on your business plan, I would encourage you to do some strategic planning. A thorough strategic plan will allow you to hammer out all the pieces of your business plan in a direct and focused way. A great book to start with in terms of sound strategic planning is *Deep Dive* by Rich Horwath. There are many creative tools in his book that you can use to stimulate your mind when developing a business plan.

This brings me to another incredibly important point: Always include the negatives in your business plan. Don't leave anything out. You have to show who your competition is, who else is out there. In all my original business plans, when I was first shopping around Rock 'n' Roll Fantasy Camp and the various tours I've done, I put down that I had some competition, who else had tried it, and what else was out there on the market. You have to put in the information about the negative stuff, too; otherwise it will come back to bite you. Protect yourself.

Do investors expect to see some of the challenges in your business plan? Absolutely. In all the big Wall Street plans you see, they always talk about how this thing could potentially not work at all, that it's a big risk. And they explain that they also have money in the project, so they're risking something, too. Investors expect to be told the truth. If you write all positives, people aren't going to believe you. They'll think you're delusional (think Charlie Sheen). But if you write everything, you show people that you've done your full research, and they'll be more apt to give you money.

You also have to tailor your business plan for who your potential investors are. If your potential investors are friends and family, your business plan can probably be shorter and less formal. If your potential investor is a big banking company, you'll probably need something longer and more in-depth.

Putting together a business plan for a big bank or corporation can definitely be intimidating. But before you get too terrified, unless you're looking to raise millions, you can keep your plan on the shorter, simpler side. After all, projections are essentially informed guesses.

In my business, tickets can get unexpectedly hot overnight. For instance, when I did The Monkees tour in 1986, I originally projected selling 3,000 seats per venue. Then, almost overnight, I was selling out 18,000-seat venues. It can also happen in reverse: I projected my Mortal Kombat tour to sell 8,000 tickets per arena, but it ended up selling approximately 3,000 tickets per arena. I projected Ringo's All-Starr Band to sell 4,000 tickets per venue during the first tour, and he sold 8,000. As much as you put these numbers together, as much as you see these fancy business plans with all these projections, you have to be prepared for the unexpected to happen. But you have to do it because investors will want a piece of paper that states where the money is going and projected expenses.

I've discussed how important a business plan is, why you have to do it, and what goes into it. "Well, that's all great, David," you may say, "but what if I don't have any kind of business background? How am I supposed to know how to come up with a business model? Where do I start?"

First of all, don't worry—you are definitely not alone. A lot of people who come up with great ideas don't have a business background and are not business-minded at all. I've met many artists over the years who want to write songs and create music, and they don't want to think about the business side at all. Many times they end up hiring managers and agents who completely rip them off, because they don't pay attention to any of the business that's going on. Or the artist will deal with honest representation who tells him something he doesn't want to hear, and the artist ends up not listening. I always tell the artists I work with that there's a reason it's called "show business." It's a show, but it's a business, too, and they have to remember that. Artists need to be responsible for their own careers at the end of the day. Managers and agents cannot be held completely responsible for the successes and/ or failures of artists.

That goes for any field. If you're creating the newest kind of software, then you're in the software business. If you've created a new kind of soda, you're in the beverage business. The word "business" is really important and, therefore, you have to educate yourself about it. Now, there are a lot of programs and people out there that can help you. There are computer programs that will help you format a business plan and create a business model. There are people you can sit down with and firms that will help you put it all together. But you still need to educate yourself about business.

A man once asked Rabbi Hillel to teach him the entire Torah while standing on one foot. Rabbi Hillel replied, "What you don't like done to you don't do unto others. This is the entire Torah; the rest is commentary. Go and learn." Well, here is my MBA class on one foot: "You manufacture low and you sell high." You have to be able to create your item, whether it's a product or a show or a record, for as cheap as you can, and then sell it for higher, so you make a profit. There's no sense in making something for $10 and selling it for $10. You have to create an item for $8 and sell it for $10. That's business at its simplest.

But I'll also echo Rabbi Hillel on this: Go and learn. Educate yourself and find out what it takes. Don't be afraid to return to school—just a couple years ago I went back to Fordham University to take a refresher accounting class. There are also some great books out there that I found very helpful when I was raising money. But whatever your method of education, it's something you have to do—something you have to keep doing over your career, as I did at Fordham. You'll forget over the years, and you always have to stay sharp on the business side of things. The Learning Annex offers online classes on almost every subject you can imagine. Lynda.com is a great Web site that has a library of over 40,000 video tutorials for learning software applications and more.

Keeping current in your field and always working on your business plan will also force you to answer the questions you might not have thought about. Staying up-to-date in your field of expertise and constantly reorienting your business plan are healthy practices. The constant review will force you to answer questions that you might have missed the first time around. It has certainly helped me over the years. When you're selling something, you're so into making sure the item or the show or the project is going to work, that you don't think about all the nuts and bolts. It can be really helpful, as you are working through it all, to sit down with a nuts-and-bolts person. No great idea was brought to life by one person. Oracle, Facebook—they were all started by more than one person. Sitting down with someone who has a different background and perspective than you can really help get all the necessary questions laid out.

Bon Jovi (left) saves his band money by keeping overhead low. Here he talks with me and Phil Simms (right) at a charity dinner.

ROCK OUT IN THE REAL WORLD
Bon Jovi

Jon Bon Jovi is best known as the lead singer-songwriter of the Grammy-winning rock band Bon Jovi, purportedly the second richest band in 2011 with earnings of approximately $125 million. Collectively, he's produced eleven studio albums with the band and two solo albums. As a solo artist, Bon Jovi's hit "Blaze of Glory" received a Golden Globe and an Academy Award nomination for the soundtrack he composed for the film *Young Guns*. Bon

Continues

Once you've got your business plan all written out, it's time to present it to investors. I think in the world of business you have to get as many people interested in your product as possible. You can't rely on just one person or one company.

I was negotiating for a long time with a major publishing company to buy my company. I was absolutely sure that I was going to be sold out to them. But in the end, they felt that my product wasn't an area they wanted to expand their business into, and we didn't make the deal. That experience taught me that if you rely on one company, you could get into a situation where they turn you down, and your whole project can get messed up. I believe you should be out there negotiating with four or five different companies, four or five different types of investors, to see who is going to give you the best deal. Until someone signs a contract or puts a check in your hand, it should be a free-for-all. Then, when someone comes to you with the best offer, an offer that you want to deal with, you take it.

Once you've sold your business plan to an investor, be careful not to fall into the common trap of spending the money too fast. This is a mistake I made once when I raised money. It happens because investors will pressure you. They'll say, "You have all this money, now what are you

Continued

Jovi ranks thirty-first in the list of top Metal Vocalists of All Time by *Hit Parader* magazine.

According to *Forbes*, the band played seventy-four gigs in fifteen nations in 2010, grossing $203 million in ticket sales and $20 million in merchandise. According to veteran concert promoter Ron Delsener, they're one of the highest grossing bands year after year. After decades of experience, the band members are touring pros and run a tight ship. While they may not have started out this efficient, over the years, they have learned how to be most efficient and utilize their band time to gross a large ticket revenue as well as earn a large sum through merchandising sales.

Here are some of their efficient methods: The band usually plays with only six musicians and utilizes only a dozen trucks to carry their gear. By carting their own circular stage and specially designed double-sided LED video screens, they can sell thousands more tickets. They save hundreds of thousands of dollars in setup and breakdown expenses by playing consecutive nights at the same venue. They also figured out a way to market to the select VIP crowd. At $1,275 per ticket, these VIP packages include fold-up, take-home seats in the front row and autographed lithographs.

Continues

Continued

"Jon is a businessman," says co-manager David Munns. "He knows what it takes to have a great-quality show, but he also knows how to be efficient with money."

"It wasn't some conscious decision to be penny-pinching. I think it's just wise to be efficient," says Bon Jovi. "I know big bands where each of them has personal assistants on the road, each of them has a security guard. We don't have a security guard. Take your own friggin' bags!"

Now, the Jon Bon Jovi band probably didn't emerge onto the scene this business savvy and begin grossing millions upon millions the moment they started playing. But after years of playing, understanding the way ticket sales works, understanding venue booking, etc., the band was able to create business plans for themselves as a collective band. They eventually figured out how cost effective and timely it would be to tote their own venue set-up with them, and this saved time and money, which turned into them earning more from their ticket sales and merchandise.

Jon Bon Jovi is just one example I am giving, but the important thing to understand with this section is that it is important to grow your business plan as your idea, your company, etc., begins to

Continues

going to do with it?" I would say, "I want to keep the money in the bank until the right opportunity comes, until I'm ready to do something with it." And the investors would say, "Well, money in the bank only earns 1 percent, and if your business is going to have returns of 20 percent or 25 percent, you should spend the money now."

Investors want their money invested. This happened all the time during the dot-com boom. Companies were forced to spend their money way too fast because investors wanted action. And the companies went down like flies. You have to be up front with your investors. Tell them, "Listen, I'm trying to build up so that when the right opportunity comes, I will be ready." That's a big part of business—you have to strike when the iron is hot, and not just because you have money.

You can have all the mini–business plans in the

world, but you can never be sure of what will happen. Who knew that the economy would break down in 2008? Who knew that after 9/11 the business to be in would be private airplanes because people didn't want to deal with airports anymore? Who knew Lady Gaga would turn out to be such a huge star? I

Continued

grow. It is important to always start out with a plan and know where you want to head, and continue to grow and develop from there. Figure out the loopholes and ways you, and your teammates (whether band mates, coworkers, or employees), can make the most out of your time and money.

bet you that when promoters were projecting her tour, nobody thought she would reach the numbers she grossed. I'm a huge fan of Warren Buffett through my business advisor, Bruce Berkowitz of the Faireholme Fund. Buffett always has lots of cash to use when the time is right, like when he bought into Goldman Sachs and made billions when the company recovered. Jason Fried, in his opinionated and insightful book *Rework*, says, "Unless you're a fortune teller, long-term business planning is a fantasy." What I believe he's saying is that your career necessitates a business plan, but you must go in realizing that it all can change in a heartbeat. There are many factors that may drive you to rewrite the script. Be ready for that possibility.

It won't just be outside factors that cause your business plan to change. Your plan can and should evolve as your idea evolves. As you meet people and pitch your idea, it's going to change, over and over and over again. This is something I wish I had read when I was first coming up with ideas and creating business plans. You wake up one day and you think your idea is one thing, and then it evolves—and your business plan has to evolve along with it. If you start getting the feeling that your business plan today is totally different than the business plan you wrote three months or three years ago, don't worry—that feeling is totally normal.

Your plan can and should evolve as your idea evolves. As you meet people and pitch your idea, it's going to change, over and over and over again.

I always had this plan to have Rock 'n' Roll Fantasy Camp as part of a casino. But when I was doing a camp at Atlantis, I saw all my customers gambling away. Ace Frehley from KISS was at the casino every night; the great guitar player George Lynch lost $2,500; these six ladies from Austin, Texas, were gambling and eating at Nobu; and all these campers were drinking all night with the rock stars. I said to myself, "Wait a minute. I am bigger than just Rock 'n' Roll Fantasy Camp at x casino—I am the casino!" My idea evolved into something else entirely: not just having a camp at a casino but having an entire casino of my own based around the camp. Don't be afraid as your idea evolves. Just be ready to write up a business plan, and a month later change it, and a month after that change it again. That flexibility will take you far.

Your business plan will continue to be important to you as you reach success. It will help you stay on target and reach your goals, despite whatever distractions and temptations may be thrown in your way. I have certainly faced my fair share of temptations as my career has progressed. There was one day when an executive at a major label called me up out of the blue and asked me if I was interested in managing a big-name star who was a major sex symbol at the time. He told me that they had made a record and a video with this vixen star and that she was looking for management. I said,

"Well, I'm not sure if I'm interested in managing her, but I would sure love to meet her!" So I made an appointment for her to come to my office.

Well, let me tell you, when she walked into my office in her beautiful Gucci outfit with her big sunglasses, I just about fell over. Then she sat down and started ranting and raving about how the executives who signed her for this record deal weren't doing anything to help her now that the record and video were finished. I could immediately surmise the problem: The people at the label were selling Bruce Springsteen and Billy Joel to the radio stations—the last thing they wanted to sell was this record from this sex symbol movie star. But there she was, going on and on about these executives, making fun of them—I'll never forget, she said, "That executive is so fat and ugly, the only way he'll ever get a woman is if he sticks an American Express card to his forehead!" She was so angry, every second word out of her mouth was a curse.

But hey, I thought, I was in the presence of this star, and I was loving it. I decided to call my friend Jeff Rowe, the head of VH1 programming at the time. I asked Jeff if he had any plans to play the star's video on his channel. He said he didn't know anything about it and that he'd call me back in a minute. He called me back a minute later, and I put him on speakerphone, not telling him that I had the star herself in my office with me. Jeff said, "David, I've seen the video, but we have no plans to show it at this time." I said, "Would you do me a favor, Jeff? I've got the star in my office right now, could you give us some airtime and spin the video?" Jeff said, "I'll call you right back." He called me right back, and said, "I programmed it." He had programmed it to run six times a day.

We hung up the phone, and well, that star, she thought I was the greatest manager in the world; I was her hero. We scheduled to meet again a few days later, and we had dinner until three in the morning. It was one of the most fun nights I ever had. I opened my heart up to her, and it was great. Then, I was supposed to meet her again, but I was a little over-whelmed—I had realized that this was not the direction I wanted my career to go. I had my business, I had my clients, and I had a plan to move a different way in the world. And I had heard from everyone that she was difficult to work with. I knew I couldn't afford to be dealing with trouble if I really wanted to get where I wanted to go. So I never followed up with her.

It was hard to let that go, because it was an amazing experience. But I had a plan for my business, and it did not involve sex symbol movie stars trying to start music careers. So I bid good-bye, and I'm glad I did, because it allowed me to follow the business path I truly wanted. But Jeff Rowe will always have my gratitude for making me a hero to her.

Even if you don't have major sex symbols knocking on your door, you still have to stay focused. Get your business plan together because now is the time to act. Ironically, even though the economy isn't strong, it's an excellent time to start a business, for two reasons. One is that we've now started to finally climb out of our recession, so there's going to be years on the positive side of the business cycle. The second is, there's a ton of money sitting on the sidelines with nowhere to go. People want to invest money in ideas, and there's a lot of money out there for people who have an idea.

Today more than ever, it's easy to run a business. You can operate a business out of your house and look like you're a big company—or even if you don't look like a big company, people don't care today, because everyone is doing it. A good part of business today is done by e-mail, cell phone, and e-fax; it's amazing what you can run out of a computer. Between Linked-In, Facebook, and Hoovers, you can find anyone you need to get your project off the ground. It's much easier to reach the world with your idea than it was ten years ago.

Take advantage! Write up your business plan and bring it to the world. With that selling tool, you'll be amazed at who you find out there to help you on your way.

Chapter Four's Greatest Hits

- It's not about luck. It's about preparing a good business plan.
- With any project, you always need a game plan.
- Having a business plan also helps you get the most out of your project.
- Your investors are going to need your detailed business plan.
- The first thing everyone wants in a business plan is an executive summary, outlined below:
  - Show what the concept is.
  - Keep your business plan on the shorter side.
  - Always include the negatives in your business plan.
  - Adjust your business plan so that it hits the right investors.
  - Make use of all the great resources currently on the market to help you draw up a business plan.
- Don't be afraid to take your business plan to four or five different people/companies.
- Be ready to shift your business plan if the need arises.
- Be careful about spending your investors' money too fast.

Like a Virgin:
CHOOSING THE
RIGHT PARTNER

I once advertised on my Web site that we'd be holding a Rock 'n' Roll Fantasy Camp in London, culminating in a recording session at Abbey Road. Next thing I knew, there was a cover story on the upcoming camp in *The London Times*. My phone started ringing off the hook from a dozen different production companies and television people, all of whom were now interested in doing a TV series. I hired a lawyer to find me the best deal, and I ended up meeting with Elizabeth Murdoch, Rupert Murdoch's daughter and the woman who put *American Idol* on the air.

Elizabeth and I did make a deal but, unfortunately, it eventually fell through. Back in Los Angeles, I held another camp to drum up more interest. The highs and lows had reached fever pitch as my camp gained ground. Then I got a call from another big-name Hollywood talent agency, who said they wanted to represent me. I met with the producer they recommended, but we just didn't click. He wanted to do the series in a very different way than I had envisioned it. At our second meeting, when we were supposed to make a deal, I walked out. I was frustrated and discouraged. After coming all that way, it looked like it was never going to happen. *It's never going to get made*, I thought. *Maybe I should just give up.*

Not more than ten minutes later, I got a phone call from Mark Burnett's office. Burnett is the king of reality TV. He's the guy who created *Survivor*, *The Apprentice*, *The Voice*, and *Shark Tank*. His partners include Donald Trump and Joel Osteen. That same week, I was sitting in Mark Burnett Productions with David Eilenberg (Head of Development) and Clyde Leiberman (Executive in Charge of Music) making a deal for a Rock 'n' Roll Fantasy Camp TV series. After thirteen years, it was finally happening.

In 2010 my dream of partnering with Mark Burnett (far right) came true when the VH1 Classic TV series *Rock 'n' Roll Fantasy Camp* aired beginning in October of that year. Also pictured here are my daughter, Ilana, and Scott Cru, an executive at Mark Burnett Productions.

Once Mark Burnett and I agreed to a deal, I started looking into moving to Los Angeles. If you have an idea, sometimes you have to make a move to get it done. I started to realize that living in New York would make it very difficult for me to continue to follow my dream of producing a TV series. I needed to be in a place where those dreams would flourish. I knew it was time to finally live the dream and move to Hollywood.

The show premiered in October 2010. The week before was the longest week of my life. My brain was buzzing with thoughts, concerns, and just about everything else you can imagine. *How was the show going to do? Would people watch it?* Well, after just the first airing it broke every record for the

Here I'm shown with bass player Rudy Sarzo (left), who's worked with Whitesnake and Quiet Riot, among others, and musician Kip Winger (right), who started out with Alice Cooper before going out on his own.

network, and VH1 Classic renewed it for a second season. VH1 launched billboards in Times Square and Los Angeles. Cheerios signed on as a national sponsor. The buzz was incredible. But it happened. By building off of my one successful idea, Rock 'n' Roll Fantasy Camp, I was able to create another great idea and fulfill my dreams to start a Rock 'n' Roll Fantasy Camp TV series. Most importantly, I saw my dreams become a reality because I never gave up. I did not stop trying. Things didn't work out with Elizabeth Murdoch and things fell through with another potential partner, but I did not shelve my idea and walk away from it. Although I had to go through a couple of people before finding the perfect partner, I stayed true to what I really wanted in my dreams. I had my vision, and for thirteen years I chased it until I found somebody who understood my vision and helped to grow it into what it is today.

Team Player

If there's one thing I've learned over the years, it's that it's impossible to do business without partners. I pride myself on my partnerships. I've got great partnerships with music magazines like *Guitar World*, *Guitar Aficionado*, and *Modern Drummer*, in which they barter with me for an agreed-upon number of ads in exchange for putting them in touch with my customers. I just entered a partnership with Citibank that allows their customers to exclusively purchase a spot at an upcoming camp before it goes on sale to the general public. Citibank even took it to another level by producing a major TV commercial in which a woman buys Rock 'n' Roll Fantasy Camp for her husband with her Citi card mileage points. Citibank spent $25 million on ads, with spots airing on

American Idol and *Oprah*'s final episode in 2011. My business would never be where it is today if I had tried to do it alone.

My business would never be where it is today if I had tried to go it alone.

Many people think "partner" means 50 percent, but it doesn't have to be fifty-fifty. There are no definitive ground rules as to what a partnership deal should be, so you can be creative. I have asked many people, "What kind of deal did you make with this person? What kind of deal did you make with that company?" I've seen partners receive from 1 percent to 50 percent. Elvis Presley's manager, "the Colonel," took home 50 percent of the King's income. When I did a contract for my NFL players, I got paid 3 percent. When I did an MLB contract, it was 3 percent again. This may sound like a small percentage, but 3 percent of multimillion-dollar deals is nothing to frown at.

A Gridiron Partnership

I first learned about partnership when I was a sports agent. In the '80s, I was Phil Simms' agent. He was the Giants' longtime quarterback, and I learned what it truly meant to be somebody's partner thanks to Phil. I was his agent, but he treated me like his friend, his loyal business partner, and somebody with whom he truly valued a relationship. We worked together for more than twenty years, and he always said to me, "Fishof, I load the gun and you shoot the bullets." This outlook allowed us to have lots of fun together rather than live a life of strictly business, politics, and money. It became a very symbiotic relationship, and it was one of my first lessons in forming rock-solid partnerships.

It started in 1986, when the Giants were on their way to the Super Bowl. Just a couple of weeks before they were scheduled to play, I was having a dinner with Phil and his fellow teammates, Phil McConkey, Jim Burt, and Brad Benson, all three of whom I also represented. My instincts were to congratulate them continuously and discuss their future game, but I knew I had to act now and plant my seeds as their partner and agent. I began to discuss with them how we could create a new vision of themselves for their fans. But, as their partner, it was important for me to hear out their own ideas for their vision.

The four of them began tossing ideas at me. McConkey said he wanted to take a white towel and wave it to the audience and get them riled up with just that towel. And that's exactly what he did. Jim Burt climbed into the audience to slap high fives with the fans. I supported each of their ideas and kept my ears open for more. That's when Disney called me. Disney proposed the idea that the winning quarterback should be asked, "What are you going to do next?" the minute that they walked off the field. And the answer would be, "I'm going to Disneyland!" The Giants ended up winning the Super Bowl, and Phil Simms and I made this deal together with Disney, kicking off their famous "What's Next?" campaign.

My reasoning for suggesting to them that they needed to come up with a new vision was not just for me to establish myself as their business partner or agent, but also because I wanted to be able to sell them for endorsements and promotions. However, without our symbiotic relationship, we would have had a very hard time working together. If I had only wanted to do things my way and they only their way, we were bound to have clashed and disagreed. This was the first lesson I had learned: Listen and absorb your partner's ideas and visions and integrate them with your own vision. The result can really pay off (for both parties!).

The second lesson I learned about how to treat your business relationships and partners also came from Phil Simms. Leading up to the Super Bowl, Phil asked for my help in dealing with the sponsors, but I was working in Hollywood at that time on The Monkees performance at the American Music Awards. Instead of turning Phil down, I put in all the more effort into both of my relationships and started shuttling back and forth between Hollywood and Costa Mesa. I spent all of Friday with the Giants, but had planned to spend Friday night in my hotel room in Beverly Hills to observe Sabbath (I couldn't be with Phil, or be in contact with him for the next twenty-five hours!). I told Phil that anybody could leave messages with my hotel, and I would call them back on Saturday evening. I will never forget what happened next.

Phil turned to me and said, "Hey, don't worry about anything. It's going to be okay. Your Sabbath is more important than the Super Bowl." To this day, this is one of the most moving things somebody has ever said to me. To have the quarterback of the Giants, who would go on to win the Super Bowl and become the MVP, tell me that my Sabbath, my faith, was more important than one of the biggest sporting events, averaging about 106 million viewers, was something that just blew me away. This really resonated with me and became very influential in my future business dealings and partnerships. I worked really hard to help Phil during the week when I was working with The Monkees as well, and he came back with the same care and compassion for my own life.

Phil Simms turned me to and said, "Hey, don't worry about anything. It's going to be okay. Your Sabbath is more important than the Super Bowl."

In working with Phil Simms (back), I appreciated that he was a family-oriented man who respected my values. Here he is with my father and daughter, Shira, when she was 12.

That year, after the Super Bowl, the players and I worked together on all kinds of crazy deals. One of those was to film an exercise video like the popular Jane Fonda videos. We spent a week filming a workout video in Costa Mesa, California, that featured Phil Simms, Phil McConkey, and seven other NFL greats. I even got to work out with them!

All of these ideas we had, from the towel waving to the high fiving to the exercise video, created a memory of these players off the field and directed focus away from just the game. Although all these ideas were great, if it hadn't have been for the trust and openness the players and I had in our relationship as business partners, we probably would not have gotten very far together. I could have lost endorsements with them or lost them altogether had I not listened to their ideas and then organized a common vision that worked for us both (as players and as agent). Thanks to Phil Simms and the Giants, I gained a clear understanding of how relationships and partners should be treated and, most importantly, I learned how much better two heads (or three or four) are than one!

Partnerships Should Be Win-Win

In previous chapters I've talked about working with other people, the importance of a great relationship, and how the dynamics of a relationship can mean everything in business, but in this chapter, I want to discuss exactly why having partners is important, and how you can choose the right partner for you. I want to start by saying something very plainly: There is no template for partnerships. As I noted earlier, they can be 50/50, 60/40, 99/1. The important thing is that it's a win-win for all partners.

When I was twenty years old and working as a sports agent, the manager Phil Shapiro called me up and said, "Can you get me baseball great Steve Garvey to do a motivational speech in New Orleans?" I called Steve, and he told me his price was $3,500 and he'd pay me a 20 percent commission. I called Phil back, and we immediately booked Steve for a specific date.

After the appearance, I went to Phil's Manhattan office to collect the check. Phil said to me, "How much do you have to give Steve Garvey?" I said, "I have to pay him $3,500 less 20 percent—so that's $2,800." Phil wrote a check to Steve Garvey for $2,800, and then he proceeded to write a check to me for $1,100.

ROCK OUT IN THE REAL WORLD
Rocking with Tequila

Rock stars are often negatively associated with booze. Sammy Hagar, Rock and Roll Hall of Famer and former front man for Montrose and Van Halen, definitely has a relationship with booze . . . a business relationship, that is. Hagar is the founder of Cabo Wabo Tequila.

It started out as an idea to have a little tequila bar in Mexico. Hagar dreamed about having a cozy, relaxing spot to hang out with friends and play music while enjoying really good tequila. He realized that dream back in 1992 when he opened the Cabo Wabo Cantina in Cabo San Lucas, Mexico.

In 1996, after firsthand research into the handmade premium tequila business, he launched his own tequila under the Cabo Wabo label. By 2007, sales had reached approximately $60 million. The demand was so high that the business grew unexpectedly fast, forcing Hagar to make a major business decision. He knew he needed a partner to help him shuffle through all the demands and business, so he began searching for the right person to help him with global distribution without sacrificing the quality of the product.

Continues

"What's this for?" I asked.

Phil responded, "I sold Steve for $5,000 to the client, and I'm going to give you half of what I made."

I said, "You don't have to do that. Just give me my $700. It was *your* client."

"No, David," he said. "I want to take care of you. This time, you only had to make the phone call, and I had to wine and dine the client. Next time, you'll find the client, wine and dine the client, and I'll make a phone call—and you'll share your profit with me."

> *"This time, you had to make the phone call, and I had to wine and dine the client. Next time, you'll find the client, wine and dine the client, and I'll make a phone call—and you'll share your profit with me."*
>
> —Phil Shapiro,
> talent agent to
> the stars

It was a great lesson for me to learn—in order to be successful in any business, all sides of the partnership need to make money and feel as if they were treated well at the end of the deal. People always ask me, "How much should I pay a partner?" The answer is that it really comes down to what you negotiate. You have to make the right deal. We'll talk more about negotiation in chapter 12, but the object is that both sides should be happy with their deal. Again, there's no template for it, so always aim to settle on a deal that you can both agree on.

Letting Go

Even if you get the hang of negotiating deals, it can be hard to bring a partner in on your project. When you're working on bringing your idea to life, it's very difficult to relinquish even the tiniest part of it to a partner. Most people with an entrepre-

Continued

Hagar makes a shrewd analogy between the music business and the expansion of his tequila business. "I knew I had to approach this like the record business. Like the record business, the spirits business calls for placement. If you're not being played on the radio, you're not going to get into the stores. If you don't get into the stores, you're not going to sell any records. Trying your product is like hearing your song on the radio. If you're not in the bars, they're not going to try your product. If they're not trying your product, they're not buying it in stores."

"I realized that I was being a small independent label that had a hit record," Hagar says. "And now I needed a big label."

After fielding inquiries and offers from a slew of investors, Hagar sold an 80 percent stake in Cabo Wabo to the established liquor company and international distributor Campari/Skyy for $80 million. Offers were being thrown at him left and right, but to Hagar, making money from a possible sale wasn't the driving factor. His focus was to find a partner he could trust to respect the integrity of the product and make it as big as it could be. He still maintains involvement and actively promotes the brand he is proud to have founded.

Continues

Continued

"It's like, would I want to make a brand-new CD and have them tell me, 'It's going to be great, but we're just going to put it out for some of your friends?'" Hagar asks. "No. This is a great CD, this is my music. I want the whole world to hear this music.

"It's the same thing. I look at Campari like Warner Brothers or MCA or Universal. I needed one of the big record companies to get my record out to the whole world. I signed deals with those people. And that's what I'm doing right now."

neurial bent have a bit of control freak in them. They want to, *have* to, do everything themselves. I know because I'm the same way! I've learned over the years the importance of delegating. It's crucial to assign work to others and share responsibilities so you don't stretch yourself too thin.

I see this all the time with the executives who come to my Rock 'n' Roll Fantasy Camps. I once saw a top executive walk into the studio and say to his counselor Bruce Kulick of KISS, "I REALLY want to play the KISS classic 'Rock 'n' Roll All Nite.'" Bruce turns to him and says, "Well, that's very nice. But we're part of a band, so I have to teach the song to everybody to make it work. If you want to do it, I have to teach the parts to the guitar player, the drummer, the keyboard player, and the vocalist. Then we can do the song correctly." It's a team effort, and as much as you want to do everything yourself, all at once, you have to trust other people to work with you and help you achieve your end goal.

It's not uncommon for some of my campers, who are high-level executives, to approach me at the end of a camp and say, "You know, you've got the best team-building program in the world. I walked into my band with an attitude like it's all about me, and I learned that in order to be in a band, you've got to trust other people, and you can't be a control freak."

The same thing goes for your business. You've got to trust other people, not only because they can share the load, but also because they offer a fresh perspective and advice from their experiences. A partner can give you a new vision of your idea, one that can help you make your dream come true. I've had so many different visions for Rock 'n' Roll Fantasy Camp, and I will be honest—after I meet and work with certain people, I change my mind. I've learned the value of staying flexible and getting input from other sides. I have even made my lawyer a partner so he can give me the best legal advice.

"Surround yourself with smarter people than you, and you'll be successful," said Dick Clark. It's doubly true for partners. Once you surround yourself with people who are more successful than you and have a bigger reputation, it will push you to go further. For the past year, I've been consulting with Paul Caine, now the executive vice president of Time, Inc. I have the utmost respect for him, and he's been pushing me to take the next step—the previously mentioned permanent location for my business. He says I need it for my business to reach its full potential—and he's right. So I'm listening to him and taking his advice.

Once you surround yourself with people who are more successful than you and have a bigger reputation, it will push you to go further.

Changing gears based on other people's insight is challenging because you have a vision of one thing in your head, and it can be really difficult to modify that vision. But unless you can take advice from the right people, you're not going to be successful. There's no question that Bill Gates had a vision.

There's no question that Steve Jobs had a vision. But it's the people you don't hear about, the people who were right below them who really guided them into making their visions come true.

It's also important to remember that the people who advise and guide you aren't your only partners. Anyone who has a financial interest in your idea is a partner. Micky Dolenz of The Monkees once said to me, "David, I look at all the following as partners: the record label, the retail store, everyone who's ever made money on us—they are a partner." That is an excellent way to think about it. I even look at all my customers as partners. Without them, the label, your consultants, whoever it may be, it would be difficult to make your vision a reality.

Former Monkees drummer Micky Dolenz and I are jamming at one of the Rock 'n' Roll Fantasy camps.

If your idea is creating a new record, you need partners. You need partners because you can't make the record, produce it, manufacture it, deliver it, put it on the shelves, and advertise it all by yourself. The publicist has to be the right partner; the distributor needs to be the right partner; they're all partners. You need partners to do all these things in order to make your idea a success.

Keeping Your Word

We've established that partners are vital to making your idea a success. But that doesn't make it any less difficult to get out of the control-freak mentality and get into the idea of sharing responsibility, risks, and rewards with others. I've certainly faced that challenge many times over. But what I've discovered is that once I find someone who really works with me and gives me the confidence that they can handle the situation, it's much easier to hand over that control.

I had a client on Wall Street who asked me to get Joe DiMaggio for an event. I did. The event was all arranged, and everything was ready to go—until a week before the event when Joe called me up and said, "I can't make the appearance. I'll do it some other time." When my client heard this, he asked me to come down to Wall Street to see him. So I went, and he said, "You see this room out here? I've got a hundred brokers here who are trading millions in currency. And when a bank calls me and wants to make a trade of a hundred million, we turn to them and we say the word 'Done.' And when that word is spoken, it means you're going to do it. I told people that Joe DiMaggio is going to be here for lunch next week, and you told me 'Done.' So you've got to make sure that Joe DiMaggio is here."

Well, I got right on a plane and flew out to The Sands Hotel in Las Vegas, where Joe DiMaggio was golfing. I said, "Mr. DiMaggio, I'm David Fishof. We spoke on the phone, and you agreed to do this appearance. And I need you to come and do it." I persuaded him to come and do the event because I had told my client, "Done." And that's what I look for in my partners. If I get people who can tell me the word, "Done," and I get the confidence that when they say, "Done," they mean it, then I'm fine with sharing the responsibility.

It's not all on your partners—you have to take the responsibility of fully explaining your idea to them. Being able to articulate an idea in a way that's inspiring and contagious is one of the keys to success in business. One of the things I admire so much about Paul Caine is that he has a huge staff, and they all work congruently. Every time I speak to him, he's very specific in explaining what needs to be done. He's learned to trust his staff to do things for him. He has that trust because he explains things so clearly. Once you've explained your idea and what needs to be done, your partners are responsible for fulfilling that idea.

Pairing Up

How do you find the right partners to take the responsibility? The key is research. Reputation is an important quality in a partner. Before you hand over any responsibility, find out everything there is to know about your potential partners. Interview people who've done business with them, and get a feel for who they really are and how they do business. There are a lot of con artists out there, and the best way to avoid them is by really taking the time to get all the information. Be thorough, be careful—it will keep you from getting burned.

You're going to find partners who are unscrupulous, there's no question about it. I'd like to share a few of those stories with you, to give you an idea of what kind of partners to avoid and to illustrate what can happen if you're not careful about choosing the right partner.

Some of my most frequent partners over the years have been rock promoters. I create a show, and then I sell the show to a local promoter who promotes it for me. Although I sometimes get a higher offer from a new promoter, I usually go with a person who has promoted me in previous years. I know they know how to promote my show, and when my artists come to town, I know they'll make my artists feel comfortable. If I'm in a new place, I sell my shows to well-known promoters because I want to be sure that when my artists get to the venue, everything is set up right and everything will go smoothly. Just because someone offers you more money, it doesn't mean you have to make the deal. And it certainly doesn't mean they are more qualified for the job.

Only a few times have I gone against this judgment, and most often it has not ended well. One time I did so completely unwittingly—it was an old associate who actually made the deal. She worked for me for many years selling concert dates. I would create the tour ideas, and her job was to find local promoters and negotiate a deal for them to partner with us and promote our shows. It was my associate's job to make sure that we were getting booked five or six times a week for the tour because that was the only way we could make money. We were guaranteeing all these artists and production people money, and it would take about four shows to pay them. The fifth and sixth show was our profit.

One night in 1985, when we were working on the Happy Together tour, my then associate was sitting alone in the office. She used to work late hours, from noon to 8 or 9 at night.

That night, around nine o'clock, the phone rang. She answered, and it was a guy who wanted to buy a Turtles greatest hits record. He had called us because the Turtles were part of the Happy Together tour.

She started talking to the guy and learned that he was from Sioux Falls, South Dakota. This got my associate very excited, because we had a booking in Chicago one Saturday and a booking in Los Angeles the next Saturday, and she was desperate to find gigs in between for Tuesday, Wednesday, and Thursday. So she said to the guy, "Listen. We have a Turtles concert coming up. How would you like to be a rock promoter? All you have to do is pay me $15,000, and I'll sell you my Happy Together tour. You put it in a 10,000-seat arena, charge $15 a ticket, and gross $150,000. You pay for the rent of the building and the advertising—and you keep the rest." So, she went on to tell the guy about all the chicks he'd meet as the hot new promoter in town, how they'd want tickets and backstage passes. The guy was a school teacher, and it wasn't too long before my female associate had persuaded him to leave that life and become a rock and roll promoter, not only for the show in Sioux Falls, but for one in Fargo, North Dakota, as well.

The guy was thoroughly convinced that he was going to make it rich. He mortgaged his house and bought a new Cadillac. He sent us a $15,000 deposit for the two shows. It all seemed to be going well. But the next thing I knew, it was two months later, and we hadn't heard a thing. Then, the day after the first show, I got a call from the local South Dakota newspaper, asking, "What happened last night? How come the concert never took place?" Well, it turns out, the guy ran out of money, didn't sell any tickets, didn't know what he was doing, and ran away from his obligations. He didn't put up the rent money, didn't pay the bills, and when the act showed up, they found the theater locked and the promoter nowhere in sight. The show never happened.

I called her into my office. "What is going on here?" I asked. "What happened? Where'd you get this promoter? He's not a real partner; we've never used him." She said to me, "Well, the guy called up and he wanted to buy a Turtles record, and I persuaded him to be a rock and roll promoter. And then he ran away."

I always advise individuals who want to go into promoting rock and roll that they should just take $100,000 and burn it on their front lawn. It's that hard of a business.

> *I always advise individuals who want to go into promoting rock and roll that they should just take $100,000 and burn it on their front lawn. It's that hard of a business.*

During my years representing the Giants, I was approached by New York City club promoter Lloyd Bloom, who wanted to partner with me in recruiting professional athletes. Although he assured me that he could sign many top-draft college football players, I didn't feel that he was the right person to partner with. After I turned Lloyd down, he approached an agent, Norby Walters and convinced him that they could copy my strategy of representing both entertainers and sport players. Next thing I know, they were out signing all of the top-draft players and calling me constantly for advice and encouraging me to partner with them. One day, I walked into my office to find two FBI agents waiting to speak with me.

The *Daily News* had just done an exposé on Lloyd Bloom and Norby Walters and how they had become so successful so quickly. When asked why he had gone into the sports business (Norby was already representing major artists like New Kids on the Block and Luther Vandross), Norby responded with something like "if David Fishof can go from representing acts from the Catskills to representing major athletes, there is no reason I can't!" The *Daily News* article prompted the FBI to investigate, which is why they wanted to question me as to my involvement with these two men. It turned out that one of the agents was a former spotlight operator at Kutshers Hotel in the Catskills. I told him how Lloyd had approached me and, when I turned down a partnership with him, he had approached Norby. Later that year, both Norby and Lloyd were indicted for paying off players in order to get them to sign. Very illegal. A few years later, Lloyd was fatally shot in his home office; I believe it probably happened from pissing off people by making bad business deals.

Another promoter I worked with on a Ringo All-Starr Band date called and said he wanted to come to my Rock 'n' Roll Fantasy Camp to help me out, driving, volunteering, whatever. He wanted so badly to be around rock and roll, so I said, "Sure, if you want to come up and work at the camp, we'll be glad to have you."

Well, he came, saw my operation, and after he got back to Florida, he called me up drunk and said, "I want to do a country camp. Do you want to be my partner?" Naturally, I was already thinking of doing a country camp on my own—after you do a rock and roll camp, people say, "Oh, next you should do hip-hop, R&B, country." I was interested, but I was not interested in doing one with him. I knew what he was really trying to do. He had seen my camp, and he wanted to steal my idea. Sure enough, he proceeded to call all my contacts and tell them that I'm not interested in doing a country camp, but that he was going to do it. My contacts all told him, "This is Fishof's idea; you're stealing it!"

But he went ahead anyway and tried to start a country camp called Camp Nashville. He raised money and advertised, and he tried to hire my people. In the end, the camp never happened, and he lost $800,000. He had a million-dollar pension from being a fireman, and he blew $800,000 of it. Eventually he flew to New York to apologize for trying to steal my idea. But it taught me a valuable lesson about who you can and cannot trust.

Partnerships don't always fail because one partner is unscrupulous. Sometimes it's just a matter of not meshing and not benefiting from each other. I had a partnership with Dick Clark, working on an American Bandstand tour. It started when I stopped by his office one day to say hello. He said, "Come in, David, let's talk."

Dick and I started chatting and eventually decided to do a show around American Bandstand. Dick said he'd have his business manager, Fran LaMaina, call me. But when Fran called me, he said, "David, we want to do this deal, but it would be eighty-twenty—Dick Clark gets 80 percent and you get 20 percent." I said, "Fran, I'm not doing that deal. I'm doing all the work, producing the tour, and I'm licensing Dick's name because of his expertise. I'll do a more equal partnership with Dick." But the business manager said it had to be eighty-twenty.

A few years later, I walked into Dick Clark Productions again. Dick Clark Productions owns all this great footage of early rock stars, and I needed some to shoot TV commercials for my Dirty Dancing Live Concert Tour. I went in to visit my friend Larry Klein, who's one of his big TV producers. "Let's go say hello to Dick," Larry said.

We walked into Dick's office, and Dick said to me, "David, what happened to our Bandstand deal? We were going to do the Thirty-Fifth Anniversary of American Bandstand Tour." I said, "Fran won't do a fifty-fifty deal, so I'm not going to do the deal." Dick called Fran in and said, "Fran, I want to do the deal with David fifty-fifty. That's it. Let's make the deal." So Dick Clark and I partnered up and decided we were going to do an oldies tour that would take people through the last four decades of *American Bandstand.*

> *Dick Clark and I partnered up and decided we were going to do an oldies tour that would take people through the last four decades of* American Bandstand.

I decided to go out and sign one act from each decade, and, in between these decades, we would show footage of *American Bandstand.* We ended up booking sixty dates on the tour, and we got a corporate sponsor, Canada Dry. On the day that Dick was getting ready to go on *Good Morning America* to promote the show, we went to have coffee beforehand at a café on West 67th Street, outside ABC Studios. As we had our coffee, I said, "Dick, I've been doing these tours for many years now, and they've all been successful. But this tour is not taking off. I mean, I'm not selling many tickets. Something is wrong."

Dick replied, "You know what the problem is, David? When two hustlers get together, they out-hustle each other. I told you how great the Bandstand brand was going to be, and you told me you could promote it, and we out-hustled each other." He was right. My idea of playing one band from the '60s, '70s, '80s, and '90s didn't work—most people's musical tastes are too narrow to buy tickets to a show they only liked a quarter of! Dick out-hustled me by telling me that *American Bandstand* was a huge name, when he had just announced his retirement, which really hurt his brand. And so, as it turned out, our tour was not very successful.

Now, I will admit—all these partnership stories I've been telling may be a bit alarming. They're probably reinforcing your ideas that if you get in bed with someone else, bad things are going to happen. But for every horror story, I've booked thousands of shows with promoters that went off brilliantly. I tell the promoter horror stories because that's the 1 percent you have to watch out for, and if you aren't watching for it, this will most likely happen to you. Don't let anybody pull the wool over your eyes.

The vast majority of my partnership experiences have been positive, from my amazing fifteen-year partnership with Ringo Starr to my current partnership with Mark Burnett Productions. I'll say it again: The only way I've been able to make my business successful has been by having partnerships.

Seeing Eye to Eye

Once you've found a partner who is trustworthy, responsible, and who meshes with you on a business level, you have to make sure he or she meshes with you on a visionary level as well. Part of choosing the right partner involves staying true to your vision. Everybody will have a "better" plan for your idea, and sometimes you can be so eager to get a deal moving that you compromise your basic idea. This almost always leads to disaster. It's your idea, and you have to be vigilant, protecting your vision against meddling by others. Most people know that Sylvester Stallone wrote the original *Rocky* screenplay and insisted on playing the role himself. Producers loved the movie but would only buy the rights if Stallone wouldn't play the main part. Stallone, to his credit, refused to compromise and turned down serious money because he believed he was destined to play the part. He was so broke that he even had to sell his dog! But he finally found a producer who would let him play the part . . . and the rest, as they say, is show business history. Although I applaud Stallone for standing up for his idea, I do think that it's very important to realize when you need to compromise. Compromising can bring the right rewards and can kick-start your independent career; Stallone could have just been lucky, landing that final producer who let him play the part. But if he hadn't, he might have never landed a deal.

A perfect example of compromise can be seen in the music industry. I've had many songwriters say to me, "I've written this song, and only I can sing it." My feeling is, you can sit with that dream for twenty years, or you can take this song, sell it to an artist, and let them record it. Then you'll get the credit for being the songwriter and you'll own the song rights. When it's your turn to record something, you'll have this great reputation: "Hey, I wrote this song for Barbra Streisand" or "I wrote this song for so-and-so rock act." That credit will help you reach success as a recording artist. A lot of times, artists or promoters will negotiate and barter deals with each other, just like this; this can create a major win-win for both parties because the barterers know they will get something they want in the end, and they also know they are offering something the other party could see as a positive on their end. We will go more into detail with bartering and negotiating to create win-win situations in the next chapter.

There are many recording artists who have forged incredible careers by following this exact path. It's how Barry Manilow got started; he was Bette Midler's piano player. It's how Neil Diamond got started; he wrote "I'm a Believer" for The Monkees. It's how Carole King got started; she wrote songs for others before becoming a performer in her own right—in fact, her tour with James Taylor was the country's number-one tour a few years ago. It's also how Lady Gaga got started (she wrote songs for Britney Spears!), and she's one of the biggest pop stars today. It's important to remember that sharing your idea, being willing to take the other side, can also lead to fulfillment of your dream. It's better to have 50 percent of something than 100 percent of nothing, especially if it serves as a step toward making your idea come to life.

> *It's better to have 50 percent of something than 100 percent of nothing, especially if it serves as a step toward making your idea come to life.*

In 2005, after my aforementioned meetings with big-name producers regarding a TV series, I called Roger Daltrey and told him about one of the offers—one that didn't jibe with my vision.

"Don't do it," Roger said. "You've got to believe in the way you want to do it. Go back in there and tell them you want to do a documentary on the actual camp, and I'll do it for you."

So that's what I did. I told them that I was turning down the series, but if they were open to doing a documentary, so was I. To my surprise, they came back to me and said they'd do a two-hour documentary.

In 2008, Mark Burnett and I discussed how the camp should be portrayed. He understood that it had to be all about the music, and that's how the show actually was made. He kept it authentic, and as a result, it's the best possible portrayal of the camp. The first season of Rock 'n' Roll Fantasy Camp broke all records on VH1 Classic and was renewed for a second season; hopefully, the show will be around for a long time. If you stay true to your vision, you can and will ultimately find even more success.

Do Unto Others

Another thing to keep in mind is that if you are generous and you share, it will help you in life. There's a great story my father used to tell about a gentleman who had worked in the clothing business for many years and had an amazing clothing store. One day, the store burns down. The man comes home to his wife crying, saying, "What do I do?" His wife says, "Why don't you call your wholesaler, the guy who supplies your store, and explain the situation?" He calls his supplier and sets up an appointment to speak with him. The man goes, and there's a beautiful meal waiting for him. He sits down, and the supplier says, "Why did you come to see me?" The man explains what happened, and the supplier says, "Don't worry. I'm going to set you up in business again. Don't worry about the money you owe me—I know you will pay me back one day. You're going to be fine."

The man goes home to his wife and tells her the good news. The next day, he tells his best friend, who also owns a store, what happened. The friend decides he's going to do the same thing. He calls up his wholesaler and says, "Can I come see you?" The friend goes to see the wholesaler and says, "Can you help me out like you helped my friend?" But this man had not had a long-standing relationship with his wholesaler, and the wholesaler throws him out and says, "Your friend has been doing business with me for more than thirty years and has always been a good customer. You've placed a few orders with me here and there. I will not help you."

You always get out of a relationship what you put into it, and the same is true in partnerships. In a great partnership, one plus one does not equal two; it equals five. If both partners are putting in their all, your product will be greater than its parts. Your business will flourish, and your project will move forward. You need to find a partner who can make that equation work. If you and your partner have a 1+1=2 relationship, then there's nothing you are doing for each other.

Of course, without a partner, you're just a "1" standing by itself, going nowhere. You can't grow a business at all unless you have partners. It doesn't work alone. Mark Burnett has a whole chapter in his book, *Jump In: Even If You Don't Know How to Swim*, about partners. All of his success has come from making sure he has the right partner. One of the reasons I love working with him is because he works with all these amazing partners, and I'm honored to be one of them.

You always get out of a relationship what you put into it, and the same is true in partnerships. In a great partnership, one plus one does not equal two; it equals five.

When former Chicago Bulls coach Phil Jackson said to Michael Jordan, "There's no letter 'I' in 'team,'" Jordan responded, "Yes, but there is an 'I' in 'win.'" And it's true—if you take yourself out and work with a team, you as an individual will still win in the end. But without the team, you can't win. You have to have partners to make your dreams come true.

Chapter Five's Greatest Hits

- Be a team player, because it's impossible to do business without partners.
- To be successful in any business, all the sides of the partnership need to make money. It needs to be a win-win.
- Delegating is critical. Share responsibilities to avoid stretching yourself too thin.
- A partner can help you formulate your vision.
- Research and reputation are the keys to discovering a good partnership.
- Just because somebody offers you more money, you don't have to take it.
- Partnerships don't always fail because one partner is unscrupulous. Sometimes it's just a matter of not meshing.
- Once you've found a partner who meets all your needs, you have to make sure they mesh with you on a visionary level.
- You always get out of a relationship what you put into it, and the same is true in partnerships.

Lean on Me:
THE BARTER SYSTEM

O ne of the most intimidating things about bringing a new idea to life is the money. As someone with a new idea, you may not have a lot of capital to get it going. Many people sit with their idea, saying, "I have no money. What do I do?" They feel they can't become successful unless they go out there and somehow raise a million dollars to fund their idea. It seems so impossible that many people just give up.

Well, I'm here to tell you there's another way to go: bartering. If you have a good idea, people will trade and barter with you, especially in today's economy. If you don't have the money for advertising, making a trade can mean the difference between exponential success and devastating failure. Bartering is a fantastic way to bring in partners, goods, and services that would otherwise be too expensive to buy with cash. With bartering, you don't need cash because it is centered around an exchange of goods or services, not money.

I told the story in chapter 2 about how I partnered with Bob Pittman and MTV when I was putting The Monkees tour together. This was one of the first big barters I'd ever done, and one of the most successful. With MTV already doing a Monkees marathon and myself already at work on the tour, it was a match made in heaven. Both partners stood to benefit hugely from the deal: Bob would gain additional publicity for his fledgling network, because with me putting a simple "Watch The Monkees on MTV" advertisement in all of my print ads and radio and television spots, I helped Bob promote his new network. I would gain exposure for The Monkees, helping my tour and concerts gain a major following and market base.

In exchange, MTV also publicized my concert schedule. Sure enough, it worked like a charm. Once I had airtime, I was able to sell out a 25,000-seat amphitheater in a matter of hours. And MTV was rapidly gaining viewers. It was the perfect barter deal, with both sides scoring big. Recently, Bob took on the presidency of Clear Channel Radio, and he mandated that the radio stations organize major contests and opportunities tied to artists, performances, and events, similar to what he did to build up MTV. Building up Clear Channel, he would gain attention from individual markets and huge fan bases.

Now, you see what I got from this deal that helped me so much: free marketing for my product. That's the key to how bartering can bring your idea to life—you can get necessary services without having to shell out huge amounts of cash. By bartering, you can get just about any service you need. This is what Google+ is trying to capitalize on. Google+ is designed as a social media tool promoting, above all else, shared resources.

The truth is, it's much easier to get services than to raise funds. In today's economy, more and more people who are doing these kinds of deals, be it marketing deals or sponsorship deals or what have you, are doing strictly barter deals. When I first started, this wasn't the case. There was a time when there was a lot more money out there for sponsorships. It used to be that I would go to VO5, Glade, Coca-Cola, Pepsi, or 7-Eleven and make sponsorship deals wherein they'd give me vast sums of money in exchange for promotion. Now, companies are more conservative with their money. They're saying, "We'll promote you, we'll promote your brand, we'll promote your venue, we'll promote your concert, but we're not going to pay you. We're going to use your brand to promote our own ends, and you'll get the exposure you want."

Guitar Center began a competition in 2010 for emerging artists to have a chance to win a recording with Slash.

ROCK OUT IN THE REAL WORLD
Deals with Strings Attached

Guitar Center is the world's largest musical instrument retailer. Darren Feldman, VP of Creative Services at Guitar Center, has been a friend of Rock 'n' Roll Fantasy Camp for many years and shared the following thoughts about bartering with me:

Barter has been a regular practice for Guitar Center. In fact, it has been for decades. Why? Guitar Center's advertising budget has to work hard, driving traffic,

Continues

Continued

sales, and margin dollars. Not only is it quite often difficult to show a quantitative return on ad spend, the ad budget falls lower on the company's expense hierarchy than hard costs required for the business to function. Compared to things like store leases, utilities and fixtures, associates' salaries, point of sale equipment, and inventory, ad spend is more "discretionary." Enter barter. Barter is an additive, or supplement, to the advertising budget that serves and benefits multiple parties: the individuals/companies partnering, and depending on the scenario, customers as well. It costs little to no budget because most barter is centered around an exchange of goods or services with an implied "value."

For the reasons above, Guitar Center continues to play a part in the barter and partner system. We utilize heavy barter for our contests of skill (talent competitions) and contests of chance (sweepstakes) that happen throughout the year.

How Guitar Center benefits: Aside from differentiating us from our competition and building brand affinity, these promotional opportunities give our customers a reason to come to our stores,

Continues

For example, six months ago Macy's approached me about doing a promotion to support the store's "Men's Style" sale. Macy's asked for a camper spot in Rock 'n' Roll Fantasy Camp to use as a sweepstakes prize. It was a win-win deal for both Macy's and me. As a sweepstakes prize, Rock 'n' Roll Fantasy Camp would be featured in a direct-mail piece sent to 1.5 million Macy's customers, in newspaper advertisements in approximately 500-plus markets, and in press materials given to local media. This type of exposure would have cost me thousands upon thousands of dollars, but because I bartered, it only cost me the entrance fee of one camper. And Macy's gained extra foot traffic that weekend as more and more people came in for a chance to gain entrance to my camp.

Helping Each Other Out

When you're starting out, it can be really hard to market your product successfully. By bartering, you can get a big company, like Corona or Procter & Gamble, companies that already have a huge marketing budget, to market your product for you. I've been making these kinds of deals for years.

One night, a friend of mine, who works with acts such as Aerosmith, Ringo Starr, and Hanson, was having dinner with Steven Tyler, and Steven—who is a huge Beatles fan—questioned him about his Yellow Submarine jukebox. Now, the Yellow Submarine jukebox is a limited-edition jukebox made for friends of the Beatles to purchase first. There are only a hundred in existence, and Steven Tyler really, really wanted one. He asked if he could have my friend's. "I'm

Continued

even if they don't happen to be in the market for musical equipment at the time. Best-case scenario, they see something they like/need when they come in to enter/participate and we get a sale. Worst-case we capture their name/address enabling us to remarket to them and hopefully capture their sale when they are in the market for gear.

How the partner benefits: Guitar Center has a formidable palette of marketing tactics (direct mail, Web, e-mail, radio, TV, in-store/on hold audio, etc.) that have a broad and extending reach to a large and attractive audience. These are used to deliver sales announcements, launch new and exclusive gear, and promote value-add contests. By including partners as sponsors in the latter, we receive dollars and prizing to support the contest while they get a fully integrated marketing campaign to our customers—their potential future customers—at a fraction of the cost were they to do it themselves. Depending on the nuances of their participation, sponsors can also get their product into potential customers' hands via prizing or seeding opportunities.

Continues

Continued

How the customer benefits: By entering/participating, customers have the chance to win experiences or goods. From a VIP experience at a concert to recording with a world-famous artist and producer to a home studio or installation of one-of-a-kind musical instruments, many of the prizes are things "money can't buy." A few examples of barter in play at Guitar Center:

- In 1999, Ford and Fender partnered with Guitar Center for our August Anniversary Extravaganza—a monthlong sales event featuring a commemorative sweepstakes. Our 35th Anniversary aligned with the 35th Anniversary of the Fender Stratocaster and the Ford Mustang. Ford manufactured a custom "35th Anniversary" Ford Mustang convertible (including a built-in guitar amp) and Fender provided a (1 of 35) limited-edition "Mustang" Strat (to go with the in-car amp) to give away as the grand prize of our customer-facing Anniversary Sweepstakes. In exchange for the prizing, Ford and Fender were promoted in all sweeps collateral

Continues

not giving you my jukebox," my friend said. "But you know who else has one? David Fishof. And if you go and do a Rock 'n' Roll Fantasy Camp for David, I bet he'll make a deal with you." The next thing I know, my friend called me and said, "Steven really wants your Yellow Submarine jukebox." I said, "Well, if he does the camp, I'll make a deal with him. I'll give him my jukebox. So Steven Tyler came and did Rock 'n' Roll Fantasy Camp. It was great for him—he loved his experience working with amateur rock stars. He went on to take the *American Idol* job, in part because he enjoyed working with these amateur musicians so much. I, of course, got the great Steven Tyler at my camp! My Yellow Submarine jukebox now sits in his kitchen. You may not have a Yellow Submarine jukebox to barter, but you have something of even greater value—your services.

Whether you're a lawyer, an accountant, a writer, or whatever your profession or skill set may be, there are people who will be willing to barter their services for yours.

You may not have a Yellow Submarine jukebox to barter, but you have something of even greater value—your services.

This kind of bartering is incredibly easy to do, thanks to a slew of bartering Web sites. These sites work in largely the same way. You create an account, and it allows you to barter your wares and products. You put up, say, $10,000 worth of services for barter. Someone "buys" your services, and then you have $10,000 in your "bank" on the site. You can then use that $10,000 to buy whatever service you need from someone else on the site. The only catch is that, like eBay and other

Continued

during the month, including national direct mail, radio, and in-store posters/POP.

- In March 2001, ESPN reached out to Guitar Center to help promote its inaugural Action Sports & Music Awards. In exchange for promoting the event and telecast in GC direct mail, radio, in-store signage, Web, and more, ESPN provided a winner and guest a trip to LA to attend the event, including round-trip airfare, hotel accommodations, and spending cash.

- In June 2001, Tim McGraw and Bud Light asked Guitar Center to team up. Tim had a new album out and had a tour scheduled to support it. Bud Light had signed on as a tour sponsor. In exchange for marketing the album and tour in-mailers, in-store (posters), online, in radio spots, and more, Bud Light funded a sweeps that sent one of our customers to become Tim's "roadie" for a week, a signed guitar, Bud Light swag, and Tim's CD catalog.

- In 2002, multi-platinum band Limp Bizkit and its management

Continues

Continued

company approached Guitar Center about a nationwide guitar audition to find a replacement for the band's recently departed axeman. The ensuing "Put Your Guitar Where Your Mouth Is" Tour saw thousands of guitarists (and fans) flock to 22 Guitar Center stores in key markets throughout the country in hopes of landing the gig. In exchange for marketing the "tour" and audition venues (Guitar Center stores), Guitar Center benefitted from all the in-store traffic and national and local PR.

■ Over the years, Guitar Center has partnered in similar ways with such brands as Nike, Levis, Skechers, Jagermeister, New Line Cinema, The Gravity Games, MGM Home Entertainment, Bose, Scion, Jim Beam, Sirius/XM Satellite, 20th Century Fox, and Adidas and artists including Slash, Motley Crue, Run-DMC, and Keith Urban.

sites, you have to pay 6 percent of what you barter to the site—that's how the sites make their money. If you barter $10,000 worth of services, you have to pay the Web site $600. But if you are using the service strictly for business, you can write it all off on your taxes.

There are many of these Web sites that cater to different services. There are a ton of barter companies out there, and they are generally regional. I found a lot of good ones listed on the directory page of the National Association of Trade Exchanges' Web site (www.natebarter .com) and have worked with a company named ITEX with good results.

Although bartering your services and whatever exciting wares you may have is an excellent way to get goods and services, the absolute best and biggest thing you have to barter is your idea itself. What do I mean by that? I mean you exchange a piece of ownership in your company in return for services. You go to someone and say, "Listen, here's my idea, here's my invention. I'm willing to give you x percent of this product in return for barter." Or better yet, go on the Mark Burnett TV show *Shark Tank*, sell off a piece of your idea to a mogul, cash out some, and get the expertise of these business sharks.

Say you've got a great idea for a smartphone app. You can go to a company that makes apps and say, "I've got this tremendous idea for an app. I'm willing to give you 25 percent of the revenues if you will build my app." If you need sponsorship, you can barter with a company and give them a piece of your business. If you need legal services, you can barter with a lawyer and give them a piece of your business. You can give an accountant or a public relations firm a piece of your business. As long as you are willing to give off a piece of your idea and not necessarily collect money, you can get anything you need.

Bartering percentages of my ideas is how I make many of my deals. When I was doing my Dirty Dancing tour, I knew I would go bust if I spent too much money on advertising. I just couldn't afford it. I went to the head of programming at VH1. I started out with a small barter, saying, "Hey, I'll give you fifteen or twenty tickets to every concert I do in return for a TV spot." This got VH1 associated with my brand. The network thought my Dirty Dancing tour was a great idea and wanted VH1 to tie it in with a live show.

"But David," you may say, "if my company or idea or invention isn't proven yet, why would somebody want to take a piece of it?" The answer is simple: Because it's a good idea. If you have a great idea, people are going to want a piece of it.

A Litmus Test

Bartering is a great way to test if your idea is good—if enough people have interest and say, "Hey, I'm willing to take a little piece of this company to do this," then you know your idea is good. If I'm a lawyer, or an accountant, or a radio station, and you come to me with a bad idea—"Hey, I have this idea for a radio show about mental maniacs!"— I'll say to you, "It's not a good idea. I'm not going to barter you my services." When I was producing Mortal Kombat, I couldn't find anyone to barter with me. Nobody. I should have known the show would be a bomb because if it was a good idea, people would have been willing to barter with me.

I did mention before that you need to move forward without constantly worrying about everybody's perception, but that doesn't mean you should ignore the fact that nobody else is interested in your project. No man is an island, and sometimes you're going to need a little help from your friends.

A barter deal is no different than a contract where you're paying for a service. When you're bartering, going through a Web site like those I mentioned above can help you avoid disagreements because the company knows who the people on the other side are and they have certain protections in place. However, it's always good to do your research, just like you would with any partner.

I once bartered with a caterer using a Web site and used $15,000 of my credit to hire his services. But the caterer did not do a good job for me, which was my fault. Why? Because I should have gone and checked him out, made some phone calls, or gone to a tasting instead of relying solely on the bartering company. It's just like buying anything else—you should always do your research and you can always make a mistake. Just because you're getting it as a barter doesn't mean you can skip out on the same research you'd do if you were paying for it. The one difference is, if things do go sour, at least you're not out the cash!

The prospect of things going sour can be intimidating. But it's important to get past the fear because bartering is one of the most important tools you have. Bartering is how the big companies get bigger and how the smaller businesses get big. It's by bartering that you can really get going. One of the biggest international barter agreements to ever take place was between PepsiCo and the then government of the Soviet Union. Pepsi became the first foreign product to be sold in the USSR in exchange for the rights to Stolichnaya vodka in Western markets—a huge win-win on both sides.

Bartering does more for you than just net you the things you bartered for. It also nets you extra confidence. I know it's true for me. If I can get Gibson guitars and Citibank to barter with me, then I know my idea is good, and I know it can go somewhere. If you get the right people to barter with you, it will give you the confidence to keep moving forward with your idea. If you can find the right lawyer, the right accountant, the right business partner or media partner, who is willing to barter with you on your idea, that gives you a lot of validity that your idea is good.

Your resources aren't meant to be hoarded. They're a tool. We're all given, or have developed, a certain skill set that can better the world in some way. America was built on the concept of mercantilism. Mercantilism is the notion that exporting more resources than you are importing keeps a country strong. The same is true with our own gifts. If you are not giving—engaging in bartering—at some point you may lose your support base.

> *Mercantilism is the notion that exporting more resources than you are importing keeps a country strong. The same is true with our own gifts. If you are not giving— engaging in bartering—at some point you may lose your support base.*

In this economy, you need that confidence. But many people blame the economy for their failures and use it as an excuse not to follow their ideas through. The ones who are going to be successful in this economy are the ones who are confident and creative, the ones willing to take their idea and wave it around to be noticed. It's a glass-half-empty or glass-half-full situation. You can look at the economy either as an excuse to fail, or as an opportunity to be more creative than other people.

If you are creative, you can really get a step above those who are just sitting around making excuses. Some people will go to companies with their ideas, and when they're told there's no money, they just go home. Don't be one of those people. You have to take your product to a lot people, and you have to keep knocking on doors and showing your product. Inevitably people will say, "I have no money." Instead of giving up, your next question should be, "How can we find a way that we can work together? How can we barter it out?" If you can barter with the right people, you'll be well on your way to executing your idea.

Chapter Six's Greatest Hits

- When money is short, bartering is the way to go.
- Sharing resources is much easier than raising funds.
- Take advantage of the numerous bartering Web sites on the market.
- Besides bartering services, you can barter a piece of your idea as well.
- Bartering percentages is a good litmus test to see if your idea is a good one.
- Your resources aren't meant to be hoarded. They're a tool.

You Ain't Seen Nothin' Yet:
CRAFTING THE
PERFECT PITCH

There's an old adage in Hollywood: "Just show up there and make a pitch." It sounds overly simple, but it's remarkably true. You can have the greatest idea in the world, but if you can't pitch it, it's worthless. You need to be able to sell your idea, because you need to deal with other people, and you need to get those other people excited about your project. Whether you're looking for a sponsor to invest in your project, or you need a partner to get on board, or you're trying to interest a company in bartering services with you—it's all in the pitch.

What exactly is a pitch? And how does it differ from the business plans I discussed earlier? Well, if your business plan is the book report that you hand in to your teacher, your pitch is the presentation on the book you give in front of the class. It's an oral presentation of all the information about your idea, and it has one goal—to sell your idea to your audience. Just like a TV commercial, you have to get them excited enough about your idea that they will buy in.

Learning how to pitch is essential to bringing your idea to life. But you don't necessarily need a class to learn how to pitch. Lessons can come from anywhere in your life. As a child in synagogue, the son of the cantor, I talked to people who were older than me all the time, and I became very comfortable around them. This served me later in life when I pitched ideas. I don't allow myself to be intimidated by people who are older, more experienced, or in a position of power.

If your business plan is the book report that you hand in to your teacher, your pitch is the presentation on the book you give in front of the class.

I also learned a great deal by watching people pitch. I watched people pitch on TV, in stores, at business meetings. I watched every salesman who pitched a product to me to figure out what he did that worked and what he did that didn't work.

Lessons from Amway

What really taught me how to pitch was working with Amway. Amway is a direct selling company that specializes in health and beauty products. As an independent business owner with Amway at the age of nineteen, I sold Amway products directly to consumers, and I also recruited other people to become independent business owners with Amway.

Here's how it worked: I would go up to people, from friends and family to people I stopped on the street, and say, "Hey, do you want to make some money?" Inevitably, they would say, "Yeah, I'd love to make some extra money. How do I do it?" And I would say, "Come by my house tomorrow night. Bring your wife or significant other, too. You'll enjoy it."

The next night, with all these people in my home, I would pitch them on being Amway salespeople. The trick was, I didn't focus on getting them interested in being soap salespeople. I focused on getting them enthusiastic about team building and being part of this amazing organization, and most of all I focused on Amway's biggest concept: being your own boss. I focused on the freedom that Amway could provide, by helping you make money on your own time, in your own way. I had a brief amount of time to make this huge pitch. If I was able to sell people these Amway starter kits, I knew I had been successful.

Trust me, I'm not pitching you to sell Amway—I only did it for a few months before I took the ideas and used them in my own business. One of the biggest lessons I learned was that when pitching, you have a short amount of time to get your point across. This is essential to remember when you start forming your pitch. The second lesson is the most important thing about pitching: A pitch is about answering the other side's needs. In the case of Amway, I wasn't pitching the product; I was pitching financial freedom, more time with your family, more time to do something for yourself—everything that people want. A basic sale strategy is, in a way, identical to making a pitch. A strong salesperson knows that you first must create "pain." You present to prospective buyers a compelling emotional reason why not having your product gets in the way of living their best life. Once that pain has been generated, the power salesperson swoops in and shows how her product or her idea will make that hurt go away. Take a look at magazine headlines the next time you're checking out at the supermarket, and you'll see what I mean.

This is the key to any great pitch. You have to make it entirely about the other side. Don't make it entirely about the product, and definitely don't make it about you. What makes a good pitch is showing the other side how your product is going to work for them. If you want their money or their input, if you want something from them, you've got to worry about what they want and need. You can't be thinking self-ishly. Your product should be a solution to a problem.

In order for your product to be a solution to a problem, you yourself have to truly believe in your product and that it is beneficial to all. It needs to be a sincere thought—you can help solve a problem. It can't be a product made solely to benefit you or your wallet. Whomever you're pitching to already knows that the product is going to benefit you; after all, you're the one pitching it. They want to know how it's going to benefit *them*. If you can focus on the other side in your pitch, you'll be successful.

> *Whomever you're pitching to already knows that the product is going to benefit you; after all, you're the one pitching it. They want to know how it's going to benefit* them. *If you can focus on the other side in your pitch, you'll be successful.*

You obviously can't give the same pitch to everyone. How you craft the pitch depends on the type of person you're speaking to about your idea. If you're pitching to an investor, he doesn't necessarily care about the idea itself. All he's interested in is the money. You could be creating water for all he cares. What he wants to know is what will his return on the investment be. So the pitch to him is, "If you invest in my idea, you're going to make five times your money. This is who we're going to sell it to, this is how the revenue will get made," etc. Lay out your idea, but emphasize how he's going to get his money back and how he's going to make future money.

If you're pitching to somebody who needs the product itself, it's not about the money. It's about how it's going to help him on an emotional level. He's going to be more interested than the investor in the idea itself. You can tailor your pitch and say, "This is how this particular product or idea is going to help you with your particular problem."

To know how your product will benefit the other side, you have to do your research. Just as I discussed in previous chapters, you can learn about your audience by going on LinkedIn and Google. Find out what their interests are, what they're looking for. Your pitch has to answer their questions and pertain to their needs, particularly their unmet ones. You need to get across how your product and idea can work for them. You really only have one chance to make a pitch to someone—first impressions count—so anticipate the questions they may have. Have all the information they may want to know about your product—the price points they may be concerned about in today's market, how much you're going to sell the product for, how you're going to market the product, what it's going to cost you to produce it. For example, I was in contact with 7-Eleven about sponsoring my American Gladiator tour. The convenience store needed to find a retail partner to pay for the promotion and approached Coca-Cola, which bought a sponsorship from 7-Eleven in exchange for shelf space at the front of its stores. In the end, 7-Eleven received branding from Coca-Cola, which in turn received prime shelf space for its product, which in turn helped promote my tour. If I didn't think through possible options, I might have lost 7-Eleven at the start when the store said it needed a retail partner to pay for the promotion. I could have just thought, *Who would do that?* But we approached Coca-Cola and used the barter system: shelf space for promotion. If I hadn't considered the idea of bartering with a bigger company, I might have given up a good deal of my own money to promote with 7-Eleven. If you think through what the questions or obstacles to your product will be before you get in the room and have the answers already in the pitch, you'll be covered, and potential sponsors and partners will be far more likely to say yes.

Along with researching people's and companies' professional interests, it can be really helpful to get to know them personally as well. I was having dinner with a friend who is a salesman, and he told me that he keeps a record of every conversation he has with his clients. If a client says, "My son John went to the Lakers game last night," he makes a note of that. Then the next time he speaks to the client, he says, "How's your son John doing? Is he still following the Lakers?" That kind of attention to personal detail is really, really important. People think about themselves all day, and when you show that you're thinking about them, too, it forges a stronger connection.

How do you find out this kind of information? In this day and age, it couldn't be easier. You can often look a person up on Facebook to see what their interests are and if they have family. You can find interviews or articles about people in which they mention details that you wouldn't learn just from researching the company. I have used these tools constantly throughout my career, and I can tell you from experience, it makes a world of difference. Plus, getting to know the people you are working with on a more personal level tends to make doing business much more enjoyable for all involved. It can also make for a loyal partnership. Clients, partners, all like feeling welcomed and like knowing that whom they are working with is somebody they would hang out with outside of work.

Once, when I was a sports agent, I sent a letter out to a hundred top draft picks, pitching them my services as an agent. I encouraged them to call me collect, as I would love to talk to them. Now, there was no way I was going to remember a hundred players. So when I got a collect call from a "Robert Hubble," I knew it was one of the ballplayers because they had called collect. I picked up the phone. "Robert, how are you? I'm so glad you called me. Are you going to be around the next ten minutes? I'm in a meeting with a client, and I want to call you right back. Do you mind?" And he said, "No, that's fine!"

I hung up and gave myself fifteen minutes to get on the Internet to read everything I could find on Robert Hubble. I remembered that he was a tight end at Rice University, and I went over all his statistics. In one article, I saw that he was quoted as wanting to name a stadium after himself, called "Hubble's Bubble."

After my fifteen minutes, I called Hubble back. "Robert," I said, "you had a great year this year, and you really, really improved from your junior year. And one of the things we should do when we get you signed to the team is insist in your contract that they name their new stadium 'Hubble's Bubble.'" When I said that, he started laughing and laughing. He loved it. What did it show? In his mind, it showed, "Wow, this guy really knows me." I took that fifteen minutes to learn some details about him, and he signed with me as a client right away.

Of course, when you're bringing your idea to present in a more formal setting, it's important to do all that research and collect all those details beforehand. Preparation is key. Rehearsing the pitch as many times as you can, whether it's to a friend or your spouse, whomever you can get to listen, is very important.

Part of why practicing your pitch over and over again is so important is because it will help you condense it into its

Eric Clapton says he succeeds through discipline and practice.

ROCK OUT IN THE REAL WORLD
Clapton's Discipline and Practice

Leaders of the corporate world can rightly be compared to entertainers, as both must engage their audiences in an effort to influence, persuade, and pitch their ideas.

There's always an element of performance in sales. Most of us can generally acknowledge when we're in the presence of a great salesman or corporate speaker because they entertain us, whether we agree with the content or not.

Continues

most concise, to-the-point form. That's what you have to do—you have to pretend the cameras are on you and the clock is running down. Because that's how it will be, with any pitch, just like it was with Amway, just how it is with pitching movies in Hollywood: You have to say the most you can say in the least amount of time. People don't have long attention spans, and if you take up too much of their time, you're going to bore them.

Preparation is key. Rehearsing the pitch as many times as you can, whether it's to a friend or your spouse, whomever you can get to listen, is very important.

Instead of going on and on, you have to be straightforward and to the point. People get pitched ideas all day long, especially on Wall Street. Every day, they hear ten new ideas. They aren't interested in listening to you talk for hours. But if you can walk in and knock it out, lay everything out quickly and clearly, you'll be a step ahead. Being prepared and practicing your pitch will help with that immensely.

Making It Personal and Real

Of course, with all the pitches people are hearing, you'll need more to stand out than just brevity. This is where your prototype comes in. As I discussed in previous chapters, having an actual product that people can see or hear makes all the difference.

For me, that product has often been a radio spot. That was one of the best ways I pitched earlier in my career. When I was getting ready to pitch a tour to a promoter, I would call my friend Nick Summers, who's a radio DJ and does all the commercials for the WWE and rock concerts. I'd barter

Continued

Whether it's a one-on-one encounter or in a stadium of thousands—the necessary principles of a great performance for the executive and the rock star are the same: engage, entertain, evoke. In order to effectively engage and entertain your audience to evoke an emotional response, the most important thing is to dedicate yourself to practicing for perfection.

Legendary rock star Eric Clapton is a great example of dedication through hard times and adversity. Somehow even during his darkest and most challenging days— surviving the death of his son, battling his addiction, roller-coaster romances—he found the discipline to rock on. In his book, *Clapton: The Autobiography*, he makes it clear that two things are responsible for his celebrated career and ongoing success: discipline and practice.

This guitar hero still practices finger placements and chords! Even as a rock star who "arrived" decades ago, it's not beneath him to continue to learn and practice relentlessly. Clapton is a seasoned guitar player (obviously!), but continuing to master the basics provides him with superior flexibility for musical improvisation.

Corporate leaders and executives can take a lesson from Clapton: You're never too smart to keep learning, and

Continues

Continued
you're never too perfect to keep practicing your pitch. Just like Clapton keeps practicing the basics so he can wow his fans, corporate leaders have to keep practicing the basics of good leadership if they want to "wow" their audiences and deliver a winning pitch to employees and clients.

with him, saying, "Hey, you do this commercial for me for this pitch, and if I make the sale, you'll do the commercials for my show in every town." In return, he would create a commercial for me. I'd go to him, and we'd write up a commercial together, and he would prepare a sixty-second spot with the sponsor's name, the talent's name, and a made-up date and venue—usually a big one, like Madison Square Garden. Then I would walk into my meeting and pitch this commercial like it was actually happening.

I used this tactic repeatedly when I was looking for corporate sponsors for The Monkees. I would have Nick and his radio crew put together a commercial, and then I'd use the same commercial, just with a different sponsor's name in it, and send it out. I'd say, "Hey, play this in your meeting." It was a great way to show companies what the tour was about. I'd present these people with what I thought the radio spot should sound like, and get them excited.

These days this method has become much more popular—but it's still just as effective. When people can hear it or see it, it's easier to make a decision. People hear countless pitches, countless people laying out their ideas. But if you put in the time and effort to create that TV spot or radio spot or newspaper ad, it really stands out.

Just by having that prototype, you can help plug any holes that your audience might have questions about. An important thing to remember in pitching is that you can't leave anything up to the imagination. If you really want to get something done, the more prepared you are, the easier it will be to sell ideas. If you just go in and verbalize it, and you don't put the time into it, you won't get the result you want. I truly believe that there is no limit on what you can and should spend—both in terms of time and money—on a pitch, and there is nothing you should leave out.

Tell a Story

Along with all of this, there's one other thing to remember about your pitch: It has to tell a story. It can't just be scatter-shot information all crammed together. It's important to shape your pitch so it tells the story you want it to tell—to explain your product, to show how your idea will benefit the other side, to get the other side excited about your idea. For each audience, the story will be different, because it will need to include the specific interests, needs, and details of each specific person or organization.

Brien Meagher, executive producer of *Shark Tank*, sorts through three to four hundred pitches a year from entrepreneurs who want to appear on the show. His staff winnows those proposals down from the thirty thousand submissions *Shark Tank* receives annually. So my question for Brien was what makes an idea jump out at him—what makes an entrepreneur right for *Shark Tank*?

Brien explained that an idea can be something entirely new—in which case Google keywords related to the entrepreneur's idea reveal that there's nothing else like it out there. In that case, the sheer newness and inventiveness of the idea carries the day. Alternatively, the idea might be something as familiar as barbecue sauce, but the entrepreneurs are so nimble and effective that their concept is irresistible.

An example of the latter is Pork Barrel Barbecue Sauce, the brainchild of two Capitol Hill staffers who were talking late one night about pork barrel politics and hit on the idea of creating a barbecue sauce with that same name. These two young guys had incredible enthusiasm, a knack for getting on TV, a sense of humor, and the relentless work ethic that marks the successful entrepreneur. They appeared on *Shark Tank,* and their business exploded, which is what happens, Brien says, to pretty much every business that appears on *Shark Tank.*

"We always tell the entrepreneurs," Brien says, "your Web site is going to crash from all the hits you're going to get. And they never believe us, and the Web sites always crash."

> *"We always tell the entrepreneurs, your Web site is going to crash from all the hits you're going to get. And they never believe us, and the Web sites always crash."*
> —*Brien Meagher, executive producer,* Shark Tank

In the case of Pork Barrel Barbecue, the product went from something manufactured in the basement of one of the entrepreneurs' mom's house and sold in three stores to a national product featured in major catalogs and with a new line of related products—including a barbecue-smelling cologne! Crazy ideas, and they generated crazy money.

Brien says that if you've got a new-concept product that can generate excitement and enthusiasm, your path is even easier. Brien says he's astonished by the number of bathroom-related products, as if too many entrepreneurs had a fascination with the excretive function. Those things are a tough sell, simply because if that's what you're thinking about, so are a lot of other businesspeople. (Maybe all of you ought to find something else to ponder!) But if you do have a new idea, one that doesn't exist on Google, you will find the money and you will find success . . . as long as your presentation is solid, according to Brien. That's because there simply aren't that many eye-popping new ideas at any given time. The term Brien uses for such ideas is "loud"—you can practically hear the entrepreneurs shouting about it even as you read the pages of their business plan.

If you're looking to get a television show produced, Brien adds, the key to success is what he calls access. Sure, lots of people are pitching ideas about reality shows involving police departments, ride-alongs, and the like, but you're the only one who can guarantee access to the New Orleans Police Department and exclusive video of how they cleaned up the city after Katrina. If you've got access, you'll get an audience.

It's even better if your idea can be sold not just in the United States but in markets around the world. That's when a show really makes huge dollars. *Shark Tank*, for example, was initially a Japanese show that traveled to England then to the United States, in different formats in each country, of course.

Peter Guber wrote a fantastic book titled *Tell to Win: Connect, Persuade and Triumph with the Hidden Power of Story*. In it, he discusses how a great pitch is all about the story, and how you tell it. If you can tell a great story with your pitch, you will bring the other side along with you. If your story is concise, well-researched, and stays focused on the other side, you'll have yourself a killer pitch.

As I have shown, a good sales pitch is a combination of many factors. Here's a boiled-down version of a few essentials you should keep in mind. First and foremost, when you pitch you should be oozing with confidence that your product or idea has the potential to make your investors' money. If you don't have that confidence, you probably need to rework your ideas and financials. Also, know who your audience is. If you're pitching a technical product to somebody without a technical background, you have to use language that will easily be understood. Remember, investors are investing in you as much as your product or idea.

As a basic rule, the following five elements should be included in your pitch:

1. A description of your product and what niche it fills or what problem it solves.
2. Who your product or idea benefits and what demographic you are targeting.
3. Who your competition is and how your product is different or superior.
4. What your projected earnings are.
5. What type of investment you need (time, money, expertise) and how you plan to use it.

Chapter Seven's Greatest Hits:

- Learning how to pitch is essential to bringing your idea to life.
- When making a pitch you have a very short window to get your idea across.
- A pitch is about understanding the other side's needs.
- Remember to diversify your pitch based on who you're presenting to and use language the audience will easily understand.
- Prior to the pitch, make sure to do your homework and research.
- Incorporating a prototype into your pitch is very effective.
- Your pitch has to tell a story.
- Work on your "elevator pitch"— that brief hot-flash explanation of your vision.

The New Kid in Town:
HOW TO STAND OUT
IN A CROWD

There are countless new products and ideas entering the market every day. When you are ready to send your idea out into the world, you have to ask yourself: How am I going to draw attention to my product? How am I going to make my product stand out from the crowd?

The key is publicity, and when I say publicity, I really mean hype.

What is hype? Hype is introducing your idea to the world and getting people excited about it. But hype is not just advertising. Hype has to be beyond advertising. Consumers know who pays for the advertising that claims your product is great. Hype is buzz about your product that people read or see beyond the ad—a review, or a news report, or an article in a newspaper. I find that third-party endorsements are the absolute best way to sell your product. I can spend all the money I want on advertising for my Rock 'n' Roll Fantasy Camp, but what will really get people interested is a great article or review. People read and take in information, and they believe what they read. You want to try to get as much editorial as possible.

How do you get that press? You have to be as creative as possible. One of my greatest hype successes was the Dirty Dancing Live tour. I talked about it briefly in previous chapters, but I want to share the story more completely here.

I went to see *Dirty Dancing*, the movie, when it came out, and it really touched a nerve in me. I started my career as a waiter and a busboy in the Catskill Mountains, as many successful people did back then. Working in the Catskills was an opportunity to make a lot of money in a short amount of time. When I saw *Dirty Dancing*, it reminded me of working as a waiter/busboy at the Lake House Hotel in the Catskills. As the movie became a box office hit and the soundtrack topped the charts, I thought: How cool would it be to make this into a live show? If we got the original dancers and the original choreographers and used the original songs and dances, I saw the potential for a great road show.

No one had ever done a movie as a live show before, but I thought the music and dancing were so amazing, I knew it was worth trying. So I contacted Vestron Pictures, which distributed *Dirty Dancing*. I figured they'd be interested because the film was such a huge success—after all, it was a film they spent $5 million on, and it went on to gross vast amounts of money around the world.

I got a meeting with the president of Vestron, Jon Peisinger, and pitched my idea, complete with a radio spot and print ad. Jon thought it had potential, but he saw it primarily as a club touring show. But I knew that *Dirty Dancing* was a cultural phenomenon that had a deep appeal: It played to older audiences who remembered the music from the '60s, and to younger audiences drawn in by Patrick Swayze and the sexy dancing.

I obtained the rights from Vestron to do the show, I think in part because they knew of my previous successes with The Monkees and the Happy Together tour, and as a sports agent. They trusted that I knew what I was doing. In return for the rights, I would give them 10 percent of the gross and a percentage of the merchandise.

Next I had to figure out how to promote the show. First, I partnered with my friend Dennis Arfa, who represented Eric Carmen, whose song "Hungry Eyes" is featured in the film. We decided that Dennis would book the show, and I would produce it. Then I went to seek out a press agent to help me figure out how to build hype for the show.

In those days, it was very popular to go to a location, such as a restaurant, call a press conference, and hope that all the media would come and the venue would get lots of media attention.

You have to be careful when you have reporters around that you don't get the wrong kind of coverage. At one of my recent camps, I got a call from the *New York Times* reporter Larry Rohter, who wanted to write an article on my New York camp; he asked if he could just follow me around and observe the camp.

Now, that's sort of dangerous, to just let someone walk around and see what's going on behind the scenes. The camp is very similar to being on tour. What happens in an interview room is one thing; what happens onstage and backstage is another thing. I was aware of the risk, but I knew that an in-depth article in the *New York Times* would be great hype, so I was up for it. I said, "Okay, you can follow me." I let him go wherever he wanted to go, despite the risk. And in the end, it was totally worth it, because he wrote an amazing, glowing story for the *New York Times*.

Now, chances are, if you're just starting out, it won't be easy to get the *New York Times* to come write an article about you. How do you get the kind of coverage that will get you hype? You have to be proactive. One of the best things to do is to write your own press release and get it out to the world. Simple advice, but it's amazing how few people take advantage of it! If you put out a press release, you can use a site like Bacons. com. Bacons.com is a great Web site that, if you subscribe, provides you the name of the editor of every possible magazine. It even tells you all the different editors—music, travel, all the specialties—all the personnel of all the media. So you can send those particular editors a press release about your item. If things work out, they will call you and they will cover you.

PR Newswire is another great company for getting your product out there. You write your press release, pay them by the word, and they send the release out to the media. You don't need a big press agent; you don't need to spend a lot of money when you're just starting out. Everybody gets PR Newswire, and if you send your press release out through them, it will get in front of a lot of editors. PR Newswire is also great because you can segregate your audience and say, "I only want to reach travel editors," or "I want to reach people who are doing Father's Day specials," or "I want to reach women who deal with cosmetics."

Pitching to the press really works—it creates a lot of interest. Whether you want to sell a product or promote awareness of a Web site—whatever your project is—sending out a press release via one of these companies is a great step toward building hype. If people are made aware of your product and they feel it's a good story and a good idea, they will write about it. Once they've started to write about it, then you will start getting some credibility behind you.

A lot of the hype-building methods that come along with getting press are being usurped by our current hype engine: social media. The discussion of whether social media is effective or not has long passed. Done. We know that it's the most effective means of getting your message out there. Become familiar with Facebook, YouTube, LinkedIn, Google+, Twitter, Foursquare, and other sites to understand their unique communities and how each of these outlets can be used to get you some solid press.

Product Placement

There is another almost infallible way to get hype, besides getting press, and that is getting people—big-name people especially—to use your product. One great example of this is the clothing company Members Only. Many years ago I had dinner with Lou Piniella and the owner of Members Only. The owner turned to me and said the way he broke his company was that at every celebrity golf tournament, he would make jackets with the celebrities' names on them, and send them to the celebrities. So when Frank Sinatra was having a golf tournament, the owner would create a Members Only jacket with the name "Frank" on it, and send it to him.

Then there was a celebrity tournament called the Frank Sinatra Open. The owner found out who was going, invested $10 in a jacket, put the celebrities' names on the jackets, and sent them a personalized Members Only jacket. He made one each for Frank Sinatra, Sammy Davis, and Dean Martin, who were all going to be at this golf tournament, and sent them to the tournament.

Well, the three of them took a picture together for the press, wearing the personalized Members Only jackets, and the company just exploded. Everybody wanted that jacket. They saw Frank in it, and Sammy in it, and Dean in it, and every guy wanted to have a Members Only jacket. For only $10 a jacket, Members Only raised monumental hype.

Today, this is a very common hype technique. Instead of paying money for advertising, they just put things in movies—product placement. If you can get your logo, product, or idea into a movie, you'll get great exposure, and it's a great form of advertising.

In the same vein, gifting suites, in which celebrities are given products for free in exchange for a picture of them with that product, have become popular. If you follow gossip magazines, you will often find pictures of a celebrity like Paris Hilton holding a new cell phone and posing for the camera. These pictures are generally taken at gifting suites at big events like Sundance Film Festival, the Oscars, or the Super Bowl. These gifting suites are an excellent way to promote your products. It's the same idea as a dress designer giving an actress a free dress to wear to a big event in exchange for being mentioned on the red carpet. It's very expensive to advertise, and it is remarkably easy to get people to use your stuff. All it takes is giving it to them for free. You'd really be surprised. I remember sitting with Phil Simms and a bunch of football players in Atlantic City at a buffet, and one of the players yelled out, "Hey, you know what's better than food?" After the obligatory dirty jokes, someone yelled back, "Free food!" Even celebrities love free stuff. And giving a celebrity your product to wear or to use is a fantastic way to raise hype.

It's not only celebrities who can help your product in this way—getting industry leaders to use your product can have the same effect. I've certainly found this way of raising hype to be incredibly effective in my career. Over dinner with Roger Daltrey one night in London, I was explaining my Rock 'n' Roll Fantasy Camp concept. I asked Roger who would be his fantasy to meet, to which he replied, "Levon Helm." I told him that I could introduce him to Levon Helm if he agreed to come do my upcoming camp. Roger agreed. I hinted to Roger that Levon had been experiencing some recent financial difficulties, so Roger told me to give Levon half of his appearance fee. I called Levon, and he was thrilled to meet Roger, and they met at The Bottom Line, a famous NYC nightclub. Roger ended up doing my camp and going above and beyond during his appearance—staying for four days instead of one. I will always be thankful to Roger for his contributions to my camp and his friendship. In fact, Roger was the first person to call me after 9/11 to make sure my family was safe.

Levon Helm (right) of The Band and David (left) at Rock 'n' Roll Fantasy Camp.

His appearance gave my brand a major hype boost. When I advertised Roger Daltrey, the media exploded. Suddenly we were getting write-ups in *Fortune* magazine, *The Wall Street Journal*, and a whole bunch of other business magazines. Then we got one of the most culturally relevant nods you can get—an entire episode of *The Simpsons* devoted to Rock 'n' Roll Fantasy Camp, in which Homer goes to the camp with Mick Jagger and Keith Richards. Jane Rose, who has managed Keith Richards for years, told me the boys loved doing the episode, and it's still one of the top enjoyed episodes. They even debuted it on my first night of camp in Los Angeles.

Then Ellen DeGeneres mimicked it with Aaron Neville, Bonnie Raitt, and David Crosby on her ABC comedy show. They even wrote in a character who wore a yarmulke and only ate kosher food—me! When someone as famous as Ellen starts spoofing you, you know you're making waves. Those spots on *Ellen* and *The Simpsons* really helped my brand. Even Jay Leno got in on the action, making jokes like "for $5,000 you can jam at Rock 'n' Roll Fantasy Camp with a bunch of B-list Rock 'n' Roll stars. For $5,500, you can check yourself into the Betty Ford Clinic and hang out with a bunch of A-list Rock 'n' Roll stars."

> *When someone as famous as Ellen starts spoofing you, you know you're making waves . . . Even Jay Leno got in on the action.*

It wasn't too long before Roger recommended Brian Wilson of the Beach Boys to sign on for the next camp, and it kept snowballing from there. People came out of the woodwork with money and ideas. Soon I decided that the best strategy

Here I'm gathered with some of the Rock 'n' Roll Fantasy Camp counselors,
along with Slash (center) and Roger Daltrey (front row, to his right),
at the camp's tenth anniversary in Las Vegas.

for raising money was to go to my customers who had previously attended the camp. Because they'd all benefited from the life-changing experience, I was able to raise enough money to go out and sign bigger stars, like Slash, Paul Stanley, Meatloaf, and Nick Mason. I'd always believed in the concept of Rock 'n' Roll Fantasy Camp, but now others believed in it, too.

There's one thing you may notice about these stories, and it's one of the greatest things about hype: Hype generates more hype. Once the hype started with Roger Daltrey, it snowballed. If you can get that first credible publication, one publication will lead to another one. Once you get one celebrity using your product, others will follow.

Playboy Hype

The ultimate example of hype has got to be the Playboy empire. The whole concept of the Playboy Mansion is constructed entirely out of hype. I went to the Playboy Mansion, and it was one of the most fun nights of my career. It was 2008, and my buddy Mancow, the Chicago radio personality, was hanging out with me at my LA Rock 'n' Roll Fantasy Camp. One Sunday, at about 4:30 p.m., he turned to me and said, "My friend Kevin Burns, who produces *The Girls Next Door*, is going to pick me up and take me to the Playboy Mansion for Hugh Heffner's movie night, where he watches the new episode of the show live along with new movies. Do you want to come?"

Now, let's face it—nearly all men have fantasies of hanging out with Hef and his playmates. It's got to be on any man's bucket list. I had a dilemma: Part of me didn't want to leave the camp because we had so many stars dropping in at every meal.

My assistant told me, "I've got it covered here. Go have a great time." So I jumped in the back of Kevin's '66 Cadillac convertible, figuring that my wife would also tell me to go and have fun—but not too much fun!

As we pulled up and the guard let us in, I gathered all of the camp swag I had grabbed for Hef's girls. After all, I'm a promoter.

Once in the house, I saw Hugh Hefner come down the stairs in his robe, right on cue, just like in a scene from a movie. He greeted us. We took a photo with Hef—one of my favorites to this day—and exchanged pleasantries. Then Hef invited us to dinner.

We were introduced to others there, including Hef's daughter and her husband. Another couple approached me

The excitement I felt going to the Playboy Mansion that first night stayed with me, and I used the venue for a camp function. Here I am visiting the mansion with radio personality Matthew Erich "Mancow" Muller, on my right, and its resident guardian, Hugh Hefner.

and told me they had always wanted to meet David Fishof of Rock 'n' Roll Fantasy Camp. Now, you can imagine what was going on in my mind. Here I was at the Playboy Mansion, and *I* was getting the star treatment. Apparently this couple went to one of my Ringo shows at the Greek Theatre in Los Angeles on their first date and were now married. They jokingly credited their marriage to me.

After the movie, we said good night, got back in the Cadillac, and went back to Rock 'n' Roll Fantasy Camp. It was a fun night, made incredible by the fact that I could say I had been there and had a picture with Hef to prove it.

Recently, I went back to the mansion with my daughter Ilana—and a strange thing occurred to me when I was standing in front of it again: It was just a building. But the hype of going to the Playboy Mansion that night had made the experience unforgettable. I decided to take advantage of this hype and made arrangements to produce the final performance night of my fantasy camp at the Playboy Mansion. We ended up capitalizing on that same hype that I felt the first night I went inside, and so we sold out the camp with Paul Stanley of KISS and another one with Steven Tyler of Aerosmith.

When your product is ready to be introduced to the world, hype it as much as you can. The more hype you can get, the more successful you will be.

Chapter Eight's Greatest Hits

- Hype is not just advertising. Hype has to go beyond advertising.
- You have to be careful with reporters to ensure that you don't get the wrong kind of coverage.
- You have to be proactive. One of the best things to do is to write your own press release and get it out to the world.
- With the advent of social media, generating hype is much easier.
- Another way to create hype is to have big-name people use your product.

OVERCOME
ENORMOUS
OBSTACLES

Ain't No Mountain High Enough:
OVERCOMING OBSTACLES

I n the process of bringing your idea to life, there is one certainty: You will run into obstacles. It's part of nature; there's no way to avoid it. I always think of the Zig Ziglar line "When you leave for work in the morning, nobody calls the city to see if all the lights are going to be green. You're going to hit red lights. But what will you do with them? Will you get shut down and go home, or will you keep going?"

We all have obstacles to overcome—lack of connections, competition, and our own insecurities. If you're new at something, you're especially likely to struggle with self-doubt. "I'm not good at this," we tell ourselves. "Why would anyone want what I have to offer?" We face legions of naysayers, often our own friends and family, telling us our idea will never work. At times, the challenges facing us seem insurmountable. But if you can learn to look past the obstacles, you can unlock a world of potential in your life.

In this chapter, I want to show you how to clear the obstacles from your path and sail unencumbered into the future, whatever your field. I want to teach you about self-doubt and how to break it. Once you are able to free yourself from the fear, self-doubt, and the stories your mind tells you, there's no telling where you can go.

We face legions of naysayers, often our own friends and family, telling us our idea will never work. At times, the challenges facing us seem insurmountable. But if you can learn to look past the obstacles, you can unlock a world of potential in your life.

Dealing with Your Shortcomings

I have faced many obstacles in my life that might have prevented me from getting where I am today. A challenging obstacle I had to overcome was ADD (Attention Deficit Disorder). Until I learned to work with my ADD and say, "This is me," it adversely affected my life. I read a book called *A.D.D. & Romance* by Jonathan Halverstadt, which basically told me that if I want to succeed in my life, both professionally and personally, and reach my goals, I need to accept my condition as a part of me and treat it medically. It helped me understand that there's no weakness in using medication to help me deal with the symptoms of the condition.

I followed this up by going to see a well-known doctor, Dr. Antoinette Lynn, in New York City, who coached me on reading through magazines, contracts, and books. I had never been a reader because it was too hard to concentrate with my ADD. This needed to be addressed! At one point, I even turned down an offer of $500,000 from a license for The Monkees logo because I didn't read the entire contract, which gave me the retail rights on the logo to sell off. Not reading that contract cost me a lot of money. Reaching out to Dr. Antoinette Lynn definitely helped me take control of my ADD.

But dealing with it was still difficult—I had to find my own tools to work around it. Even today, I like to get into the office an hour and a half before anybody else to get myself organized. The real key, however, was learning to embrace my ADD and accept it as a part of myself. I've even grown to love it—without it, I probably couldn't be as creative and represent twenty ball players, produce three tours in one year, and do so much more all at the same time. My ADD is part of what makes me who I am. Have you embraced who you are? Have you seen the positive side of your perceived shortcomings?

One effect of my ADD was that I simply did not have the patience to complete college, and therefore, I never got a college degree. Many people would see that as an obstacle, but I went on to be successful—all because I persevered on some very good ideas and I was able to reinvent myself time and again, despite not having a complete college education. I recently met NFL great Herschel Walker at a morning TV show we were doing in Dallas to promote our products. Herschel was a role model of mine because, like me, he left college to pursue his career and make money, but soon after he left, he was able to sign a big contract with the New Jersey Generals and their owner, Donald Trump.

Now, I want to be clear. I don't think college is a waste of time. In fact, I think college is important for most people. My three adult children completed college, and I even encouraged them to go to graduate school. I also have two former interns who went on to achieve great things after I encouraged them to attend law school. One is Effy Zinkin, who is now the president of Marc Ecko Enterprises, a global clothing and accessory retail company. The other is Gil Goldschein, the president of production company Bunim

Murray, which produces reality shows like *The Real World*, *Keeping Up with the Kardashians*, and *Project Runway*. Striving to accrue knowledge in any way you can will serve you throughout your career and life.

However, sometimes college is about putting your life on hold and spinning your wheels for four years while others are accomplishing something. For you or your child, college might not be the right path. Or maybe you're in college when you get your big idea. If so, there is absolutely nothing wrong with leaving to pursue that idea and coming back to finish college later. In fact, I would advise it. College isn't going anywhere, but it's always best to act on your idea while it's hot. Some of the greatest entrepreneurs in the world didn't finish college: Mark Zuckerberg, founder of Facebook; Bill Gates, founder of Microsoft; and Steve Jobs, founder of Apple, to name a few. They pursued their ideas instead and found immense success. But then again, for others college is the place where they are introduced to new ideas that might help spark the "big one." You just have to go with what's right for you and have confidence in your decisions.

When I lecture, students always want to hear how I became an agent. At one particular seminar at Seton Hall University in New Jersey, I was the last speaker. My colleagues all got up to tell the students what classes to take in order to be a good sports agent. I remember closing the seminar by telling the law students, "All of these agents are full of it. If you want to become a sports agent, leave this seminar and go find a client like all of us did. The key to becoming a sports agent is to get a client. Period."

Now, whether or not you choose to attend college is completely up to you. The important lesson to take away from what I have been talking about is that no matter your choice, you need to recognize what sort of obstacles you may encounter while pursuing that choice. It may be a hard class, a tough client, etc., but whatever it is, you need to figure out what sort of solution works best for *you* in that situation. Work with the resources you have (a study group, friends in the business, etc.), and work to overcome that hurdle. At some point in life, almost everybody will experience shortcomings, failures, personal struggles, and eventually success. Sometimes going against the grain can lead you to reap great success, but other times, it just isn't the right thing to do. I can't pick and choose when that time for you is—only you can.

However, I do recommend that you first talk to other people when making these big, intimidating, life-changing decisions—people who you trust and respect. Their opinions and advice could carry weight and give you valuable insight as well as help you gain the confidence you need to pursue your idea.

No Doubt About It

The single biggest obstacle anyone can face, and almost everyone does, is self-doubt. Self-doubt alone has killed more ideas and inventions than any other factor. Therefore, it is one of the first areas you need to work on if you are going to be successful.

Napoleon Hill, a pioneer of personal success writing, writes in his book *Think and Grow Rich* that the human mind tends toward the negative. Everyone has those negative feelings about themselves and their abilities—it's part of the human condition. That negativity and self-doubt is passed down to you from your parents, as it was from their parents, and is compounded by incidents that happen to you over the course of your life.

Self-doubt alone has killed more ideas and inventions than any other factor. Therefore, it is one of the first areas you need to work on if you are going to be successful.

As a kid growing up in Galveston, Texas, I was taunted for being Jewish. When I was four years old, I had a kid throw a brick at my head and yell, "You dirty Jew!" I remember going to the hospital to get stitches. That experience stuck with me and made me feel like I was a less significant person. I ended up using that negativity as fuel to create success. I had to show the world that I wasn't a lesser person for being Jewish, or for any other reason.

Our interactions with our parents can affect us the most. Almost all sons and daughters are, on the deepest level, looking for parental approval. It's a universal feeling, from my son, Mordechai, who shoots a basket and shouts, "Daddy, did you see?" to Nicole Kidman winning the Best Actress Oscar in 2003 and saying in her acceptance speech, "Mommy, are you proud of me now?"

So when a parent says, "You'll never amount to anything. You'd better be an accountant. Get security. Don't pursue your crazy dreams," it deeply affects a person. Parents have a responsibility to be really careful about what they say to their children. But no matter how careful parents are, they're bound to say something that their child will hear differently than what was meant, and that stays with the child.

Everyone is, on the deepest level, looking for parental approval. It's a universal feeling.

I was lucky in that my parents were incredibly supportive of my ambitions. They didn't try to stop me when, at seventeen,

I wanted to buy a bar near Brooklyn College called Grandma's to make money. They always made me feel like I could achieve anything. But there are many parents who are insecure about taking risks, and they pass that on to their children. They discourage their children from trying their ideas, and their children grow up full of fear. You need to find freedom so that you can become who you are, not someone who your parents, or anybody else, wants you to be.

Tips for Overcoming Self-Doubt

The truth is, neither the craving for parental approval nor self-doubt are likely to disappear entirely. But you don't have to let these obstacles continually manifest in your life. If you learn to understand how they affect you, you can learn to manage them and eventually they might even empower you. There are a lot of different paths you can take to turn your self-doubt around and build confidence. Here are a few:

1. Think Positively. I find that having the right attitude really helps your outlook. Sports and entertainment agents will have clients come to them and say, "I can get another agent who can do it cheaper." You hear that kind of thing all the time, especially in today's economy, when everyone is so money conscious. In my opinion, the best response when clients say something like that is, "Yes, this agent's good, and that agent's good—but I'm the best." The same attitude works in sales—"Yes, this product is good and that product is good—but mine's the best." If you have that attitude, you will not only make others believe it, but you will make yourself believe it. By saying it, you make the decision that you're going to deliver on that promise—and you therefore drive yourself to become the best you can be.

To have that upbeat, can-do attitude, it's important to fill yourself with positive energy regularly. At a point when I had just finished two amazing tours (The Monkees and Ringo Starr and His All-Starr Band) and my business was booming, I still couldn't help but feel like something was missing from my life. I had to find some kind of balance. That's when a friend recommended I try the Hoffman Process in Northern California. The Hoffman Process is an intensive course in personal discovery and development that allows you to examine your life and your behavior while empowering you to make lasting changes.

Through the Hoffman Process, I learned how much our parents and our past can control the way we live in the present. I always believed I was entirely my own person, but the Process revealed how much my parents' past was still looking over my shoulder every moment of my life.

The Process taught me to take all that negative energy and turn it into a positive force. Before, I didn't really enjoy any of my success. I was so driven to succeed, so focused on the next bit of business that I couldn't enjoy what I was creating. I strongly believe that you should be able to enjoy all parts of your life. The Process freed me from the self-doubt that hindered me. Every once in a while, when I see the Hoffman Process is offering their weeklong seminars and classes, I will join in and take it.

There are many tools like the Hoffman Process that can help you achieve the next level. One technique that I learned and use often deals with negativity. I imagine writing the negative thought in the sand on a beach. I visualize the words in the sand, and then I wait for a wave to come in and wash the words away. Then in their place, I write a positive thought. That's just one way of visualizing. I've also visualized shooting the thought out of the air, or crumpling it up and spreading it over a bed of roses. These are my particular tools, but it's important to find your own way of taking negative feelings and turning them positive. These tools are very important when you're just starting out with your idea.

I'm a big fan of Tony Robbins. He has a great line: "You cannot control what happens to you, but you can control what it means to you." This mantra, along with many of his other teachings, have helped me tremendously. Just the other day, I listened to a Tony Robbins seminar before a meeting I had. It was unbelievable. I walked into the meeting after listening to Tony's inspiring words and made a killer presentation. I had them eating out of the palm of my hand. They booked my show in Las Vegas because I came in

Tony Robbins (left), with his encouraging
talks, has been a great inspiration to me.

with all the confidence I needed. Tony talks a lot about how our greatest performances come when we take action while we are in a peak state. In peak state, you are at your strongest emotionally and physically. It also means that you have total, unwavering focus.

Whether you find your personal freedom in a program, a Tony Robbins talk, or any of the many positive books you can read, it is vital to becoming successful. Here's a quick list of people you can listen to for inspiration: Zig Ziglar, Earl Nightingale, Eckhardt Tolle, Catherine Ponder, Norman Vincent Peale, Jim Rohn, Deepak Chopra, and the grandfather of the personal development movement, Napoleon Hill. For specific titles, visit my Web site, www.davidfishof.com. Once you make your way through some of these books and commit yourself to implementing their paradigm shifts, you'll be a changed person!

2. Get Physical. One of the best things you can do is take care of your health. When I start working out and getting into shape, I feel like a superman. When I don't take care of my health, I could come up with the greatest idea in the world and still feel poor and inadequate. If you take care of yourself and keep yourself in good health, there's nothing in the world you can't do. It's such a simple step, but it's the number-one thing you can do to create that positive feeling that will help you overcome your self-doubt.

If you take care of yourself and keep yourself in good health, there's nothing in the world you can't do . . . it's the number-one thing you can do to create that positive feeling that will help you overcome your self-doubt.

3. Make Good Friends. I've always taken criticism from my wife, who says, "All your friends are famous. You only hang around with celebrities!" Although many of my friends are musicians, athletes, and show business people, just as many are lawyers, doctors, salespeople, or in medical billing. I surround myself only with what they all have in common: success and positivity. I strongly believe that surrounding yourself with successful people will make you want to be successful yourself. Being around them, with their success and strong work ethic, will prompt you to grow personally and reach for the high-hanging fruit. It's important not only to surround yourself with people of excellence but also with people who are creative and who want to share their knowledge with you and help bring you up in the specific community and industry you're interested in so that you can become a part of that community.

Conversely, if you fill your life with people who are self-doubters, it will only perpetuate your own self-doubt. As a parent, I see it more and more—you can raise your kids as well as you possibly can, but if they're hanging around with a bunch of bad kids, it will influence their actions and decisions. We're influenced by the "vibe" around us, so pick and choose your friends and associates carefully and intentionally. You don't need hundreds, but you do need people who are on the same wavelength as you, or are ahead of the game and can teach you. Look around, see who your friends are, and evaluate whether they are a positive or negative influence on your life.

Look around, see who your friends are, and evaluate
whether they are a positive or negative influence on
your life.

Networking Opens Doors

Another important aspect of surrounding yourself with the right people is that those people will often introduce you to others who will play an invaluable role in your life. For me, this happened when I was working on my ill-fated American Bandstand tour with Dick Clark.

Even though the tour wasn't as successful as I had hoped, Dick taught me a very important business lesson: networking. It's one thing to be with a celebrity who is recognized by fans who want his autograph or just want to say hello. It's an altogether different experience to be with a celebrity who recognizes nearly everyone who recognizes him. In airports, guys in suits would say, "Hi Dick," and he'd say, "Hi Charlie, how's business?" Or "Hi Fred, how's the merger going?"

He'd tell me, "He's a VP at Procter and Gamble . . . He's with Volvo . . . He's a big pharmaceuticals guy."

Dick was one of the world's great business networkers, and it's one of the reasons he has had such enduring success. Our partnership just didn't work as well as we'd hoped, as I have discussed. But the lessons I learned from Dick were absolutely priceless.

The Naysayers vs. the Backers

What about that other form of doubt—doubt from others? Chances are, when you are just starting out, you will get many people telling you "No." Whether it's your friends and parents, industry leaders, promoters, or backers, you are probably going to hear "no" over and over again. But you can't let that discourage you. It happens to everybody with a new idea.

As I mentioned, I was lucky because I grew up in a very supportive environment. My parents were largely accepting of my creative endeavors. Being a younger child definitely helped with that—my older brother was the guinea pig. He was the one who had to find a secure job, who had to finish college and become a rabbi, who couldn't be a rock star even though he was a very talented drummer. I am eternally grateful to him because he was, in a sense, the sacrificial lamb for me. Because of him, my parents were willing to indulge me when I wanted to try out my crazy ideas. At age ten, I was the kid copying the Sunday newspaper in my basement and selling the copies to my neighbors at a discount. I sold seeds, advertised in the back of comic books, and when I won prizes for sales records, I would raffle off the prizes. My parents' attitude was always, "Let him do it—at least he's being creative."

But there are many other kids whose parents wouldn't even give them the opportunity to set up a lemonade stand. In my family, I was allowed to pursue my dream of going into show business, rather than following the traditional path of men in my family, who all became cantors or rabbis. But many other kids are too afraid to risk their parents' approval.

My Rock 'n' Roll Fantasy Camp is filled with people who have been told no. That's the reason it's so successful. It's filled with people who had the dream of being a rock star but were told by their wives, girlfriends, parents, "You can't go for it," "You have to go get a job," "You have to get off the road." One camper in particular who comes to mind is John Ferriter, who was head of television at the William Morris Agency. Before taking that position, he was a full-time touring musician. But when he got married, he suddenly had to find a "real" job and give up touring. But he went on to find success, being hired as the head of television and representing such celebrities as

Ryan Seacrest. He's a typical camper—someone who was told, "No," but who went on to find success in another area of his life. The same is true of my TV producer, Lee Metzger, who is the executive producer of *The Voice* and so many other TV shows for Mark Burnett. He and his brother wanted to be full-time rock stars. That's why he's perfect for producing our TV series.

> *My Rock 'n' Roll Fantasy Camp is filled with people who have been told no. That's the reason it's so successful.*

The Input of Others

We often lack confidence because we lack knowledge. This is why talking to others is so important. Talking to others, especially others whom you trust and think of highly, will help you figure out the best path. Your friends and family can, or should be, brutally honest with you, and you should digest their opinions and advice as you form your own.

When I first had the idea to create the Ringo Starr and His All-Starr Band tour, I went to my friend Dave Hart, who was booking the amphitheaters for the Nederlander Organization in New York. I said, "Dave, I have this idea. I'm going over to London to see Ringo, to pitch him the idea of putting together an all-star band that he would lead. Can you give me some ideas of who you would put into an all-star band?" We batted names back and forth, which is the reason I went to him, as he is a talent buyer. When we finally settled on a dream list, he said, "I'll tell you what. If you can put this band together, I can pay you 150 to 175 thousand dollars a show." With that guarantee, I was able to go to other promoters and say, "Hey, I've got these other guarantees. If you want the show, this is what the cost would be." That was a huge help in putting the tour together. Dave continued to buy my tours each and every year since 1986. Fifteen years later, after I've stopped doing the touring, he's taken over.

It's not always industry people who give you the best advice—sometimes spiritual guidance can be just as, if not more, important. There's a rabbi in Jerusalem called the Amshinover Rebbe. It's very hard to get appointments to see the Rebbe; he's the kind of man you have to visit at three in the morning. But my friend Mordechai Ben-David got me an appointment to see this great Rebbe. I flew to Israel, and I got a call at three in the morning from his assistant, telling me to come over and see him.

I met with the Rebbe, and I told him about my interest in producing the American Gladiators Live tour. I told him that I would have to put up hundreds of thousands of dollars to do the show and that I was doubting myself, questioning whether I should do it or not. I remember him shaking in front of me for twenty minutes before he answered. He told me that in the Talmud, it says you should have a third of your money in land, a third in cash, and a third in your business— so I should go ahead and make the investment in my business. With his encouragement I went ahead with the tour—and made a lot of money. Now I often fly to Israel to meet with the Rebbe because he gives me great advice and confidence.

Sometimes the input you get from others is not from the words they say but from the inspiring lives they lead. For me, knowing that my father was a Holocaust survivor who escaped from a concentration camp and spent part of the war in hiding, pretending not to be Jewish, making fake passports, and saving many lives, gave me the confidence to believe that there's nothing I can't achieve. One of my favorite stories about my father is when he took me to see the great Bobover Rebbe for a blessing. The Rebbe said to me, in Yiddish, "My entire life I have worked to keep people Jewish. And your father turned me into a Goy—a non-Jew!" My dad had provided the Rebbe with his false passport, which enabled him to escape from the Nazis. Positive examples like this encouraged me to persevere no matter what roadblocks I faced.

The Perils of Overthinking

Just as you can paralyze yourself with self-doubt, you can also paralyze yourself with overanalysis. What I mean by that is, you can spend so much time and energy analyzing your idea from every angle that you will never bring your idea to fruition. Instead, think of the old Nike slogan, "Just Do It." You can learn as you go. Many people came to this country to escape the Holocaust, and they were able to build up business from nothing because they just went for it. The pain was too much to dwell on, so they simply moved forward.

There was a story I read recently about a father who runs a small grocery store on the Lower East Side of Manhattan. He raises three children to be a lawyer, a doctor, and a PhD from the Wharton School of Business. The three children come to their father one day and decide they want to analyze his business and help him make it grow bigger by inviting in some big accounting and law firms. They suggested it to their father, only to have him say, "Your mother and I raised three amazing kids, paid off all your schooling, and will be retiring soon. All thanks to this little grocery store. I don't think I need any big-shot advice." He certainly didn't!

Barriers of Money and Location

A lot of people ask me about the obstacles of money and location. Strange as it may seem, I would actually count these among the smaller barriers to success. There's no question that money is a big issue. But in today's world, it's very easy to find ways to get things done with little money. It's easy to be resourceful. And you can find a partner to work with, to help you fund your idea—in fact, you should. All you have to do is find the right people and make a great presentation. It's called the "friends and family" round of financing, and I'll talk more about it in a later chapter.

As for location, I have always been very thankful that my parents left Galveston, Texas, for New York. They said the reason they did so was because they wanted to give their kids more opportunities by living near a big city. For many years I really did believe that you had to be near a big city to have the kind of opportunities that lead to success—and for a long time, it was true. However, today you can really live anywhere. With the Internet, Skype, and cheap airfares, you can connect to anyone you need, anywhere. There are so many different franchises and industries in so many different cities. You have investors everywhere. Even in the entertainment business, many people have moved out of LA and New York and are living all over the United States. They just find a way to get where they need to go for the next gig. Connecting to anybody anywhere is what has made a modern success out of Justin Bieber. Years ago would anybody have noticed his talent while he was tucked away in Stratford, Ontario? Bieber was discovered by talent manager Scooter Braun, who was surfing YouTube.

Fleeting Ideas

You may also hit the same obstacle I've hit several times in my career—someone else coming up with and implementing your idea before you have a chance to. When we finished up the first Ringo tour in Las Vegas at the former Aladdin Hotel (now Planet Hollywood), I decided to have a few drinks with Levon Helm and Joe Walsh on the final night. As we were hanging out, I said to Joe and Levon, "We should build a rock and roll hotel here in Las Vegas!" But I had so many other things going on that I didn't pursue it at the time. Then Hard Rock went and built a huge and super-successful casino. But I didn't let it stop me from trying to do something else with Joe. While in Vegas, Joe Walsh shared with me an idea to host

My daughter Shira was able to meet Joe
Walsh of the Eagles during the Ringo Starr
and His All-Starr Band tour.

his own syndicated radio show. He didn't want to depend on a DJ any more to play his own records. I pitched his idea to radio syndicates, and he ended up hosting a show for many years.

If McDonald's and Burger King can coexist, there's no reason why your idea can't compete with others like it.

As a side note, it definitely paid off that I continued to look into my rock and roll hotel idea mentioned above. Someone else's success with a similar idea—like the opening of the Hard Rock Hotel on Paradise Road, Las Vegas—didn't scare me away, even years later, from bringing my own rock and roll project to Las Vegas, and it shouldn't scare you away, either. If McDonald's and Burger King can coexist, there's no reason why your idea can't compete with others like it. In fact, I did pitch my idea, and my Rock 'n' Roll Fantasy Camp will have a permanent location in Sin City at the MGM Grand Hotel & Casino. It's slated to open in the fall of 2012!

The Power of Music to Heal

Rock 'n' Roll Fantasy Camp has also introduced me to some remarkable people who have overcome tremendous challenges in their lives. They learned to move on from their painful past. One man, whose story was reported in *USA Today*, had a son who had been murdered around the time of the JonBenet Ramsey case in Denver. His other son committed suicide a week afterward. A couple of years later, his friend saw how much he was still suffering and knew he needed some kind of outlet. So he said, "Come to Rock 'n' Roll

Fantasy Camp with me." The man came to the camp to play guitar and afterward told *USA Today* that by expressing himself through music, he was able to overcome this tragic incident, get engaged, adopt two children, and continue to play music every day. That's what it is all about—letting go and freeing yourself so you're able to follow your dreams.

There was another camper at the New York camp who had tragedy in his life. His son was getting ready to go to college, where he was set to become a football star. But one night his son got drunk and killed two people and himself in a drunk-driving accident. This happened seven years ago, and all these years this father had been living with the pain every day, trying everything he could to overcome it.

One day at the New York camp, I was checking in at Gibson Studios and saw this man sitting quietly by himself in an empty studio, writing lyrics and crying. I asked what was going on, and he said, "Can I read you these lyrics?" I said yes. He read me his lyrics and asked what I thought. "Go back to Rudy Sarzo," the bassist for Ozzy Osbourne, who was heading this guy's band. "Go back to your band and create some music for it," I said.

On the last day of camp, I brought Roger Daltrey, the lead singer of The Who, in to see this guy and his band. I told Roger, "This gentleman has written a brand-new song." Roger said, "I'd like to hear it." I said to the man, "Before you sing the song, tell Roger what it's about." The man explained the story about his son. When he finished, Roger walked over to him, grabbed him, and hugged him for five minutes. As Roger hugged him, he said to him, "Let go. Let go. You have to let go."

The band played the song, and we were all in tears. Afterward Roger hugged the man again and again said, "Just let go." That night, the band performed the song at B.B. King's, as the last song of the concert. The next day, this man, who hadn't really smiled in years, had a huge smile on his face. He said, "I can let go. I was able to write a song, be creative, and although it will always be in my mind, I'm not going to let it stop my life."

Believe in Your Dream and Persevere

The strength that these two men had to overcome the tragedy in their lives is truly inspiring. But the strength of conviction to pursue your dream until it becomes a reality is also vital to finding success. The stories are amazing that come out of each camp. The reason the camp works is because the rockers get emotional meeting the people, too. The late Levon Helm, drummer for The Band, always had this dream and idea of doing concerts at his house in Woodstock. He hated touring, so he wanted to do shows from his home. I told him it was a brilliant idea, but everyone else said it wouldn't work. He was having all sorts of problems, financial and personal—but he had this dream, and he wouldn't let it go. He persevered in pursuing his idea, and now most Saturday nights, he does a show in his house called The Rambles with Levon Helm. He sells tickets for $200 apiece and grosses $20,000 to $30,000 a show. Despite all the naysayers and obstacles, he followed his dream, and it's turned out to be a fantastic success, and now many top rockers go up there to jam with him. Since starting this venture, Levon has won two Grammy Awards! One in 2007 for Best Traditional Folk Album for *Dirt Farmer* and another in 2010 for Best Americana Album for *Electric Dirt*.

Giants legend Phil Simms had a similar story. He always dreamed of becoming a sports broadcaster. He shared that vision with me when he was just a rookie, so I contacted a local college, Bergen Community College, with a cable TV station in New Jersey. I got him his own show on the channel and found him guests each week so he could get some broadcasting experience. When he ended his playing career and wanted to step into the broadcast booth, he had all that background behind him. Today, Phil is the top NFL analyst on CBS. Was it luck or preparation that propelled him immediately to the top? You tell me! Luck is when preparation meets opportunity, and if you are persistent and willing to take your dream and really go for it, you'll find it's easier to overcome the obstacles that face you.

Luck is when preparation meets opportunity, and if you are persistent and willing to take your dream and really go for it, you'll find it's easier to overcome the obstacles that face you.

Stoke the Passion Flames

As long as you have passion behind your focus, you will find success. About fifteen years ago, I told the film producer Sam Goldwyn Jr. that I wanted to go into the movie business. I asked him, "How do I produce a movie?" He answered, "The number-one thing is passion. You really have to believe in your project. You can't just casually say, 'Oh yeah, I have this idea.' You have to have passion for it, and the passion to constantly sell it. You have to be passionate enough about it to make everyone else passionate about it, too."

A recent attendee at rock camp, Scott Rosenbaum, decided after 9/11 to pursue his dream and make a movie about rock and roll. Although it took him nine years to get his movie off the ground, with lots of stop-and-go along the way, his passion took him to the end, and now Warner Bros is distributing his movie called *The Perfect Age of Rock 'n' Roll.* What a great rock and roll flick. It was his unwavering passion that got it to the screen.

Passion is the key to success in more than one way. My philosophy is, if you can make a living doing something you're passionate about, you're successful. Whether you make your living writing books, or being a musician, or selling baseball cards, or collecting coins (like a camper I had)—as long as you have a passion for what you do, whatever it is—you are successful.

My philosophy is, if you can make a living doing something you're passionate about, you're successful.

Why? Because to me, there are greater indicators of success than money. Your goal shouldn't be to make a hundred million. Your goal should be to find happiness and passion—to do something that you totally enjoy doing, to wake up every day and make your living because you want to do it, not because you have to. One of the clearest examples of how chasing money instead of passion can ruin success is the Boeing story. Bill Allen was the CEO of Boeing from 1946 to 1968. He imbued the company with clear vision: "We must eat, sleep, and breathe the world of aeronautics." Under CEO Phil Condit, however, things took a total turn. The company became about profit. That was its new vision. Slowly but surely Boeing lost out to Airbus. When money became everything, Boeing lost its way.

And there are far greater outcomes your idea can have than just making you a profit. My main motivation today is leaving a legacy: changing people's lives through music. I've been a man of creative ideas, and now I want to give back my success to others. Creating something that can change the world, whether it's a charity or a profitable business, is the greatest achievement you can have. You don't need to beat the other guy or make as much money as someone else. If you concentrate on that, you will get nowhere. You need to focus on being your own best possible self.

There's a great Hassidic tale about Rebbe Zushya. One day, Rebbe Zushya is sitting and crying. God comes to him and asks, "Why are you crying?" Rebbe Zushya replies, "Because I'll never be as learned as Rabbi Hillel." And God says, "That's okay. All I want you to be is the best possible Rebbe Zushya." And here's the secret: If you follow that advice, be the best possible you and do what you're passionate about, the money will follow. There's no telling how much money, but if you do the absolute best you can, you're going to be successful. If you can change the world following your passion, doing what you love, and being the best you can be, then you have truly reached ultimate success.

Getting in from the Outside

One of the big hurdles people face in launching their ideas is getting a foot in the door. "How do I get started?" people ask, "How do I take the first step?" They build this huge fear within themselves, like a kid getting scared to jump off the diving board into the pool. They fear taking that first step of finding the right person to present their idea to.

But here's the secret: That first step is incredibly simple. All you need to do to get that first meeting, that first presentation—is ask! Sometimes you have to do it over and over again, but all it takes is asking. Don't be afraid to reach for the sky—no idea is stupid.

You can't underestimate the power of a simple phone call. It was a simple phone call that really launched my career as a sports agent to a new level. While I was representing baseball player Lou Piniella, I heard about an amazing ad campaign that Sasson Jeans was launching, using NHL players. They had booked four players for these ads, including Phil Esposito, who was a client of mine. I knew this was going to be a hot commercial, and I wanted to get Lou involved. So I called Phil, and asked him about the ad.

"David," Phil said, "the lady who's doing the advertising doesn't like to deal with agents. She came straight to the Rangers to book us for the ad. I'm going to pay you the commission anyway, but she won't want to deal with you."

How was I going to get this commercial booked for Lou if the lady wouldn't deal with agents? Lou was very hot in New York at the time, so I knew they'd want him, but how was I to make the connection? I would have to be a little tricky about it. I decided to call the lady and pretend to be Lou Piniella.

I made the phone call and said in my best Lou Piniella voice, "This is Lou Piniella, and I'm very interested in the commercial you're making with the Rangers. My teammates and I would actually love to do a commercial."

"Lou Piniella?" asked the lady.

"Yes, ma'am," I replied.

"Is this you?" she asked.

"Yes, ma'am," I said, afraid that the game was up.

"You know," she said, "we're thinking of doing a baseball commercial. Can you come and see us?"

I was in! "Sure," I said, still in my Lou Piniella voice. "I can be there tomorrow if you want."

"Can you come in at noon?" she asked.

"Sure, I'll be there," I replied. She gave me the address. My plan had worked.

I immediately called up Lou, who was already coming in from Florida for another meeting.

"Lou," I said, "you've got to catch that six o'clock plane in the morning."

"What's this about?" he asked.

"Just catch the plane," I said. "I'll tell you when you land."

Lou took the plane and arrived in New York. I picked him up at the airport and said, "Don't get upset with me, Lou. I did an impression of your voice and got us an appointment at Sasson Jeans."

Lou started laughing and laughing. He thought it was great. Then he said, "Well, how am I going to take you in? Who are you going to be?"

"Just tell them I'm your driver," I said. "Tell them I'm your best friend!"

We went to the meeting, and they offered us the commercial, which would shoot in Los Angeles a week later. Lou turned to me, I nodded, and Lou said, "Yeah, let's do it."

We went to Los Angeles to make the commercial. While we were there, Lou introduced me to Fred Dryer, and my whole career took off—all because I had the chutzpah to take a chance, do an impression, and make a simple phone call.

If you have an idea, pick up the phone, write an e-mail, send a message on Facebook—with technology today, it's amazing how many people are easily reachable. There's a great Web site called Hoovers.com that has a list of every corporation in the world, along with the various officers and executives and their phone numbers. There are a lot of people out there who are insulated, but there are other channels to utilize as well. A letter, or better yet, a FedEx, will get someone's attention. If you send a FedEx, it is almost certainly going to be opened—so for $25, you can get your idea in front of somebody.

The idea of just picking up the phone and calling is certainly intimidating. But more and more people who have ideas and want to present them will take the step of contacting the person directly. You don't want to be left behind. If you pick up the phone and call, the worst thing that can happen is that they will say no. That's not too scary, is it? And it's worth the risk. Mark Burnett writes in his book *Jump In!: Even If You Don't Know How to Swim* about how he contacted Donald Trump's office to sell him this idea about a reality show called *The Apprentice*. The secretary told him to call Trump's agent, who rejected the idea. So Mark went back and contacted Trump and set up a meeting with Trump himself. Trump was delighted with the idea, said yes to Mark, and fired his agent.

Don't be afraid of an initial rejection. You just have to give it due diligence. Sometimes all you need is an audience with the right person. You also have to have the right presentation, but we'll talk more about that in chapter 10.

One of my favorite lines that I live with every day is something Lynn Hoffman from A&E said to me: "Life is 10 percent what happens and 90 percent how you deal with it." I always write down good sayings like this because they're always helpful in the future. This saying in particular always reminds me that what's important is not the obstacles you face, the fear and self-doubt you carry, the incidents in your past, big or small, that hold you back. What's important is how you deal with those obstacles. Take advantage of the programs and books out there that can help you overcome your self-doubt. Consult your trusted advisors and surround yourself with people who influence you positively. Seek inspiration in the example of others. Find the confidence to put yourself out there and keep knocking on doors. If you develop the right tools, you can free yourself. And if you are free, you will be successful in your life.

Chapter Nine's Greatest Hits

- We all face challenges. How we deal with those challenges can bring us abundant success.
- Self-doubt is one of the biggest obstacles in our way, but there are ways to overcome it and move forward in confidence instead.
- Our parents' approval plays a huge role in how we operate.
- Your fears will be a part of you, but you don't have to let them take over your life.
- There are many useful tools to master our fears. I personally have worked with and like the Hoffman Process and talks by Tony Robbins.
- If somebody else is doing your idea, don't fear the competition.
- Surrounding yourself with other successful people will make you want to excel yourself.
- Fears can be broken when you get the courage to make that first move.
- Believe in yourself to overcome all obstacles, even when you haven't set a foot in the door yet.

CHAPTER 10

Every Rose Has Its Thorn:
TAKING FEAR OUT OF THE EQUATION

I have found that fear in the entertainment business is much stronger than in any other business. The reason for that, I believe, is because when you are in the entertainment business, your life is, unfortunately, like an open book. Everything you do, everything you say, every move you make is open to scrutiny by the press, the public, and your peers; and it is magnified by those people to a much larger degree than in other businesses. You are watched like a hawk, and there is not much to do about it. Inevitably, this creates fear—fear of being exposed, fear of public failure, fear of even wearing the wrong outfit! Rock stars and other people in the entertainment industry are constantly fearing something that could, would, or might happen.

It is this fear that constantly makes artists want to be ahead of the industry or on top of what is going on. They schedule way too many tours and/or appearances to keep up. But this can, in the end, cause great distress and lead to failure, simply because it is too much pressure. Take Michael

Jackson for example. Before he died, he was rehearsing for a fifty-show run at the O2 Arena in London, and he hadn't done a tour of this magnitude in years. As a result, he needed a medical doctor at his side twenty-four hours a day to constantly care and watch after him. It isn't just Michael Jackson. Nearly all artists experience the need to prove themselves to their audience day in and day out because of the constant judgments they face from the outside world.

I applaud and respect artists who have the muster to put themselves out there daily, and nightly. But for me (and probably for you), fear is something I need to get past so I can move forward rather than make myself sick over it. The one thing I always tell myself is that all, or most, problems I encounter in my business will be gone by the following week, so don't stress over it.

Don't stress. Tomorrow is a new day; next week is a fresh start. Remember that. I hope this chapter will help you alleviate fear as best you can.

Settle it for yourself right here, right now: Not everything you do is going to be successful. But unsuccessful efforts aren't necessarily failures. Sometimes apparent failure can lead to success in unexpected ways, as it did in my case.

I had my first rock and roll fantasies when I was sixteen. They weren't grandiose. In fact, they went no further than my immediate family. I wanted to be in my older brother's band.

It was perhaps the world's first openly Jewish rock band: The Ruach Revival. "Ruach" is a Hebrew word meaning spirit. My brother, Joey, was the leader of the band, the drummer, and my hero. Joey, who is six years older than me, was a natural. He couldn't read music and never took a lesson. The girls loved him, of course. I envied him. I took guitar lessons in hopes of joining his group. But two things made it difficult: One, I had no musical talent, and two, my brother didn't want me in his band.

My father, Mark, stepped in as a peacemaker. "David, my son," he said, "instead of being a performer in the band, be the guy who books six bands a day." That's how I began to follow my career path. If it hadn't been for my failure to join my brother's band as a musician, I may never have found my true career path and reached the success I have achieved.

The problem for many people is that when they encounter failure, they think, "I failed, it's over, it's never going to work." When you fall flat on your face, it's easy to walk away and say it's not going to work. But I've always found that when one door closes, another one opens. I've been beaten down and turned down over and over again in my career. You're going to get a lot of no's before you get a yes. But you only need that one yes to see something happen and to get to the next level—or perhaps a no will direct you elsewhere, like my musical "path" took as a youngster.

When you fall flat on your face, it's easy to walk away and say it's not going to work. But I've always found that when one door closes, another one opens.

You have to be mentally prepared and not let the no's affect you. Instead, you have to let the no's make you stronger—you have to find a way to take that negative energy and turn it positive.

Fear of Failure

Many books you read will tell you that your fears are exaggerated. That's not what I'm going to do. Many of the fears you have are very real and may very well become realized. But I want to help you learn how to take fear out of the equation, to conquer fear by focusing your energy and attention on the outcome you want to achieve.

One of the great fears we have is the fear of failure. People are afraid of royally screwing up, of falling flat on their red-tinged humilated face. They are afraid to step out of their comfort zone, because they are afraid that if they try something new, they will fail at it.

And you know what? It's not a silly fear. The truth is, sometimes you will fail. It happens to everyone. In my career I've certainly had failures. The Mortal Kombat tour that I've mentioned, for example, was a project that was somewhat of a disaster for me. When I was approached by the movie producer of Mortal Kombat to create a live tour, I really thought it would take off. But I didn't take the steps necessary to make it happen the right way. It was all very badly timed. For one, I used my young son's and his friends' opinions as the bulk of my research, and there are a million reasons why it failed. But the important thing was that I learned from the mistakes I made, and that in turn helped me reach success with other projects.

Don't be afraid of the failures you might face; know that they can be a great learning experience and that if you are able to learn from your mistakes, grow, and move on, you will have success.

Fear of Success

Being in show business, I have seen many artists blow opportunities and deals because they subconsciously fear success. Sometimes, people self-sabotage when they find themselves out of their comfort zone, even if they've moved forward in a positive direction. This is one reason why many people who win the lottery end up blowing the money in a short span of time. I've seen people who have gotten hot so fast that they get completely overwhelmed. They get freaked out because they just don't know how to handle it. In some cases, they completely blow it the first time around, and then people don't want to work with them again. In others, when they try to regain their success, they botch it themselves because they are, deep down, afraid to regain it.

It's a fairly common occurrence in our business. We all have heard the story of a famous musician who was enjoying great success but becomes an alcoholic and completely sabotages his career. Unfortunately there is almost no end to the number of musicians with this story. This kind of thing happens so frequently in the music business that it's almost become a running joke. Riding around in the van with the All-Starr Band, we would all say that every rock story sounded like a story from the *VH1 Behind the Music* TV series: A band makes it big from nothing, loses all their money and publishing to a bad manager, then regroups and tries to make a comeback—just insert the band or artist's name.

Sometimes, people self-sabotage when they find themselves out of their comfort zone, even if they've moved forward in a positive direction.

Roger Daltrey was generous enough to come to my son-in-law's synagogue for a Sabbath dinner, and he had a brilliant line about becoming famous, and what it was like for him when The Who got big: "Before success, I was walking with traffic, with all the people. All of a sudden, when I got successful, I was walking against the traffic, toward everybody,

POWERFUL WAYS TO CREATING AN IDEA AND FOLLOWING THROUGH

"Fear stops us from being successful." Bill Zanker, founder and president of The Learning Annex, and one of my good friends, understands fear. For Bill, fear is rooted in everything we do. But he never let that stop him from achieving success. The Learning Annex began in 1980 and has since become the leading producer in adult education. Experts in business, leadership, the arts, and so on participate in online classes, seminars, workshops, and expos to give practical, powerful insights into their careers as well as to teach individuals how to improve the quality of their lives.

However, the idea for a cheap, simple, yet very effective way to get people educated did not come to Bill with the snap of his fingers. Just like each and every one of us, Bill experienced fear of failure and had to jump many hurdles before deciding to move forward with his project. As Bill told me, "Everybody has [something], but we all get tripped along the way." A big part of being able to look your fear in the eye and shove it aside for your chance to be successful is to recognize what groups of people to surround yourself with. Establishing that group of people, that strong support sys-

Continues

and everybody was looking at me." That's a hard shift to make, and it takes a while to get used to.

Fear of failure is hard, too—and it doesn't go away once you're successful. You still have to run that gamut every day. When you are successful, you come to the point where you start thinking, "Oh no, I'm not going to be successful anymore." So really, fear of success can be an aspect of fear of failure, like an endless cycle. It's easy to fall into the trap of equating your success with your financial success, with being "on top." You forget about other more important things, like being a parent. I try to live by the following motto: A hundred years from now, it won't make a difference how much money you had, what kind of car you drove, or what house you lived in. The only difference will be what effect you had on the life of a child. That's the most important responsibility we have. If you keep yourself grounded in the true, important things in life, you won't get swept away by the giant fears of success and failure.

You also can't be afraid to move on from your past to bigger and better things. It can be hard to leave behind what you're used to, what you've already had success with. I had to make that shift when I moved into representing rock and roll artists. It was Ringo who told me that if I was going to work with him, I would have to lighten my roster and focus exclusively on him and a few other classic rock bands.

So I made the decision and I told my right-hand guy, Howie Silverman, that he could have all my old pop acts. He went on to open his own talent agency, called Paradise Artists in Ojai, California, and made lots of money—and I'm very happy for him. Meanwhile, I moved into the rock and roll

Continued

tem, comes over time. You will likely come across those friends who tell you "No, no..." and the ones who find criticism in every move you make. Don't let the fear of rejection, or the fear of being shot down by your peers (the people who often matter the most to you), turn you into a quitter. Bill argues that the first important step to facing the fear of rejection is to become confident enough in yourself and your ideas that everything else around you suddenly doesn't matter as much—you continue to pursue what you want. As you grow more confident in your success, you bring in others whose thoughts are reliable and trustworthy.

Bill Zanker did exactly that. First, he figured out what he wanted in something (a product, an event, a Web site, etc.). For Bill, his needs were more education and more learning resources. He researched and found that there wasn't much out there to satisfy those needs. After his research, he began to write his ideas down and create a step-by-step plan—a map. "It's nothing formal," he says. Bill insists that keeping everything in your head will only cause more fear to build up; every idea becomes somewhat scarier when it is floating around your head with no direction. Bill's advice? Write it all down on one index card. "If it's more [than that], it's not simplified enough. If

Continues

Continued

it's all on one index card, it's not scary anymore." Make it a point to carry that card around with you—it's easy to manage, easy to access, and easy to understand.

After you have figured out what you want and how you are going to achieve it, then you are ready to move forward and gauge what the public's wants are. Bill stresses that it's important to ask experts—a lot of experts. However, it's important to remain strong and confident in what you created; again, don't let the fear of what others will say about your product stop you from pursuing your idea. Don't ask people if you should move forward with the project; you want their input, but be confident that you are moving forward with the project. All you are asking the experts for is advice on how to get the product out there and if they or people they know would need something like what you're offering. Always remain confident that what you are offering is a good product; you just need to find for *whom* it is a good product.

After doing all of this, it's time to prepare to pitch your product to investors. Bill started his company in 1980 with just $5,000, sold it in 1991, and came back and bought out all of his partners in 2001. Although Bill started his company on his own, many of you may want to get investors or start partnerships. Bill explains

Continues

business. It was a lot harder and more demanding, but the loyalty of the following is second to none. It was a big, hard decision to leave my former success behind to try this new thing, but it was without question the right choice.

Behind the Fear

To truly overcome a fear, we have to understand the root of it. What is at the heart of it? *Why* are people so afraid of failing, even if they know that failure is a good opportunity to learn and grow? The chief reason is bad publicity. People are afraid that if they fail, they will be thought of as a failure; they will lose face.

One of the biggest lessons I had to learn years ago is not to care what other people think of me. I wasn't the hippest of rock promoters. My pal Kip Winger told me one night that people consider me an outsider in the music business because I came from the world of sports. But I didn't (and still don't) let that bother me. Sometimes there's an advantage to coming from the outside—you are not doing things the same way as others. I've been lucky to work with hundreds of the greatest musicians in rock and roll from the biggest bands. Hip—what's hip? If you can make a living in the business you love, that is what counts, not what people think of you. Other people's perception of you is only relevant in so far as it can advance your business—there's no value to perception for perception's sake.

Take Gene Simmons for example. He and his band, KISS, can be considered one of the most lucrative rock and roll bands in merchandising, and Gene Simmons is proud of it. Once while I was visiting Gene at his home, I was able to sneak a peek into his famous room of

Continued

that there are four major points that sell your product and will help convey your confidence in your product to the investors, which will in turn, make them confident to invest in you:

- The first is passion. This, for Bill, is the most important part of your pitch and your presentation. If you display passion in your idea, you show that you are confident in the product. As Bill tells me, "If [the presenter] is passionate, they'll stick with it and see it through."

- Second is the idea itself. Make sure you put in due time in the preparation phase—the time for you to build your idea and expand on it so that it is the best product on the market, meeting the needs you established in the beginning.

- The third point will be to discuss the market for the idea, product, etc. If you aren't confident here, your idea will fall through the cracks. You need to be absolutely sure of the kind of audience you will market to and how you will gain their following.

- Fourth, you will need to figure out beforehand how much of the market's needs would be solved through your product.

The fear of being rejected at any of these steps can definitely consume you and halt

Continues

Continued

your drive. But, as Bill argues, "Once we accept [fear], and understand [fear], we can be successful." Even when you are up and running and well on your way to success, fear can wiggle its way into your thoughts and prevent you from moving forward. It can still strip you of your confidence to take things to the next level, pursue other options for your product/company, and expand on your idea. Bill Zanker is no stranger to the fear of moving ahead. When he decided to take his company to the next level, he wanted to lock in Donald Trump to speak, but Trump was very expensive. Bill says he offered Trump two different amounts, but both were rejected—Trump was asking for $1 million! At that time, Bill didn't have that, but he didn't let that scare him into backing down. Instead, he remained confident in his product and committed to Trump. "I remember going to the bathroom [feeling very ill]," Bill recalls. "It was that hard, putting everything I had on the line. But it was the right decision because I believed he was the right guy to headline my real estate seminar, so I took the leap, and booked Trump for all that he asked."

Looking back, Bill feels that his decision was one of the best he has made. It was worth every penny to him. The passion and confidence Bill had in himself

Continues

licensed products that he has partnered with, one of them being the famous "Hello Kitty." But Gene doesn't care if people think it's hip or cool of him or not cool; he becomes a part of what *he* feels is successful for his brand, and he becomes a part of what *he* sees as successful—not what anybody else defines it as.

Hip—what's hip? If you can make a living in the business you love, that is what counts, not what people think of you.

This fear of what people will think can easily grow out of control as you achieve success. The more successful you are, the more visible you are to other people. Ironically, this is also at the heart of what people fear most about success. People think, "Everyone will look at me differently, everyone will want money from me." It's true, becoming successful, making a lot of money—it's a lifestyle. You will have more people in your face, and everyone will want something from you. This is widely acknowledged in the field of sports. The NBA has even created a Rookie Transition Program, an orientation to help rookies ease into the NBA's demanding lifestyle. It's funny to see how many new relatives these athletes meet. But they learn how to stay grounded through all of it. That is key—you have to learn to stay grounded. One of the most important lessons I can teach about staying grounded is to always be aware of how you are growing. Every once in a while, take a step back and look at your success; you need to be ready for anything, from small to large growths in your business. And be warned—it doesn't come on schedule and success won't wait for you. It just happens.

Continued

and his product drove him to book Trump and continue to take his company to the next level of service. That type of passion, Bill says, is one of the most important qualities you can have. "You have to have a lot of passion to take your business from a few million to over 100 million—which is what we did."

Before you start questioning if you have the right kind of passion, drive, or the right skill set, stop! What you need to have, as Bill reminds me, is certainty in the different goals you set out to accomplish. He argues that nobody is born with a different skill set, and that entrepreneurs are no different from the "average Joe." As he put it, "I think we all have it. It's a skill set. It's that desire to say, 'I'm not going to quit.'" This is something that's in us all—to take an idea, run with it, and see how far it can go.

It isn't easy to look fear in the eye, but we are all capable of doing it. Like Bill Zanker, we have needs and wants that manifest themselves in our thoughts. Just remember what Bill says, "What you need is to say, 'I can do this, I'll just keep moving forward.'"

Legal Matters

As I became more successful I also learned the importance of proper legal protection. I spoke with a colleague the other day who said to me, "In order to run a successful business, you've got to earmark a certain amount of your money that's going to go to legal fees. You've got to count it in your budget because if you're successful, people are going to come after you. And especially if you've created a new idea, people are going to come after you."

How often do you hear about a movie deal being made and somebody filing a lawsuit against the studio? Usually saying something along the lines of, "I brought that idea to you first!" On your road to success, you have to get as much protection as you can. One way to do this, economically, which I recommend, is visit a site like Robert Shapiro's www.legalzoom .com. Through a service like this, you can trademark your ideas and get the legal protection you need to move forward. My friend Patrick Riley just used the legalzoom.com service and was very happy with it when it came to trademarking "Rock Star trainer." As a personal trainer to many famous musicians, he felt it was important to trademark the reputation he had worked so hard to obtain, and legalzoom.com made it easy.

More on Success

Success can affect you in more personal ways as well. I recently watched the Oscars and thought, *How many of these Oscar winners, these major celebrities, are now faced with people saying cruel and hurtful things about them, are faced with stalkers, or are faced with all sorts of other negatives? How many of them*

must sometimes think, "Why am I doing this? If I wasn't in the
public eye, I wouldn't have a stalker."

On top of all of these hardships, the ordinary ups and
downs of life remain—they don't magically disappear when
you become successful. I represented Trevor Berbick, who was
known for beating Muhammad Ali to become the World
Heavyweight Champion. He had a fight in Atlantic City with
Renaldo Snipes. Berbick was favored to win, but in the first
thirty seconds of the fight, he got knocked down. I came up to
him and said, "What happened?" He replied, "My wife called
me an hour before the fight and we had a big argument." It
completely threw him off his game.

When people start getting successful, they often get discouraged by all the negativity, and this contributes even more
to their fear. It's something that once you're successful, you'll
have to deal with for the rest of your life. But trust me—the
success you will achieve is worth it. You just have to learn how
to overcome all the negativity, which I'll get to in a minute.

I remember an incident during one of the shows I put
together at the DTE Energy Music Theatre in Clarktown,
Michigan. A woman in the audience had won the two front
row seats from the local radio station. She was very excited to
be there, but next to her was her husband—and he was reading a book! The musicians performing were incredibly upset.
Here they were, playing a show, with ten thousand screaming
fans. But because of the lights, they could only see the front
row, with this guy reading his book.

But that's how it can be—even if you've got ten thousand fans, it's often that one person bringing you down,
whether it's your significant other or a stranger in the audience. Even the most successful people are not immune to feeling down—they are human, too, and they are just as affected
by it as anyone else.

Some people find creative ways to prevent this kind of negativity from affecting their performance. Billy Joel's tour manager, Max Loubiere, has a brilliant tactic. He gets eight tickets in the very front row, right in front of Billy. Then, at the show, he goes to the last row of the theater and finds eight screaming fans who really want to be at the concert. Then, Max will say to them, "Tonight's you're lucky night—you're going to sit in the front row." So it's those eight ecstatic fans who Billy sees when he performs, and it's those vibes that he plays off.

Power of Persevering and Adapting

In chapter 4 I talked about my disappointments with my British Rock Symphony idea, as I faltered in my game plan. But even from that failure, I pulled success. I came up with the concept for the symphony when I saw the talented Zak Starkey, son of Ringo Starr, playing drums on the Ringo tour. He's a great drummer and now plays for The Who and Oasis. When I saw him play, I thought, *How amazing would it be to put an orchestra behind him and play rock and roll with a symphony?* When I told my idea to Zak, he told me that Roger was very interested in merging symphonic music and rock and roll. He had actually just done a symphonic show of the music of Pete Townshend, with legendary orchestrator and conductor Michael Kamen. The show had just finished a tour of the United States with a packed house at Carnegie Hall.

So Zak introduced me to Roger Daltrey. I went to meet Roger at his home in the English countryside and shared with him my vision. Roger was skeptical at first, then he liked it and helped me launch the British Rock Symphony by helping me find a conductor, singing on the album, and agreeing to do a twenty-five-city tour for me.

After the music was written, I contacted Peter Frampton as well, and he agreed to do three shows. I then approached Lisa Altman, who originally signed Andre Bocelli to Universal Records. She introduced me to the label head, Costa Pilavachi. Costa was great and gave me a record contract. I then hired producer Ron Nevison, who had worked with such amazing acts as Heart, Led Zeppelin, and Alice Cooper. Rory Johnson, who worked for Phillip Glass, was also in on the record.

We pulled together a vast amount of talent. We had the great violinist Nigel Kennedy doing a version of "While My Guitar Gently Weeps." Paul Rogers of Free and Bad Company did a Beatles medley. Alice Cooper sang "Another Brick in the Wall," while Nancy Wilson of Heart belted out Led Zeppelin's "Kashmir," and Roger Daltrey did "Let It Be" and "Pinball Wizard." It was a great CD.

As I've explained, however, the tour was not successful. Simply put, we didn't get the response we hoped for from American audiences. Now, I could have pulled the plug on the British Rock Symphony early on. But I was determined to do this symphonic rock concept. So I reworked the tour a bit based on some of the feedback I got and relaunched it to great success in South America, Australia, Spain, and other places.

In Australia, I brought together on one stage Alice Cooper, Paul Rogers, Peter Frampton, Roger Daltrey, and Gary Brooker from Procol Harum. We toured Australia, all the major arenas, and then I took the same show to South America with Alice Cooper and Jon Anderson from Yes. Roger and I went to Spain with the show and toured all the castles in England with it.

Years later, the ambassador for the United Nations to Bosnia came to see me, and he urged me to go and try to help the Bosnian government bring rock concerts to Bosnia. It was after the war, and none of the youth wanted to stay there. A year earlier, the UN ambassador explained, Bono had come over and done a concert. It was a huge success, so the government wanted me to help bring more concerts to the area.

I was intrigued, having read everything about the war and Yugoslavia. The UN ambassador invited me to Sarajevo to check it out. I agreed to go over if they would send me to Israel afterward. They agreed, and anytime I can get a free trip to Israel, I go—so I went.

It was quite an experience. I stayed in a Holiday Inn in Sarajevo, where the next room was all bombed out. The whole hotel was bombed out. All of the buildings had bullet holes; the city was so bare. It reminded me of what my poor father had probably gone through after the Holocaust, and I felt I really wanted to help these people.

At the time, Grand Funk Railroad had asked me to manage them. So I said, "I'll manage you on one condition—that we do a symphonic concert, symphonic Grand Funk, that we do three concerts, and that the money we raise goes to Bosnia." They agreed, so I went to Paul Shaffer, musical director and leader of the CBS Orchestra on David Letterman's show, and I asked if he would conduct the orchestra. He had never conducted an orchestra before, so he thought it was quite cool. We did a show at the Beacon Theatre in New York, and a show for 16,000 people in Detroit, and played the Greek Theatre in Los Angeles, where Slash came on for. It was amazing. We did these three concerts—all sold out—and produced an album.

Then I went back to Bosnia a year and a half later while I was on tour with Ringo. During a weekend off, I took Eric

Burdon of the Animals, and we did a show there with the local Bosnian symphony, which Eric writes about in his book *Don't Let Me Be Misunderstood.*

So even though my original British Rock Symphony wasn't a huge success, I pursued my vision and found a way to make it successful in a different way. And I came away from it with another added bonus—having met and gotten to know Roger Daltrey.

Ignoring Rejection

Sometimes, to make your idea happen, to get past all the no's, you have to take big risks. You also have to get used to the rejection and realize that it doesn't mean you won't be successful beyond your wildest dreams. You have to get past the fear of being rejected.

Take Elvis Presley. Several years into his career, Elvis was still a nobody. It was 1954, and in a few more years he would be a household name, but at the time no one had ever heard of him. In fact, Jimmy Denny, manager of the Grand Ole Opry, fired him after just one performance.

"You ain't goin' nowhere, son," Denny said. "You ought to go back to drivin' a truck."

However, Elvis embraced the fact that his voice didn't mimic a cookie-cutter pop or rock sound, and he was fully aware that he didn't sound like any other musician out there at the time. Elvis also knew that the way he moved his hips could get a crowd's heart racing and their blood pumping; he had the ability to build his moves and his show based on fans' reactions. Even though Jimmy Denny turned him down, he found a spot on *Hayride*, the more "wild" version of the Grand Ole Opry. After a couple of flubs and attack of the nerves, he finally got his groove and was booked for a year's worth of Saturday night appearances.

Imagine the history of rock and roll if Elvis had taken Denny's advice, given up on music, and gone back to Memphis to be a truck driver! Luckily for us, Elvis was confident in his future as a musician, and the rest is history.

Another band got its humble beginnings in Hamburg, Germany, where they lived in squalid conditions as they tried to hit it big as performers. It is said that they slept in an unheated storeroom behind the screen of a movie theater, next to bathrooms, and in an area that was heavily populated with gangsters and prostitutes. They played for hours on end, sometimes more than eight hours a night, with songs lasting more than twenty minutes. At one point, they were even deported back to their home country of England. In England, they were rejected numerous times before landing their first deal. One record company told them, "We don't like your sound, and guitar music is on the way out anyway." That band went on to become the Beatles. I imagine you've heard of them!

If they had turned away the moment they found out they had to play nine-hour music shifts, at the sight of their make-shift bedrooms behind the cinema, or even after being rejected in England, who knows how the '60s and '70s would have turned out as far as music is concerned!

You Gotta Have Faith, Faith, Faith

If I look back at a lot of my projects over the years and really think them out, I don't know if I would do them again. But, as the popular saying goes, "Little risk, little reward; big risk, big reward." You have to take the chance. Almost everyone who has achieved success with their ideas has had to take a major risk.

Of course, taking these big risks can be terrifying. So how do you get past that fear? The key is passion and perseverance—you have to have a burning desire to turn your idea into reality. In 1989, I had a burning desire—I had to do the American Gladiators Live tour (my secret desire was to climb the wall and joust). I think sometimes, when you have that passion for an idea, you just have to go blind. What do I mean by "go blind"? I don't mean ignore advice and research—I've already discussed how important those things are. What I mean is, put blinders on and don't let the road-blocks stop you.

For every great idea, I can give you twenty-five reasons why you shouldn't do it, and maybe one why you should. Don't let those twenty-five reasons kill your dream before it starts. Instead, focus on the idea itself. This focus is what will allow you to move past the negativity that surrounds both your journey to success and success itself. The best golfers keep their minds not just on the distance, but on the hole as well. You have to do the same. Yes, it may be a long, difficult journey to bring your idea to fruition. But if you focus on your idea, and stay focused, you will get there. Look to your goals—to your end results.

Focus . . . The best golfers keep their minds not just on the distance, but on the hole as well. You have to do the same.

Now I'm in the process of setting up my first permanent location for Rock 'n' Roll Fantasy Camp. It's a huge, multimillion-dollar project. As you can imagine, there are a lot of fears that go along with a project this big. I am deeply afraid that it's going to be too big for me to control. I'm creating this permanent location for a recording and rehearsal building with the intent to open more locations around the world as it gains momentum and ground, but, of course, there is that nagging, fearful thought in the back of my mind—what if this first attempt fails? To face that fear, I've brought in people who will help me control it, help me run it, and help me get it to place where I can sell it. This relates to what I mentioned in the previous chapter about surrounding yourself with the right people. When you have a good team, you can put your mind to rest that you've done everything you can to make your venture successful.

I recently hosted a camper at RRFC who was general manager of the Atlantis Hotel in the Bahamas for ten years. Her name is Nan Palmer, and she has great experience, so I know I will ask for her advice. By doing so, I'm following the advice of Dick Clark, who writes in his books that you should surround yourself with people who are smarter than you are and they'll make you successful. So that's what I'm doing!

There's clearly a lot of work to do, and there are a lot of fears. How do I deal with the huge fears that come with this huge project? I put my blinders on. Every morning, I visualize this permanent location. I close my eyes and focus on the finished product, the final goal. By the time you have this book in your hands, my Rock 'n' Roll Fantasy Camp will have its permanent location.

With that kind of focus, you will be able to overcome all the fears and negativity that face you.

Walking with the Dinosaurs

The greatest success that came out of a "failure" was when I was trying to do a Beatles reunion tour. I was on tour with Ringo, and he would always share with me what was going on with Apple and the Beatles. One day, Ringo was telling me about the Beatles anthology project and all the interviews he, George, and Paul were doing for it. The idea sprang into my head: Wow, this would be a perfect time for a Beatles reunion, without John, of course, but with Ringo, George, and Paul. I'd done The Monkees with three, and I saw how big that was, so I knew it could work. I asked Ringo, "Do you think that could ever happen?" He said, "Well, put an offer together."

On his say-so, I put together an offer. Miller Beer had contacted me about sponsoring one of my programs, so I went to them and said, "What would you do if we could get the three Beatles together for ten concerts?" Miller said, "We'd throw in ten million to sponsor."

Then I went to Del Furano, who had a merchandising company called Sony Signatures, which would later become Live Nation Merchandise. And Del said to me, "If you get the Beatles, I'll give you ten million." Then I sat with Michael Fuchs, who was the president of HBO at the time, and he said he'd give me ten million. The meetings went on, and all together, I got 110 million dollars in offers. It seemed that all of corporate America was on fire to make these concerts a reality, and I was set to make 10 percent of the entire gross. It was the deal of a lifetime.

I sent a letter and offer to Neil Aspinall, the Beatles' manager and head of Apple, for $110 million. I laid out how I would organize the tour. I flew out to London and met with Aspinall. I was sure Paul was in because he had even told *Time* magazine about the $110 million offer. We were on the verge of success.

Then, Neil got back to me and gave me the bad news— George turned it down; he couldn't do it, for various reasons that I can't discuss. George said no. It was heartbreaking to see the deal fail. I had worked so hard on it. I had to call all the sponsors, everyone who was involved, and tell them that the live reunion was not going to happen.

When I called Del Furano, he said to me, "Hey, why don't you just see if maybe we can get the retail merchandising rights?" I said, "Let me look into it." At that time, the Beatles were with a small company in San Francisco and weren't really doing much merchandising. They were just looking to protect their name. I found out that their contract with this company was up.

I did some more research, and I found out that both Warner Brothers and Disney were interested in doing the licensing of the Beatles. I would be going against some big guns to get these merchandising rights. I contacted Neil Aspinall and asked him if I could come in there and introduce my friend Del and let him pitch Sony Signatures to the Beatles. Neil said we could do it.

I went back to Del and made a deal that I would help him to deliver a killer presentation and introduce him to Neil, the Beatles, and the Apple organization. In return for my consulting fee, I wanted a percentage of whatever the Beatles made. Del said, "Fine," and we made the deal. We would fly over to London, and I would coach him.

I happened to be on the phone with Neil Aspinall at the time, confirming the appointment time for Del's presentation. Neil mentioned very briefly during our phone call that George was in charge of the Beatles' merchandising, and he believed that their merchandising should be like *Jurassic Park*'s, and it should be everywhere. In just a few brief minutes, Neil made something clear—George wanted the merchandising for the band everywhere and on everything.

Let me just impress upon you, if you don't remember, or if you are too young, how completely huge *Jurassic Park* was at the time. Spielberg came out with this movie, and the merchandising was everywhere. You couldn't turn around without buying a piece of *Jurassic Park* merchandise. When Neil told me that, a lightbulb went on in my head. I called up Del the next day and said, "Del, I know what you need to do to prepare for this meeting."

Now, at that time, I understood George Harrison would always show up to the Apple meetings in person. The other Beatles had their lawyers, accountants, and advisors at these meetings, but George would always show up and represent himself. I told Dell, "You're going up against Warner, you're going up against Disney, but I have one thing I'm going to recommend that you do, strange as it may seem, that will knock them out of the water. In the meeting, you should turn to George Harrison, look him straight in the eye, and say, 'Hey, I can do your merchandising just like *Jurassic Park.*'"

In truth, I was scared at the time that we had no chance to get the deal. I had heard that McCartney's family was in with the Disney folks, and George Harrison was recording for Warner Bros. With these competitors, how could we ever get this deal? But I coached Del, and knowing that insider information from Neil, I thought I could recommend what to say in the meeting. I knew we'd want to go in there and pitch real rock and roll—Bob Dylan and The Who—not Mickey Mouse and Bugs Bunny.

When it came time for the meeting, Neil said to me, "David, it's best if you don't come—they'll see you as being on Ringo's team, so it's best if it's just Del, who's neutral." So I didn't go into the meeting itself, which was fine—it wasn't about my ego; it was about making the deal. I was fine with whatever it took to make the deal. But I walked Del right up to the door and told him exactly what to say.

Del made his pitch. Then he turned to George Harrison, looked him straight in the eye, and said, "I can make your merchandise just like *Jurassic Park*." All of a sudden he noticed the movement, he noticed that George smiled, with a look that said, "How did he read my mind?" Del made the deal and even gave the Beatles less than Disney and Warner. I had my entitlement to 10 percent of whatever the Beatles made.

To this day, every Beatles T-shirt or other piece of merchandise that is sold came out of that deal. Live Nation owns it today, and it created a nice payday for me. Even though my original idea of a Beatles reunion tour failed, we worked hard, and something else amazingly successful came out of it.

My so-called failures have actually enabled me to write a book like this because I've seen both sides—success and failure. I hope in the end you'll see more successes, but at least a few failures are inevitable. Just remember: One failure can often lead to another amazing success—if you keep your eyes, ears, and mind open, and don't allow yourself to become depressed and demoralized when things don't initially go your way. You will be faced with incredible amounts of negativity as you work to make your dream a reality and as your idea becomes successful. You have to learn to block out that negativity and focus on your final goal. Then, if you have the true burning desire to see your idea through to the end, you will be able to blaze away all your fears.

Chapter Ten's Greatest Hits

- To overcome fear you have to get to the root o
- Don't let other people's perception of you weig
  you down.
- Being on the outside isn't always a disadvantage.
- When making deals, make sure to have proper legal
  protection.
- Don't let one person's negativity affect you.
- Passion and perseverance are two ways to get past
  fears.
- Sometimes apparent failure can lead to success in
  unexpected ways.
- You have to be
  mentally prepared
  and not let the
  no's affect you.
- Even when some-
  thing appears to
  be a total failure,
  you never know
  what relationships
  you might have
  made or what
  piece of the deal
  is going to come
  back.

We Will Rock You:
DEALING WITH
COMPETITION

O nce your idea is out in the world, and especially once it gains some publicity, there is one absolute certainty: You will have competition. There is just no way around it. I'm always thinking about my competition. To me, if you're not thinking about the competition, you're not ready to be in the business. Believe me, McDonald's is always thinking about Burger King, and Coke is always thinking about Pepsi. You have to look at your competition—find out as much information as you can about the products out there competing with yours.

It can be really hard when you are the originator of an idea and people come and copy you. Five months after I produced my Dirty Dancing tour, a show called "Dancing Dirty" popped up in Las Vegas. Rock 'n' Roll Fantasy Camp spawned a whole legion of copy cats. Look at all the TV shows out there that try to compete with *American Idol* or *Dancing with the Stars*. The bottom line is, people will try to make good off your idea. If you become successful, it's inevitable.

So what do you do about it? First of all, it's important to make the distinction between clean competition and dirty competition. Clean competition is when McDonald's and Burger King try to out-burger each other. This kind of competition is everywhere, and it's a big part of what drives the market. Believe it or not, it can really help your product. Clean competition can drive your business to success because buyers and your audience will recognize that you are honestly and genuinely trying to compete with your business rivals. You are not trying to fool your audience in the process; you are simply trying to take your rival's product and make it a better product at your own company. Hence, the burger example. In reality, Burger King and McDonald's probably use similar tastes and flavors to make their burgers, but they try to beat each other in other categories. One burger adds two patties, another adds teriyaki-glazed pineapple, etc.

Years ago, any competition with my ideas would really upset me. But people would tell me, "Imitation is the sincerest form of flattery," and I came to realize it's true. If people start imitating you, it shows that there's a demand for your idea in the marketplace. It means they're endorsing your idea and putting money into the fact that your idea is a good one. If you have competition, you know your idea is good.

But how do you beat that competition and keep your product at the top of the market? My philosophy has been to focus not on having a satisfied customer but an appreciative customer. A satisfied customer will join you but will also go to another company, a competitor. An appreciative customer, on the other hand, is one who really appreciates your company or product specifically and will show loyalty.

My philosophy has been to focus not on having a satisfied customer but an appreciative customer.

How do you make an appreciative customer? Go the extra step toward making the customers' experience better. Find out your customers' needs and personalize the service so they don't want to go anywhere else. Give them a little more time, a little more results, a little more caring—whatever it takes—to make them feel close to you and your service. Then they will not only be satisfied but also appreciative. For example, Apple, Dell, or insurance companies like Progressive all use the "satisfied customer" as a backbone for creating their products or pitching their services. They respond to the individual, whether it's the college student looking for deals, the businessperson searching for the perfect presentation tools, or the savvy saver wanting to pick something that fits her monthly budget. Each company responds to its customers' needs, making each customer feel much more comfortable buying and investing in that company's product.

Of course, as you do this, your competition will as well, which means you have to constantly upgrade your customer experience. I'm constantly upping my product, upping the talent I bring in, and upping the challenge. I'm always changing recording studios, bringing in new engineers and new rock-star counselors, keeping it fresh with every rock camp I do. Whatever your idea is, you have to do this. If you have a hotel, you have to upgrade the pillows and blankets. If you have a gym, you have to upgrade the equipment to make sure it's the latest. Make sure you give the clients towels—heck, do their laundry for them like Equinox Health Club does. Does Equinox want to do this? Not necessarily, but it must to compete with all the other gyms. You have to find a way to one up your competition. It's not enough just to think of an idea. Once you get the idea, you have to keep it evolving if you want to be successful in the business.

Howard Schultz, the creator of Starbucks, writes in his book *Onward: How Starbucks Fought for Its Life Without Losing Its Soul* about the day he closed down all Starbucks coffee shops. His company wasn't doing that well, so one day, he closed all stores for three hours and had all his employees watch videos on how to make the absolute best drink. He said, "If the drink is not good, you've got to take it back. You've got to say to the customer, 'If you're not satisfied, let me make you another drink.'" He realized that to put his company back on top, he had to give his customers the absolute best service.

Schultz could have gone a different route. He could have just slashed the prices of his coffee to compete. This is many people's first thought when it comes to topping the competition. And sometimes it does help. I'm faced with that every day because my product, Rock 'n' Roll Fantasy Camp, is a high-end product. But I'm now starting to offer camps at a lesser price (at Woodstock and weekends in Las Vegas!) because I'm trying to open it up to a wider audience.

If Schultz had just dropped his coffee prices and not enhanced the customer experience at Starbucks, it would have killed the perceived value of his brand altogether. If your price drops and the customer experience doesn't improve, then all you do is devalue your product. You're not only killing your brand—you're killing your bottom line as well! Competing on service is always the better way to go. Focus on how you can make your customer experience better without overspending, not just how you can make it cheaper. I work constantly on how I can make my brand better and better and better. That's what healthy competition pushes you to do.

Dirty Competition

Dealing with dirty competition is much more difficult than dealing with healthy competition. Dirty competition is when someone truly steals your idea (e.g., copyright infringement, stealing personal property, or impinging on a trademark). This has happened to me many, many times over the years.

When I told Roger Daltrey I was moving to LA, the first thing he said to me was, "Be careful who you trust in Los Angeles." Sure enough, when I moved to LA, a guy who'd worked at a kid's music camp sent me his resume, and I hired him to work for me. Every day, he told me he had my back. Until one day, he sold my back: He decided he wanted to compete with me and start his own music fantasy camp in Hawaii, and he stole my entire e-mail list. I had no choice but to sue him. It ended up costing me $50,000 in legal fees, but the guy lost and the judge told him he'd be thrown in jail if he ever did it again.

One of my biggest encounters with dirty competition was when I created the Quarterback Club for the NFL. One night, I was having dinner with Lou Piniella and the president of Members Only. It was the same night the president told us the story of giving the Members Only jackets to Frank Sinatra, Sammy Davis, and Dean Martin (see chapter 8). At that same dinner, the president turned to Lou and gave him a check for $50,000. "What's this for?" asked Lou. "It's a bonus," he said. "I sold more bathrobes than ever before because of that picture of you wearing a bathrobe."

I said, "What do you mean, you sold more bathrobes?" The president said, "See, women buy clothing for men. So when that picture Lou Piniella took wearing a bathrobe appeared in the newspaper—every woman bought her husband a bathrobe for Christmas." Now, that was something I didn't know. I was young at the time and didn't have a woman buying me clothes.

I went to talk to the person who was in charge of clothing at the NFL. He liked my Quarterback Club idea, so he took it back to the NFL and tried to pitch it in-house. But he couldn't get it sold. Why? The NFL at that time didn't want to promote individual players. Pete Rozelle, the commissioner of the NFL, only wanted to promote teams as a whole.

For years, once a year I'd get together with an NFL executive and he would say to me, "I like your idea, keep developing it." After about five years, he got a phone call. The NFL was negotiating against the Players Association over a collective bargaining agreement. The new commissioner, Paul Tagliabue, called the executive and said, "Remember that idea that you and Fishof discussed . . . his Quarterback Club? Let's do it. Let's go to all the quarterbacks—Simms, Marino, John Elway—and let's do it."

Now, I had previously spoken to the quarterbacks' agents and had told them my idea. My original concept was to do a line of clothes and collectables for current NFL quarterbacks; there would be two separate lines—one for all the rookie kids coming out and another, older line, with Johnny Unitas and Bart Starr, and so on. So when Tagliabue said to the executive, "Go make this happen," he went ahead and called the quarterbacks and offered them, on behalf of the NFL, a half a million each to be part of this club to get their licensing rights.

Tagliabue's whole reason to do this, why there was this change of mind, was due to the conflict with the Players Association. The Players Association was making the majority of its money by licensing six or more big-name players exclusively. If a car company or a T-shirt company or anybody wanted to license one of those players, they had to go through the Players Association.

With the Quarterback Club as the NFL's licensing program, they would be giving these quarterbacks half a million each for their exclusive licensing rights. Then the Players Association wouldn't be able to represent them. So if you're a car company and you wanted to license six of the Miami Dolphins players, you could get all the Dolphins except for Dan Marino, the quarterback—because he was signed to the NFL licensing program. Tagliabue's thought was, "If we do this, no one's going to want to license anything from the Players Association. Then they won't have any money for legal fees to fight me, and they'll have to come over to our collective bargaining agreement." That was his whole game plan for the Quarterback Club.

Naturally, if you offer a quarterback half a million, he's not thinking about what's going on, about the fact that he wouldn't be able to take any other deals. He just thinks, "Wow, I'm getting half a million through this Quarterback Club!" So all of these quarterbacks took the deal.

In the midst of all this, my client Phil Simms was waiting for me to decide what he should do. He was very loyal, because he knew that I had given them the idea. Meanwhile, I kept calling the NFL and saying, "Hey, how am I going to be included? I gave you guys this idea, and now you're running with it. What's my involvement going to be?" But they felt, that since I represented Phil Simms, I would get my piece from him via commission. Even though I created the whole overall concept, that's all they thought I should get.

The NFL made an announcement that they were going to hold a press conference at Mickey Mantle's Restaurant in Midtown Manhattan. Shortly before the conference, Phil picked me up from my New York office, and when I got into the car, he said, "They were just talking about you on WFAN," which is a sports talk station in New York. It was Bill Mazer interviewing the NFL executive. When asked, "So how did you create the idea of the Quarterback Club?" the executive was honest and said, "It was David Fishof's idea. He came to me with the concept with Phil Simms and Vince Ferragamo and the other quarterbacks, and we decided to run with it." Then when it was time for the press conference, the same thing happened: That same NFL executive got up there at Mickey Mantle's and said, "I want to thank David Fishof for creating this idea."

Well, after that, it was just ridiculous to me that they weren't going to include me in the program. I went to the NFL and said, "What about me now?" But they said again, "No, we're not going to pay you." So I went to see my lawyer. My lawyer said, "Let's file a lawsuit against the NFL."

My lawyer said, "Let's file a lawsuit against the NFL."

I had to be careful, because not only was I representing a bunch of players, but I was also booking the entertainment for a lot of the NFL Super Bowl parties. I was in a tough position. But I felt I had to file the lawsuit, because I knew the Quarterback Club was going to be big. Besides, I had evidence—their executive said that it was my idea on the radio and at the conference. They had blatantly stolen it.

My lawyer called the NFL and said, "We're going to send you over the paperwork of the lawsuit we are filing. This is what it's going to look like. Let's settle." That was on a Friday. On Monday they settled and gave me a piece of the action. The Quarterback Club went on to become the biggest licensing program in the NFL, making millions of dollars.

A Word on Lawsuits

This whole story leads me to a broader topic: When do you sue, and when do you not? It's a hard decision, because suing itself is very difficult. It's tedious, emotionally upsetting, and it can be costly. I have to say, the old line is true—the lawyers are the ones who always come out the winners. Personally, I like the way they operate in England, where they have a "loser pays" law. That means that if you lose the lawsuit, you have to pay everything—including the winning side's legal fees. I think it's a great law, because you really have to think twice before you sue somebody. People are much more inclined to just get into a room and say, "Let's straighten this out." I actually include a "loser pays all" clause in my contracts now, which basically means that if you were to lose the lawsuit against me, you pay the fees assessed as well as the legal fees I had accrued during the whole process.

We're also a very sue-happy country. Here, people's first thought is to sue. And, horrible as it is, the truth is you sometimes have to—like I did with the NFL over my licensing rights idea, and with the guy who stole my e-mail list. So the big question is, when do you sue and go all out, wanting all the money, and when do you sue and decide to just settle? It can be tricky to figure out, even for the biggest names out there.

In 1977, Steve Leber and David Krebs came up with an idea for a musical called *Beatlemania*, based on using the likeness of the Beatles and all Beatles music. They went and acquired the music rights, which the Beatles didn't control, and launched *Beatlemania* in Boston.

At the time, the Beatles were in a bit of disarray. When they heard about the show, three of the Beatles wanted to sue to stop Leber and Krebs from doing the show. They felt that regardless of whether they had the music rights, Leber and Krebs were using their names and likenesses without permission. But Paul McCartney said, "Let's not bother—the show is not going to work anyway." This was during the same time that McCartney was dealing with litigation matters of his own with the other three Beatles, so their lives were all a bit messy at the moment.

Paul turned out to be wrong. When the show opened in Boston, it was a huge hit. Shortly thereafter, it opened on Broadway to even greater success. The Beatles decided to sue. They went to a judge to try to stop the show, but the judge said, "No, you can't stop the show. You should have tried to stop the show when you first found out about it, before it launched in Boston. You can't put a cease-and-desist order on it now that it's successful. You can just continue the lawsuit."

Now, Leber and Krebs had taken a precaution before they even launched the show. They had gone to two different insurance companies to get insured. First they went to an insurance company (I'll call it "A") to get a million dollars worth of coverage to protect them against any lawsuit filed against them by the Beatles. Then they went to an insurance company (I'll call it "B") and got an additional 5-million dollar umbrella policy as further protection against any lawsuits filed by the Beatles.

Then it came time for the lawyers to depose John Lennon. Lennon was having legal issues with staying in this country and didn't want to deal with this lawsuit anymore. He said to his lawyer, "Let Leber and Krebs have *Beatlemania*. Have them pay us a million dollar down payment and 10 percent of the gross, and let them keep the show."

Leber and Krebs liked this deal, so they went to insurance company A and asked them for the million to give to the

Beatles. But insurance company A went to insurance company B and said, "Now listen, if you give us five hundred thousand dollars, if you split this million with us, then we'll settle this case. Otherwise, there's no reason for us to settle this case right now and lose our million. We can just keep the case going and let our million sit in the bank and collect interest." This is a pretty common thing insurance companies do.

Insurance company B didn't like this. They said, "No, you have to pay the first million, and then we come in." So insurance company A went back to Leber and Krebs and said, "Keep the lawsuit going. There's no reason for us to want to settle now." So the lawsuit went on. The Beatles ended up winning $10 million from Leber and Krebs, and Leber and Krebs were ordered to stop the show. Insurance company A had to write a check for a million, and insurance company B had to write a check for $5 million, and Leber and Krebs had to cover the remaining $4 million, along with shutting down the show.

Then, insurance company B turned around and sued insurance company A, saying, "We wouldn't have to pay the $5 million if you had settled the case and covered that first million like you were supposed to do." The judge said, "You're right," and awarded insurance company B $5 million, plus all the interest and legal fees.

Then, Leber and Krebs sued insurance company A as well, saying, "We would have owned *Beatlemania* to this day, and we would have been filling up stadiums and arenas, if we had made that deal. Here are the numbers to prove it." They hired me as an expert witness, along with Charlie Koppelman, who runs Martha Stewart's operation. In the end, insurance company A had to pay them back millions and millions of dollars.

Clearly, there are a lot of lessons to be learned from this story. First and perhaps most important, the time to protect your intellectual property is at the very beginning—because if you snooze, you lose. Although they walked away with $10 million, the Beatles still learned a lesson: If you don't claim what is yours at the beginning, in this case *Beatlemania*, then you could wind up knee-deep in messy, legal matters. The same thing happened with Vidal Sassoon and Sasson Jeans. Vidal Sassoon had a line of shampoo, and then somebody came out with Sasson Jeans. But Vidal Sassoon didn't do anything— until Sasson Jeans became successful, and then Vidal ran into the same problem the Beatles had faced. You need to make claim on your intellectual property from the get-go, not when something makes it big and happens to sound like your name, or be spelled like your name, or whatever it may be. Legal cases are not fun, cost a lot of money *and* time, and you risk not winning anything—if you have an idea, claim it now! Before somebody else does!

Second, if you move forward with suing, know when to settle. Even if someone is pressuring you to continue with the lawsuit, you have to look at the whole situation and decide what the best outcome is for you.

How do you know when to sue, when to settle, and when to just walk away? There's no easy answer. You really have to take it on a case-by-case basis. In the case where my worker in Los Angeles stole my e-mail list, he took personalized information, so in my mind I had no choice but to sue. But even then, I had to carefully consider. My trademark lawyer said, "Don't worry, he's not as good as you. It's not going to happen. You can leave it alone." But I went to a litigator, and he said, "He stole your personalized information with the intent of competing with you—you've got to sue."

Don't Let Lawsuits Inhibit You

Whether it's someone walking into Starbucks and spilling hot coffee on themselves or someone copying a patented idea, it's all part of the business. You just have to keep the right attitude: Lawsuits are a part of business, and the threat of them can't stop you from going on with your life and ideas. People are terrified of lawsuits, of people stealing their ideas, and of fighting the competition. These fears keep them from bringing their dreams to life.

Lawsuits are a part of business, and the threat of them can't stop you from going on with your life and ideas.

I was on a plane recently, and I asked a flight attendant if she had an idea for a business venture. She said, "I have this great idea, but I'm not telling you. You might steal it." I said, "Don't worry, I'm not going to steal it. I'm just writing a book." She still wouldn't tell me!

That happens every day. I'll be talking to a friend or a stranger in the airport, and I'll say, "I'm writing this book about ideas, and I bet you're sitting on an idea right now, saying to yourself 'I could make a million off of it.' Am I right?" And they say, "Yeah, I've got this great idea." But they're not doing anything with it. People are afraid. They're afraid someone will steal their idea, and that if someone did, it would cost too much money to sue.

But you can't let competition scare you off. Yes, it can be nerve-wracking, worrying about someone stealing your idea. Today with Google, you can find out in a minute whether someone is using your name or trademark. If someone is trying to copy your idea, it can really bother you. Initially, you get a jolt, and you say, "God, I worked my whole life, I dreamt this whole thing, and someone's coming along to compete with me." And you can feel a real sense of shock, frustration, and disappointment. I certainly feel that way.

But the next thing that happens with me is, I push ahead and I think, "Can I improve my brand?" You have to turn around and think positive, and focus on working on your product and making it the best you can make it. You can't just rest on your laurels. Competition doesn't let you do that. With competition, you've always got to be thinking ahead by being creative and keeping the competition on its toes. Competition is good because it pushes you to be the best you can be, and if your goal is to be the best you can be, then the success—and money—will follow.

Chapter Eleven's Greatest Hits

- Once your idea is out in the world, and especially once it gains some publicity, there is one absolute certainty: You will have competition.
- There's a difference between clean competition and dirty competition.
- Focus not on creating a satisfied customer but rather on creating an appreciative customer.
- Focus on how you can make your customers' experience better without overspending, not just how you can make it cheaper.
- The time to protect your intellectual property is in the very beginning.
- Always press forward with your ideas; don't worry about somebody stealing them. If they do, learn what legal action is right for you.

- With competition, you've always got to be thinking ahead by being creative and keeping the competition on its toes.

Barracuda:
NEGOTIATION

I 'll never forget what American band manger Doc McGhee, best known for working with KISS, Bon Jovi, and Mötley Crüe, once said to me, "You never get what you deserve; you get what you negotiate."

When you are bringing your idea to life, you are going to have to do a lot of negotiating. That's because you need others to help you bring your idea to life, and no matter whom you deal with, you will have to negotiate with them in one way or another. So how do you negotiate successfully?

In my experience, there are three things you need in order to be successful in your negotiations:

1. Information—whoever has more information than the other is likely to win the negotiation;
2. Timing—whoever's in a rush to make a deal is going to lose; and
3. Power—power is in the mind. If you think you have it, you have it, and if you don't think you have it, you don't have it.

ROCK OUT IN THE REAL WORLD
Negotiating with Satisfaction

"We never dreamed there was any money when we started this thing. It was idealism. It was not knowing what else to do with your life. But then, suddenly, the impossible happened."

—Keith Richards, 1989

Through concerts and continuous touring, worldwide album sales, royalties, merchandising, and film licensing, the Rolling Stones managed to turn their passion into the most lucrative brand in rock and roll.

The passion was always there, but the money wasn't. In their early years, even after sales reached 10 million from their hit single "Satisfaction," the Stones weren't exactly rolling in the dough. Truth be told, they were hardly making money at all! Touring as a money-making industry didn't exist yet. In a 2002 interview in *Fortune Magazine*, Mick Jagger attributed a lot of the band's lost earnings in the '60s to the fact that they just didn't have business savvy or the necessary negotiating skills.

A bitter experience in the late '60s with a greedy business manager could have ended the band forever, but the Stones weren't ready to throw in the

Continues

Do the Research

My first big negotiation taught me how essential the big three (information, timing, and power) are. They are truly the key to any negotiation. I want to discuss each of them in more detail.

Finding information in some cases is easy. In sports, for example, when I was negotiating a player's salary, years ago, before the salaries were public, all I had to do was call a bunch of general managers. But what if you don't have a resource like that? How do you gather information that's meaningful in a negotiation? The answer, as always, is research. I'll do anything I can to find information. You can always pay someone for information—it's one of the biggest businesses out there.

And there's endless information out there for free, or cheap, too. You can look up people's pay salaries in public records. In sports, the biggest thing the players' union did for these players was get them salary information by making everyone's salary public information. If you wonder what a vice president at a company is making, you can get an idea by going to a recruiter to look for similar jobs, hiring someone who works in the field you need information on, or by taking a job in the industry and asking around.

Of course, today the Internet is one of the best and easiest ways to get information. From About.com to Bing to Google, Web sites allow you to find just about any information you need to know.

George H. Ross, Donald Trump's advisor and vice president of Trump Organizations, recently wrote a book about how Trump negotiates, and it's fascinating. One of the things Ross points out is that most people will do the absolute minimum work possible, even

---

Continued

towel. They hired a new financial advisor and started to practice and sharpen their own negotiating skills. They became real tough with numbers, and by the '80s, the band had learned a thing or two. Walter Yetnikoff, a CBS record executive who negotiated with Mick Jagger in the '80s, says that Jagger was "very astute," with a real head for numbers.

By the late '80s, the Stones' *Steel Wheels* tour was a touring revenue phenomenon, and it became a model for the concert touring industry. By expanding into ancillary products, the Stones capitalized on almost every possible avenue to reap revenue from their tour. Under the helm of a Canadian promoter named Michael Cohl, the Stones were guaranteed a minimum of $70 million from the concert portion alone. The numbers were astounding:

- Tickets: 3 million people × $30/ticket = $90 million
- Stadium owners' and local promoters' take @ 40 percent = $36 million
- Stones' and tour promoters' take @ 60 percent = $54 million

The band also stood to make a killing on *Steel Wheels* apparel and merchandising at concert venues and via agreements with key national retail department

Continues

Continued

stores. With these agreements in place, the numbers kept growing:

- Domestic pay-per-view rights @ $6 to $7 million
- Anheuser-Busch tour sponsorship @ $6 million

The combined revenue from the *Steel Wheels* tour for the band was estimated to be in the neighborhood of $90 million! And to think that when their then business manager, Bill Zysblat, told me they were asking for a $50 million guarantee, I thought that was high!

As Ray Gmeiner, vice president of Virgin Records, notes, "The Rolling Stones are a unique brand because they've taken the business side of rock and roll to the level that few if any other bands have."

The Stones have continued to rock and roll their way to the bank by being creative in their business. In 1995, they made a deal estimated at $13 million to license their 1981 hit "Start Me Up" to Microsoft's Bill Gates, who wanted it as the advertising theme song for the Windows 95 software. *Fortune* estimated that the Stones made about $56 million between 1992 and 2002, solely for licensing their song rights for film, advertising, and radio.

"The Rolling Stones organization is a well-oiled, money-making machine,

Continues

before a negotiation. Trump, Ross writes, therefore wins a lot of negotiations simply because he out-prepares the other side. Whoever prepares the most is going to win. High-powered sports agent Scott Boras is famous for the large binders he prepares on each of his clients. For example, his binder on southpaw Oliver Perez is reported to be eight chapters long! At that length, it could be a whole book. That's what preparation means.

Trump wins a lot of negotiations simply because he out-prepares the other side. Whoever prepares the most is going to win.

You can sometimes get help preparing from very unlikely places. I learned this when I tried—unsuccessfully, at first—to negotiate a contract for Dave Magadan with the Mets. Magadan is Lou Piniella's nephew and played twelve years in the majors.

Today he's with the Boston Red Sox as the hitting coach. All the newspapers were saying that Magadan was going to get a million in his next contract. So I walked in to the Mets and right away

Continued
and to say it resembles anything less than a *Fortune 500* firm would be unjust . . ."
wrote Roger Blackwell and Tina Stephan in *Brands That Rock.*

asked for a million. And the Mets could tell I wasn't prepared. They had read the same articles I had read. So they offered me $600,000, and I couldn't get any more.

Well, shortly following the failed negotiation meeting, I was studying Talmud with my rabbi, Charlie Rudansky, as I did every Friday. But that morning, I just couldn't concentrate. And the rabbi said to me, "Something's wrong, David. You've got something on your mind. What's going on?"

I said, "I'll be honest with you. I really can't focus today. Dave Magadan is up for arbitration. Last year he was paid $300,000, and he hit .340. I thought I was going to walk in to the Mets and say, 'Give me a million,' and they would say yes. But I went to the Mets yesterday, and they said, 'No, we'll double his salary. That's all.' And I was really bummed out, because everything I read in the papers said he's going to make over a million. And I didn't get him that."

My rabbi turned to me and said, "How can I help you?" I said, "You want to help me?" And he said, "Yes! I love baseball." I showed him how to get a hold of Elias Sports Bureau, where they have all the statistics for every player. And I explained that we have to break down all of Dave Magadan's statistics, compare them to other players, and make an argument for why he deserves a million.

So my rabbi researched every single pitch for Magadan. He discovered that of the sixty-five RBIs Magadan had that year, sixty-three of them were meaningful. What does that mean? Well, for example, there was an Orioles player who had twenty-three home runs, while Magadan only had one. But the Orioles player hit a home run when the score was 12–1, making the score 13–1. Or when his team was losing 7–3, he changed the score to 7–4. But with Magadan, all but two of his RBIs were clutch. He either tied up the score or put his team ahead by a run.

A week later, after the rabbi had gone through every nook and cranny of Magadan's statistics, he came to me and said, "Magadan should be worth not only a million; he should be worth a million five to a million eight. He's better than the guy who's currently making 2.5 million." I said, "Come with me. We're going to Shea Stadium to negotiate the contract."

The rabbi looked at me. "I can't go there," he said. "I need you," I said. He was paranoid and didn't want to go, but I finally persuaded him to join me. And I'll never forget, he came with me and we walked to Shea Stadium, in the middle of winter, the rabbi carrying armfuls of Elias statistic books as though they were the books of the Talmud.

We walked into the office of Al Harazin, the vice president of the Mets at the time. He was there with Steve Phillips, his assistant GM. Harazin looked at the rabbi, and looked at me, and said, "Who's this?" I said, "It's my rabbi." "What's he doing here?" Harazin asked. "Well, he's going to tell you how come Magadan's worth a million five, and why we deserve a million five."

Harazin looked at me and said, "What do you mean, a million five? You said last time you wanted a million." I said, "I know, but I changed my mind. I did my work. And I realized that Magadan is better than half the guys out there making a million eight to two million. Rabbi, tell him."

In the same singsong language he used to teach Talmud, the rabbi started reciting all the research he'd done on

Magadan's statistics. After about two minutes, Harazin turned to me and said, "Can the rabbi leave, and can we talk, David, you and I?" I said, "The rabbi can leave if Steve Phillips leaves, and we can talk one-on-one." So Harazin said, "Steve, please leave," and I said, "Rabbi, please leave," and Harazin and I were left alone.

Harazin turned to me and said, "What are you doing?"

I replied, "What do you mean, what am I doing? I want to go to arbitration with you, and I'm going to put in a million five, because I think he's going to win at a million five. All I have to do is prove to the arbitrator that my player is worth a dollar more than the midpoint. And I can prove it." Something to keep in mind here is that in baseball arbitration, the arbitrator chooses the team's number or the player's number. That's it, period.

Harazin said, "Okay, we accept a million. We'll give you the million." But I said, "I'm not taking a million. A week ago I was going to take a million, but not now."

He said, "A million one?" I said, "No." He said, "A million two?" I said, "No. I want a million five." Harazin said, "Let me win something." I said, "Fine. 1.45 million."

We shook hands and made the deal—$1.45 million for Magadan. I called him up as I left the stadium and said, "Dave, I got you a million four-fifty." He said, "How'd you do it?" "Well, I got this rabbi. . . ." He thought I was joking, but I told him the whole story. Then he said, "You know, David, I've got to be honest with you. Every agent was calling me, trying to steal me away from you. And they'd probably be getting me a million. But you got me a million four-fifty." Magadan remained loyal to me throughout his career. And don't worry, we took care of Rabbi Rudansky as well! If it hadn't been for his help, we would never have been able to make that deal.

With the help of my rabbi I was able to get Red Sox hitting coach Dave Magadan
$1.45 million with the Mets. Pictured here with my now son-in-law
Rabbi Shlomo Einhorn, son, Mordechai, and grandson, Yisrael.

You need to get knowledge, and you're going to come out with a better deal if you do that work. So don't be afraid to look for help in the most unlikely places—if it leads to information, it's absolutely worth it.

It's About Time

When you need information, you can research. But how do you find out about the other side's timing concerns? Sometimes it's easy. In sports, you know when the deadlines are. But it can be more difficult if you're not working within an industry that has a regular schedule, so you have to work a little harder. Sometimes you can find out about timing in your research. If you look a little harder, a lot of industries have deadlines—they're just not as well publicized as in sports.

Take the car industry, for example. There are all these studies that show that if you go to the lot on the day before the thirtieth, you can get a really great deal. Why? Because all of the salesmen are trying to fill their quotas by the end of the month. And it's the same with many corporations in America. They have their quarterly deadlines, and they're all trying to get these sales in before the deadlines. If you do your research and make yourself aware of this timing, you'll know the best time to negotiate.

Sometimes, all it takes to know about the other side's timing is listening. I sold an apartment once in Manhattan. It was an apartment I had bought for $60,000 in a building on Broadway and 76th Street. When I bought the apartment, I had only seen a model apartment. I wanted to have my own co-op because in those days, everybody wanted to have a co-op.

So I went to this co-op and walked in to see this beautiful model apartment, listed for $50,000. There was a sign in it that said, "If you want an apartment on the 6th floor or up, you'll get Central Park views." Naturally, I thought for another $10,000, I'd love to be on the 6th floor. I asked, "Can I go up there and see the view?" And they said, "No, they're in construction now. You can't see it. But it's just like this apartment, except with Central Park views!" Based on what they said, and what the model looked like, I bought the apartment. I was about twenty-five years old.

I moved in, and they were right, you could see Central Park—if you were hanging your whole body out the ledge of the window! I realized that I'd made a big mistake. The apartment was dark, and it was a horrendous place to live. It was an old building, and in the middle of the night, the pipes would be rattling, and you'd think a tsunami was coming into your place. It was just horrible.

After about six months, I knew I had to get out. My goal was to get out of the apartment as quickly as possible. I went to the brokers and apparently the whole building was sold out. All the brokers said, "We can get you $125,000 or $150,000"—they just made up whatever I wanted to hear. At that point, I would have taken $30,000 just to get out of there. I hated the place.

Then, over the summer, a lady walked in with her husband to look at my apartment. I had made sure to stage it nicely, with lots of light. She looked around, then turned to her husband and said, "This place is great. There's an extra room here that we can use as a baby room, and there's a room here for our son. This is good, because he's got to start school in a month." They asked me what I wanted for it, and I said, "I want $140,000, which is the listing price. I have another buyer, but for $140,000 you can have it."

How did I know they would go for $140,000 and not try to negotiate down? I listened to what they were saying: They were in a rush to get their son set up to go to school. I knew if I put the pressure on, told them there was another buyer (and I did have another buyer, although the other buyer wanted it for less money and wanted me to hold the mortgage), they would go for it. It worked. I sold them the apartment, making an $80,000 profit on an apartment I didn't want. The mistake the lady made was giving away her deadline. By knowing her timetable, I knew I could get the deal I wanted.

This happens a lot. If you just pay attention, you'll see who's in a rush. People talk. Let them. And then listen. We're always so caught up in what we have to say that we often don't hear the other side. Listening to the other side is an important art, one you need to learn. It's like poker: A bad poker player looks at his own cards only; a good poker player looks at the other players and tries to figure out what's in their hands. One of the hardest things you've got to do is to learn to listen, but it's a skill you must master if you want to do well in negotiations. By listening to the other side's needs, you'll pick up on the information you want.

> *One of the hardest things you've got to do is to learn to listen. We're always so caught up in what we have to say that we often don't hear the other side.*

Bravo has a hit show that has finished taping its fifth season and is moving onto the sixth shortly. The show, *Flipping Out*, revolves around eccentric decorator Jeff Lewis. While the show has of late focused on his decorating strengths, his real talent is his ability to flip homes for a profit. Lewis's leverage in this area is his ability to read prospective buyers. He listens, understands their needs, and then puts all his energy into decorating a home that meets the buyer's needs.

Of course, it's always important to remember the flip (pun intended) side of this as well: Don't be in a rush to make a deal yourself! It's always dangerous, in any situation—and people will take advantage of you. Look at airline tickets. If you buy them far enough in advance, you pay one price. But if you buy last minute because you're in a rush, they've got you. Unless you've scored one of the few last-minute weekend specials to limited locations, you often pay a fortune by waiting until right before your trip. The same is true in negotiation. Never be in a rush to make a deal. Timing is everything.

You Have the Power

The third key to negotiation, power, is of course the most intangible of the three. You can't research or listen your way to power. Power is in the mind. If you think you have it, you have it, and if you don't think you have it, you don't have it. It's strictly a mental issue. Everything you can do in your mind to give yourself the feeling of being powerful will help you.

You can do "power research" by watching videos of powerful people—Tony Robbins, Donald Trump, Wayne Dyer, etc. I recommend watching them with the sound off so you can focus on how they present themselves physically. I think physicality can have a lot to do with power. The way you sit yourself down, the way you get up, the way you conduct yourself, it's all a means of conveying power.

Most importantly, you need to find a way to make yourself feel powerful in your mind. Most people don't have that level of confidence in themselves. Some do, and they feel great and come across as great. But for most people, it helps to find a way to support and enhance that feeling.

For me, a big part of it is how I feel physically. If I'm in shape I feel great about myself, and so I feel like I've got a lot more power. When I am overweight, I feel I'm out of control and I lose all my power. So you're helping your career when you exercise. When I go to the gym, work out, and eat properly, I feel powerful. Besides keeping myself in shape, I also do the Hoffman Process, which I talked about in chapter 9. Just recently, I found myself losing patience all the time. I was losing trust in myself and others, and all this negative energy was coming up in me. It happens because of my family history. When you have a father who was a Holocaust survivor, who was captured by the Nazis, it affects your life. It's what we learn from our parents. If your mother didn't have patience with you, then you're likely to lose patience with yourself and other people. I needed to work on that, and to realize where all the negative energy was coming from. So I went away to a specialized weekend study and found ways to be patient and therefore feel powerful.

Find the program that gives you the confidence you need to make you feel powerful. We're so beaten down as individuals, sometimes stemming from our childhood—not because our parents wanted to burden us, but because that's just the way it is. The more you can do to make yourself strong and powerful in the world, the more successful you will be.

A lot of people who have military training have that confidence and power just through the discipline they've been trained into. There's a fascinating book called *In Hostile Territory*. It's written by a former Mossad agent (his pen name is Gerald Westerby) who used the extreme discipline of Israeli soldiers and Mossad agents as a framework for becoming a successful entrepreneur. "Patience," "preparation," and "persistence" are the three words Westerby says defines the Mossad agent. Applying these three words to your life can bring you tons of success. Anything you can do to make yourself a powerful individual will help you in all of your work and creative endeavors.

Just a Little Respect

Now that I've gone over the three keys to a successful negotiation, there's one last very important thing to remember about negotiations: It is not always about getting the most money. A big part of it is about getting respect as well.

The amount of money people pay can influence their perception of, and respect for, a product.

The amount of money people pay can influence their perception of, and respect for, a product. I'll never forget—my first client was actor Herschel Bernardi. I was nineteen or twenty, and I got an offer for him to work Grossinger's hotel for $5,000. I told him about the offer, and he said, "My price is $7,500." I tried to talk him in to taking the $5,000, but he yelled at me on the phone and said, "Get me my $7,500!" He explained: "The more they pay, the more they're going to respect you."

Over the years I've found it to be true. You'll end up doing benefits with artists who do the event for free, and you always have a problem—with the car, or with the towels in the dressing room—it's always something. But when they pay the artist all the money, everything is there, no problems at all. In the Catskills, where I started in show business, if people got to attend the show for free, they would sit back in their seats, clap half-heartedly, and say, "I dare you to make me laugh." When they bought their tickets for $50, the same comedian could walk out and say anything, and the whole place would scream.

When you are negotiating, it's about more than the money. It's about prestige; it's about your stature in this world. You're negotiating not just to get the money, but to get the respect as well.

Creating a Win-Win

As you are negotiating for money and respect, there's something very important to remember: The best negotiations are the ones where both sides win. If both sides don't win, you don't have the best deal. You don't want to just grind the other guy down into the dust. That never works.

I got to meet outfielder Dave Winfield once and I talked to his agent, Al. Al had negotiated with George Steinbrenner and completely beat him down. In the end, Steinbrenner carried a lot of anger toward him and launched an investigation against him, his charity, everything. So what good was that deal? It was a win-lose situation, or even a lose-lose in the end. Steinbrenner gave Al the money, but he embarrassed him on another level.

Overkill deals—where one side wins and the other loses terribly—just don't work. Yet those are exactly the kind of deals they promote in the world of sports. Instead, you have to find a way for both sides to win, because that way you'll be able to make deals with people in the future. And in the long run, you'll win because you'll have longevity, and everything comes around in the end.

You have to find a way for both sides to win, because that way you'll be able to make deals with people in the future. And in the long run, you'll win because you'll have longevity.

I ran into this win-lose scenario when I was negotiating relief pitcher Randy Myers's contract and statistics. The Seattle Mariners had offered Randy two years for $10 million, an offer they eventually upped to three years, $15 million. But the Blue Jays were offering me $19 million for three years. Now, I knew Myers didn't need more than $15 million. He was never going to spend $15 million in his lifetime. Most importantly, his mother lived in Seattle, and his brother lived in Portland, and if he was in Seattle, his family could come see his games. He even runs a charity in Portland, because it was his home and he wanted to give back to his community.

But the Players Association came to us and said, "You've got to go and take that Toronto deal. It's more important for you to get the $19 million, because then the next pitcher coming up will make $22 or $23 million." The Players Association put it in his mind that you have to go for the most. He ended up signing with the Toronto Blue Jays, closing for Roger Clemens. But he didn't want to be there, and his career never took off the way it should have. He went from there to San Diego, got injured, and his career was over. (Thank goodness his contract was guaranteed.)

This is one of the things that really bothers me about professional sports, especially for free agents. I can understand the drafting a little better when you're younger and you've just come out of college—although personally, I am not in love with the whole system. I think it's unfair. Why should you come out of college and be told where you're going to play? Everybody else graduates college and can take a job anywhere they want. In sports, you come out of UCLA, and you're told, "Okay, you've got to play in Denver."

Once a player becomes a free agent, he finally gets the right to go where he wants to play—but then he's got the Players Association standing behind him, telling the agents, "You've got to get the most money." So many of these players would rather play at home, in front of their families and friends, where they actually play better because their number-one fans are there.

I negotiated a contract for Juan Beniquez, who played for the California Angels. I followed him in winter ball, and he was down in Puerto Rico hitting .440. It was amazing. So I went to the team's general manager, Buzzie Bavasi, and said, "Buzzie, you've got to pay Juan a lot of money; the guy's hitting .440." Buzz said, "David, that's his home. He's playing in front of his family and friends. Up here, they're all away games to him. Look at the statistics. Every time I gave him a contract, he hits .220 and .280 and third year .330. We give him a three-year contract, and that's what he hits when he plays for the contract. But when he plays for family and friends, he hits .400."

I firmly believe that free agents should play where they want to play, regardless of the money. I understand financial security, but how much is enough? These players are twenty-nine years old, and making $15 million instead of $19 million isn't really going to make a difference in their lives. What does make a difference, both for them personally and for their careers, is playing in front of their families and friends.

A Three-in-One Punch

When you're negotiating a deal, you have to remember that money is not the only factor in winning the negotiation. You have to negotiate not only for money but also for what is best for you and your idea. Sometimes what is best is not what makes you the most money. But whatever you are negotiating for, the bottom line remains the same: Information plus timing plus power equals effective negotiating. I learned how all three factors came together for success in the first big negotiation I ever did, which was with George Steinbrenner for Lou Piniella's contract.

When I met Lou Piniella, he didn't have an agent. He negotiated his own contracts, and they always went the same way. Lou would walk in to Steinbrenner's office, and Steinbrenner would make him an offer—say $250,000. Lou would say, "George, I want $300,000." George would say, "Okay,

$275,000. You should be happy getting that." And Lou would sign the contract for $275,000.

When I heard this, I said, "Lou, you really need to think it out, get information from the other side, and see what your true value is to the Yankees." Lou didn't realize he had the power to negotiate. Most players years ago didn't because they got beaten down so much they were afraid to go up against the management. They were afraid that if they did, they'd be out of the game, which is why today we have agents. The attitude was that you should take whatever you can get. That was years before the world of agents.

The attitude was that you should take whatever you can get.

I finally persuaded Lou to let me negotiate his contract, but his condition was that he would accompany me at the negotiation because he was afraid that Steinbrenner would be upset with him for having hired an agent. Even though it's always harder with the client in the room, I understood his concern and I agreed.

I set about preparing for the negotiation. First of all, the minute Lou hired me, I started telling him his worth and value since I had compared his statistics to other players. I proved it by getting him some endorsements almost immediately, and I think he really appreciated that. And I emphasized that even though Steinbrenner was his friend, he had to separate friendship from business.

Most importantly, I knew I had to get all my information before I went into this negotiation. I started calling around to all the teams in major league baseball and saying, "Lou Piniella's about to become a free agent. Would you be interested?" I was sure I would get offers, because Lou was a big star. Then I would be able to go to Steinbrenner and say,

"Look, here's what other teams are offering. What will you give us?"

But every single general manager I talked to said, "No, not interested." I couldn't understand it! Then I called the late Lou Gorman, of the Boston Red Sox, and I said, "You told me no a few days ago, but the Yankees are your biggest rival. Why wouldn't you want Lou Piniella on your team?" Gorman said, "It's not that I don't want Lou Piniella on my team. But Steinbrenner got up at the owners' meeting and said, 'Don't bid on any of my players. If you bid 400, I'm going to bid 500.'"

When I heard that, I called another GM, who told me the same thing, and I knew I had my key piece of information. What it meant was, Lou wasn't really a free agent. I couldn't get out there and get Lou's market value because no one would offer me what he was really worth. And that completely defeated the player's rights that Marvin Miller fought for—to be able to go out and see what you're worth in the free-agent market and to negotiate based on that information. The minute I heard that, I knew the only negotiating information I needed to go back to Steinbrenner with was, "We're supposed to be a free agent, but you made this statement."

I also knew that I had timing on my side. Steinbrenner had to make a deal with Lou in the next week or so. If he didn't, then Lou would become a total free agent and would be open to negotiate with other teams. If Lou became a total free agent, it meant that he would be able to see what his worth with other teams would be and his worth on the market, as opposed to being bid on by only one person. This would also mean that Steinbrenner wouldn't regain his negotiating rights, and his ability to sign Lou, until the end of spring training. Lou, on the other hand, was under no pressure to make a deal at all; being a free agent, with all those teams bidding on him, would be just great.

With timing and information on my side, all I had to do was walk into that room knowing I had the power. Now, I was twenty-two years old at the time. The thought of going up against someone as powerful as Steinbrenner was terrifying. So where did I find the confidence to go ahead with the negotiation? I had no choice but to feel confident—I had nothing to fall back on. This was my job. I didn't have rich parents to support me. But what my parents did give me was confidence. When I thought about my dad surviving the Nazi concentration camps, I knew if he could get through that, there was nothing I should be afraid of.

> *When I thought about my dad surviving the Nazi concentration camps, I knew if he could get through that, there was nothing I should be afraid of.*

I went to Steinbrenner to negotiate the contract, knowing the power was going to be in my mind. If I acted like I had it, I would have it. I kept saying to myself, "I have what he needs. I have the great baseball player, and I know he wants him. I have more power than he does." It was just a matter of putting it in my mind and feeling it.

When Lou and I walked into Steinbrenner's office, I remember Steinbrenner was sitting at the end of this long row of desks, and he looked very important. I didn't let that stop me. I knew I was prepared with my argument. I made my case to George and in the end persuaded him to sign Lou for a $1.5 million, three-year contract.

My Own Negotiations

Something some, or all, of you might experience at some point will be seeking investments for your business. To get the right business partner, investor, or team with the right business knowledge and outlook, you are going to need to do a fair amount of negotiating.

When you start to realize that your idea is a good one and that it could take off (for me, it was when people continuously sought me out to ask if I needed money to fund my idea), you need to start your plan for raising money for your idea. The first piece of negotiation is with yourself—do you want to get involved with bankers or investors or do you want to go to your customers, who have already tried your product? In my case, I didn't go the route of acquiring a banker or an investor because they all wanted such large pieces of my company. Instead, I figured, why not go to those who shared my vision? Those people were my customers; people who had already tried my product and had their own thoughts regarding it.

So I put the word out to previous Rock 'n' Roll Fantasy Camp attendees who had at one point expressed interest in my business plan and inquired if I needed capital. Somewhere down the road, I gained great successful businesspeople, all of whom invested and provided me with an endless amount of business knowledge that they knew would help me build and grow my business. Among them was the cofounder of Oracle, Ed Oates, who invested double what I asked for, and the President/CEO of American Seafood, Bernt Bodal (he was recently featured on the TV show *Undercover Boss*).

However, finding the right businesspeople to extend their knowledge and investments didn't take much, if even any, negotiating at all. It came quite easily for me. But, along with the great, came the not so great. At one point, I was approached by a past camper who was the president and CEO of a famous food company, and he committed to put $1 million into my company. He promised he could grow my company and take care of my finances. A couple days after we met, he sent me a check for a million dollars. A few days after I deposited the check, my lawyer, David Stone, called me to discuss this new investment. Apparently, the investor did not agree with many points of our agreement, and my lawyer made it clear to me that if we went with his version of the agreement, I might be restricted in many ways from running my business. But on the other side of things was a million-dollar check sitting in my bank account! This was a tough negotiation—I had my trusted lawyer on one side, and on the other side was the money I badly needed, but it came from somebody who wanted to alter my idea too much.

I tried to make it work so that the lawyer and the investor could agree, but in the end, I parted ways with the investor, returned his money, and stuck by my lawyer's sound advice. It might sound like it was simple, but it was one of the hardest negotiations I had to make. I truly believed that the investor's vision was not the same as mine and that he could have really controlled how I wanted to run *my* business. My lawyer understands that; he has his eyes on the business and how it can continue to grow into what I envisioned it to be.

I sometimes look back at that and wish I had found a way to negotiate a compromise between myself and the investor, but in the end, I am better off having listened to those around me who were giving good, sound advice. All my partners help to keep me and my business on the correct path, and that is the best negotiation I can ask for!

Chapter Twelve's Greatest Hits

- Successful negotiation is all about three things: information, timing, and power.
- Most people will do the absolute minimum work possible, even before a negotiation. Knowing this gives you the upper edge.
- You can sometimes get help preparing from very unlikely places.
- Pay attention to the other side's needs, and you'll find the information you want.
- Power is in the mind. If you think you have it, you have it, and if you don't think you have it, you don't.
- Negotiations are not always about getting the most money.
- You have to find a way for both sides to win because that way you'll be able to make deals with people in the future.
- Invest in trusted business partners who always have your vision for your business in mind.

TAKE IT
TO THE
NEXT LEVEL

CHAPTER **13**

Dream On:
MOVING FROM ONE
BIG IDEA TO THE NEXT

Every idea is different and deserves unique treatment. Just because I was successful with The Monkees didn't mean I would be successful with Mortal Kombat—and I wasn't. You have to remember that every idea of yours will have a different market, a different audience, and a different timing/environment, and therefore a different path to success.

Not all ideas are for the long haul either. Some ideas create short-term gain, and others offer a path to long-term success. There's that song by the Clash that asks, "Should I stay or should I go?" That's what I want to discuss in this final chapter: How do you know when to stay and when to get out? How do you know if you need an exit strategy, and if so, what should that exit strategy be? How do you know what's right for your business? And then, what idea should you explore next? One book I would recommend to help with your ideas and the growth of those ideas is *What Got You Here, Won't Get You There* by Marshall Goldsmith.

275

I honestly didn't start to think about having an exit strategy for any of my ideas until I was doing my last project, Rock 'n' Roll Fantasy Camp. Before Rock 'n' Roll Fantasy Camp, I didn't have a business I could sell. As a manager, an agent, or a tour producer, I didn't have the type of business that could be sold for much. I was offering too personal of a service. So I generally wouldn't sell my businesses. I would get the most I could out of them, turn a nice profit, and then, when it was time, I would leave. In the past few years, however, many of my associates have been able to sell management companies.

When you do your own project and you come up with your own money or you run with your own ideas, you don't have to necessarily worry about an exit strategy. When I was managing all my bands, I was running my own business. But the minute I started charging money for an event of my own, things changed. As soon as I had a brand, Rock 'n' Roll Fantasy Camp, I had to start looking toward an exit.

If you sit with any financial person, such as an investor, the first question they ask you is, "What's your exit strategy?" I've found that to be the first question everyone wants answered: "When do you exit?" Investors are looking after their investments, and they're looking to make back their money, so they want to know where your brand is ultimately going to go. For many years, I told investors that I didn't want to sell my business or take on partners who could dictate my strategy or tactics. But now, in the business of creating ideas, I've realized what a great thing it is to be able to build up your business, then turn around and sell it.

In the business of creating ideas, I've realized what a great thing it is to be able to build up your business, then turn around and sell it.

Timing Is Key

If you are going to sell your business, you have to know when to sell. You have a responsibility to your stakeholders and to your investors to sell smartly. Keep an eye on the timing. Just think of all the casinos in Vegas that were worth $800 million before the economic meltdown of 2008 and now are worth only a fraction of that! You have to know when to sell. I had a friend who owned a clothing company, and he was once offered $500 million for it. He didn't take the offer—and now his company is only worth a hundred million. He wanted to get a billion for it originally, but he lost out in the end because he had no idea what his "exit strategy" was; all he knew was that he wanted to sell for money.

One of Miami's most famous hotels is the Fontainebleau. The owners were set to build their most ambitious project ever in Las Vegas. Seventy percent of the way in on this $2.9 billion project everything just stopped. The timing was off. The money couldn't be scraped together. Analysts say that had the Fontainebleau group started construction two years earlier or two years later, it would have seen the light of day. Now it's just sitting and collecting dust. Time waits for nobody.

Know Your Buyer

It's also important to target the best buyer for what you're selling. And this is something you always have to keep in mind when you create an idea—to whom would you sell your business? Who would want to buy you out? Who would pay you the most money for your business idea? Who would be a good buyer? Who could be a strategic partner? If you're looking to raise money from investors, you'll have to have answers to these questions because the investors will surely ask you about this when they bring up your exit strategy.

And when it comes to selling your idea, sometimes the buyer is even more important than the money. If you feel like your idea can go further, can become something more, then you'll want to find a strategic partner to associate with who will make your brand bigger. That may be a different deal than just the person who's offering you the most money. Because in the case of selling to a strategic partner, you're retaining a piece of the business.

Now, having a strategic partner might be for you, especially if, like me, you don't want to sell your company outright—maybe because you love what you do or you just don't want to give it away entirely. Mark Burnett sold 50 percent of his production company to Hearst. You can contrast that with the model of Derek Sivers, the mastermind behind cdbaby.com, which is an online music site specializing in the sales of CDs from independent artists. Sivers sold the company in its entirety for $22 million to Disc Makers. He built it up and said, "Okay, now I'm done." But he also did something very interesting. He took his profits and put them into a charitable trust that promotes music education.

There's no one way to exit your business. People often think, "What's the formula?" There is no such thing as a formula. However you move on, or forward, you have to determine that on your own, based on your business and where you want it to go.

One of the best parts about selling your business is the sense of accomplishment you get. If you've sold your brand to somebody, that means they've accepted it as a valid, successful idea. It's a great feeling of success to say, "Look, someone else is buying my brand," or "They're associated with me, so I know I have a good idea." I've mentioned how I had that feeling when Mark Burnett came on board with Rock 'n' Roll Fantasy Camp. You can have an idea and know it's good, but somebody big putting real money or real resources into your idea is, to me, the greatest satisfaction, the ultimate validation. This happens when you get initial investors, and then it happens again when you have buyers interested in snatching it up.

When Not to Exit

Sometimes a business is not about money at all. Not every business needs to have an exit strategy; sometimes playing it to the end is the wisest move to make. People in show business aren't always looking for an exit, because they love what they do. That's true in a lot of businesses. You can sell your business and put that $100 million in the bank, but if you're bored and miserable as a result, that money won't mean anything to you. You have to decide when and how exiting your business is really best for you—or if sticking with your business is the best thing for you.

I'll give you an example. My father was a cantor, and at seventy-eight years old, he went to the president of the synagogue and he said, "My contract's up this year, and you're going to have to negotiate with my son. He's a big agent; he represents Phil Simms of the New York Giants."

The president said, "Well, have David call me."

Now, at the time, my dad was making $10,000 a year. He did local circumcisions as a mohel in addition to being a cantor. He didn't make a ton of money, but he felt an enormous amount of satisfaction from the roles he played in his community, even late into his eighth decade. I made an appointment to go see the president and explain to him why my father should get a raise. But when I walked into the president's office, he said, "David, we want your father to retire. He's seventy-eight years old."

I said, "My father doesn't want to retire. This is what he knows how to do. So I'll make a deal with you. I'm going to write you a check for $10,000, and I'm going to go home and tell my dad that he got a $10,000 raise, and that he's going to make $20,000 next year." I wrote the check and went home that night, and I said to my dad, "Okay, I took care of your contract, and you're going to get $20,000." He turned to my mother and said, "Edith, he should have been negotiating my contract my entire career!" My father has now passed away, and he never knew what I did. But he lived the rest of his life doing what he loved.

My father's desire to keep working was no different than why the Rolling Stones and all these other big acts don't want to retire—this is all they know how to do, and they love it. Both Paul McCartney, and Ringo Starr released new CDs in 2012, and they continue to tour; at seventy years old, they both still embrace the performer within. The Rolling Stones, my father, McCartney, and Starr are all examples of people who want to work, and they have a great work ethic to boot. I've been around many successful people, and I can tell you from what I've seen that working is a very healthy thing to do, no matter your age. If you love it, do it!

I recently met a man at an event—a beautifully dressed older gentleman, wearing a suit and tie, and he told me he was ninety-three years old. I said, "You look twenty years younger; what's your secret?" He said, "I never stopped working, I'm busy, I'm always out, I'm always learning, I'm involved in the world." I said, "What happened to your friends? Have they all died?" He said, "Well, the ones who didn't die, they just stay at home and complain about Obama!"

Continuing to work will keep you both physically and emotionally healthy. There are studies that show that more divorces happen after a business is sold. You see this all the time with professional athletes. Once they quit playing sports, they're home doing nothing. While they were playing ball, they were heroes, starting in junior high school, continuing through high school, college, and then professional sports. They had girlfriends all the time and at some point got married. But when they retire, they don't know what to do with themselves, they don't know how to do any other kind of work, and their relationships fall apart.

That's why I always worked so hard to find jobs for the athletes I represented. To me, getting them on a career path was key. At thirty-five years old, you're considered old in sports. At thirty-five, your sports career often comes to an end. But in the business world, people are just starting to mature at thirty-five. Professional athletes come out, and they have to completely start over and get their lives together, like a twenty-year-old looking for a job. And that's a very hard thing to face.

It used to be common in sports for players to start new careers *before* they retired. Forty years ago, in the winter, ballplayers had to sell insurance, work in a clothing store, unload trucks, or do something, because their paycheck from sports wasn't enough. The extra jobs they took may not have been the most glamorous, but the players were on their way to a career. Although they may not have had today's ballplayers' crazy money, at least they were building a life outside of baseball while they were still in the game. That way, they had somewhere to go, something to do, and someone to be once they retired from professional sports. Today's players make huge amounts of money, but when they retire, if they don't go into coaching and/or broadcasting, they have little else.

Baseball great Lenny Dykstra is a good example of this. Lenny, a three-time All-Star who played centerfield for the Mets and Phillies, has had endless problems with the law since his heyday in the MLB. In 2011 he was arrested for investigation of grand theft, just one day after he was charged with a federal bankruptcy crime. Although Lenny's case is an extreme example, it's not uncommon to see great talents struggle like this after their careers have died down. According to the NFL Players Association, it's estimated that within two years of retirement, 78 percent of NFL players are bankrupt or on the verge of bankruptcy.

They had somewhere to go, something to do, and someone to be once they retired from professional sports. Today's players make huge amounts of money, but when they retire, they have nothing else.

Regardless of your field, you should always remember that when you go from doing the thing you love every day to doing nothing, you can get pretty down on yourself. Yes, you can use the concepts in this book to make your idea turn into wealth and financial security, but your exit strategy should not be to sit on a beach in Rio de Janeiro and do nothing. I think that's the dream for a lot of people—making the money and then doing nothing. But that's not what I'm advocating. Doing nothing is not a dream—it's a nightmare.

Truth is, if you're smart enough to take an idea and turn it from nothing into something, you are too smart to sit and do nothing. If you're a creative person who likes to build things, you can't sit still. I know. I tried it in 1987 after my successful Monkees tour and the Giants winning the Super Bowl. I tried to sit back and retire, to do nothing but read the newspaper and go to the gym every day. It lasted about a month.

Then I found myself coming back and working harder and harder. It keeps me active, it keeps me healthy, it keeps me whole.

The exit strategy I advocate is not to sell your company, get paid, make a lot of money, and then do nothing but drink piña coladas. It's to make a lot of money and then move on to new projects. That's the real exit. Get paid, and then do something more, something new. This is the route taken by many successful people. Think about the guys in the dot-com business—they build a Web site, sell it, and then they build another one.

I have given you my recommendation, and I have also presented you with different models, such as how Mark Burnett and Derek Sivers approached their "exit." The reality is that you should do what will make you happiest and help you achieve more of your dreams. This is what Timothy Ferriss suggests in *The 4-Hour Workweek*. The goal of a four-hour work week is for you to enjoy yourself and what you do, whether it's relaxing or working. If you have options, follow the path that will work best for you.

Finding—and Following—Your Passion

The question is, what should your next idea be? Where do you find what you're going to do next? Ideas can come from anywhere. Personally, I always scour other countries for ideas to bring to America. You can get some great ideas for businesses in many foreign countries because their governments aren't as strict in allowing permission for certain products. I'm not the only one who finds ideas overseas. Howard Schultz was in Italy, visiting Milan, and he saw the way people drank their coffee—and he came back to America and invented Starbucks.

It's also important to remember that your next idea doesn't necessarily have to be another way to make money. If you have enough money from your previous business, you can create a nonprofit, invent something to help out a school system, or do philanthropic work—it can be anything. There are many nonbusiness things I want to do—teach, lecture, and keep exploring to see what else is out there.

And that's the most important thing: *Chase your dreams, not just money.* If you spend your whole life chasing money, you're going to find yourself really miserable. You have to chase the things you want to do, the things you enjoy in life. Do something you enjoy, and keep doing something you enjoy. There are so many people out there who work just to make money, money, money. That's all they think about. But you have to work to do what you love, what makes you happy, not just to make money. Otherwise what's the point?

Do something you enjoy, and keep doing something you enjoy.

Sometimes, your next idea can build on an idea or a business you already have and love, which means you're letting one great idea lead you to the next. That's what I did with Rock 'n' Roll Fantasy Camp. My ultimate dream had always been to have a TV series. My whole life I only made money if I was on the road touring or producing a camp. I wanted to get in the position where I could create a show and every night my show would be playing. It was the product of my creativity, it could play all around the world—and I didn't have to be there. So my biggest dream was to one day move to California and have a TV series.

When Rock 'n' Roll Fantasy Camp was really starting to hit it big, I had done everything in this business. I'd represented a Beatle, I'd represented athletes who played in the Super Bowl and World Series, but I hadn't yet been able to conquer television. And that was very frustrating to me, especially because I'd blown an opportunity when Kevin Bright, who went on to produce *Friends*, asked me if I'd like to be his partner. At that time, I didn't want to move to California, so I said no. Imagine if I'd been a partner on *Friends*! Even those who should know better make mistakes sometimes!

But with Rock 'n' Roll Fantasy Camp's success, I had a renewed drive to pursue television. Every day I woke up with another idea of what I was going to give my campers. The repeat business was incredible—people kept coming back. I had to constantly come up with something new—new talent, new ideas, and new ways to fulfill their rock and roll fantasies.

Rock 'n' Roll Fantasy Camp has been a journey, and here that famous rock band shows off sketches of themselves.

Zakk Wylde (right), former guitarist for Ozzy Ozbourne, has showcased
his talents at Rock 'n' Roll Fantasy Camp.

Joaquin Phoenix (left) talks with Roger Daltrey (right) at the House of Blues,
one of the venues for Rock 'n' Roll Fantasy Camp.

For ten years, I'd been trying to negotiate a deal with Abbey Road, the studio in London made famous by the Beatles, to let us record there. But the studio had consistently turned me down, telling me it didn't want amateurs. Finally, Spencer Davis of the Spencer Davis Group told me he was going into the studio, and so I asked him to tell Abbey Road about Rock 'n' Roll Fantasy Camp. Not long after that, the folks at Abbey Road called. I was able to pitch them on the idea, and they said yes.

Remain Disciplined

Whether you're building off an old idea or starting a completely new idea, there's no reason that you have to be a one-hit wonder. With the right tools and attitude, you can continue living your dreams throughout your lifetime. Creativity doesn't stop when you achieve success the first time. It can, however, be difficult, because people see all the hassle you have to go through to maintain your success. I always give credit to people who can keep going, who can write more than one big song, who have had longevity—like KISS. Year after year after year, from the '70s to now, these flashy but persistent rock musicians have been successful.

I'm a big believer in that. You don't have to stop succeeding after a single powerful idea. It's no different than a baseball player—if he had one great season, he can have ten great seasons, as long as he stays disciplined. If you're smart enough and flexible in the way you adapt to an ever-changing environment, you can keep hitting 'em out of the park.

Whether you're building off an old idea or starting a completely new idea, there's no reason that you have to be a one-hit wonder. With the right tools and attitude, you can continue living your dreams throughout your lifetime.

Discipline in business is important. I wake up at six o'clock in the morning to prepare for the day. I worked out of my townhouse in New York for many, many years, and people say, "How do you stay disciplined?" I am able to stay disciplined because I love what I do. If you love what you do, you're going to stay disciplined. If you're miserable, it will be much harder. I can tell when my employees are happy with what they are doing, and on the same note, I can also tell when they are unhappy with their work.

Very few people who are successful are undisciplined. This is true in every business, even if it might not seem so. People look at rock stars and see their long hair and tattoos and think that they are not disciplined. But I say to those people, you only see rock stars onstage. Trust me, they go home and practice eight hours a day—they're rehearsing, they're writing songs, they're perfecting their craft. That's why they are experts in what they do and why they can stand onstage and perform. They might not be disciplined in the same way most of us are—working nine to five. But they'll work from one to nine, or often much later, creating music. You can't be successful in any business if you're not disciplined, whatever shape that discipline takes.

And you have to be disciplined in everything—your physical appearance, your emotions, your spirituality, your intellectual life. When you have all of that stuff together, you can succeed. And when one thing's not working, it's going to get in the way of your success. That's why people have to work on themselves constantly. The workaholic who works eighty hours a week, who is so praised in our career-climbing society, will eventually wake up and realize he wouldn't know his kids from a milk carton and his marriage is in freefall. He'll realize he's never taken any time for himself and his life outside of making money.

You need to find balance in your life. Fit in the workouts and the time for the intellectual, spiritual, and emotional aspects of life. Only with all those things will you really have a complete life. For me, when I don't make time for those things, I feel completely empty.

You need to find balance in your life. Fit in the workouts and the time for the intellectual, spiritual, and emotional aspects of life. Only with all those things will you really have a complete life.

If you have that discipline, you will find continued success as you move from one idea to the next. And I will say, once you get by your first invention or idea, the second and so on are always easier. You just have to remember that the first one is always going to be the toughest. My mom used to say, "The first million is the hardest." Afterward, it's a lot easier to pile it on, if you're good.

It will be easier the second time you pursue an idea because you have the experience from the first and because you have the confidence—developing an idea and turning into success breeds confidence and gratification. I know in my case, there certainly isn't anything else as gratifying as watching people's lives change by attending Rock 'n' Roll Fantasy Camp. If you take an idea and you're able to see the success of it, it's the most amazing feeling in the world. And the more ideas you have success with, the more layers and layers of confidence you'll find to become the person you want to be.

I have a friend who says that confidence is a long-term proposition. It doesn't come from succeeding in a moment; it comes from succeeding over a long period of time. Think of Donald Trump—he's piled on idea after idea and success after success. Once people become famous, people scoff at them and think they're famous for being famous. With some people that might be true. But Trump is not that person. He had genuinely accomplished amazing things in the business world before he became a celebrity.

You don't have to be like Donald Trump to be successful. You don't have to emulate his swagger or have a TV show where you announce with a stern face, "You're fired." You just have to outwork the other guy, dream big, find the right partners, and follow the formula that works for you.

I hope that by reading this book, you will have learned something about what that formula for *your* success is and that you will be able to formulate many different ideas and go out and sell them. And I hope you'll be able to repeat your success, to start again and again and again. With the formula you create for yourself and by paving the path you are most likely to take, you can create anything you want.

I also hope you'll see that you don't have to follow a certain timeline for your career. Who says you have to retire at sixty-five? You can continue bringing your ideas to life for as long as you live. I feel younger today than I did at twenty, and I've never had so many good ideas. And I hope you agree that writing this book was one of them!

---

8 THINGS BRANDS AND CMOs CAN LEARN
FROM ROCK BANDS

Recently I had the pleasure of attending Rock 'n' Roll Fantasy camp, a four- to five-day rock camp for old musicians or wannabes to jam, form a band, practice and play with rock stars from the '70s, '80s, and '90s. Since the last time I played keyboards in a band was back in college, thirty years ago, I was excited not only to see if I could remember how to play but to find out what makes rock stars different from other less-successful musicians. As I got to know the rockers and talk

Continues

Continued

with them about the secrets to their success, I realized that brands and CMOs could leverage many "rock star" strategies to improve customer engagement, motivate their teams, and lead the growth agenda for their companies.

1. Like Rock Songs, Marketing Programs Are the Sum of Their Parts.

At one point during the camp, Steve Stevens, lead guitarist for Billy Idol and other great bands, broke down verse-by-verse the guitar parts for their big hit "White Wedding." Each section of the song was analyzed to determine the best guitar style to make the song more impactful. As brands, how often do we take apart each piece of a program or campaign and think about the best way to engage customers or build the brand piece-by-piece? Think of the best approach to tell your brand story at every touch point with your customers? Analyze and review each piece and timing of each piece within your branding efforts?

2. Practice Makes Perfect: Being a Gifted Marketer Is Not Enough.

I was fortunate to have Warren Haynes, lead guitarist for The Allman Brothers Band, stop by our band's practice room to jam with us and share a few stories. He shared his approach and passion for practicing every day, which many times means literally picking two notes and practicing only them for two hours. I was always under the impression that the great rock bands were just gifted musicians that "winged it" in the recording studio and at concerts. This is not the case. How much time and effort are you and your team spending staying sharp and continuing to improve as marketers and leaders? Just as hours of practice and focus separate the good from the great musicians and bands, a commitment to constant improvement defines the best marketing teams as well.

3. CMOs Are Recording Studio Mixers Assembling the Best Song Tracks.

Toward the end of rock camp, our band went to local recording studio in LA and had a chance to record our original song with a recording expert. I was impressed by the way the studio experts were able to break out

Continues

Continued

each instrument, extract the best sections, and then have a certain musician rerecord their part for a specific section—all of which resulted in the best possible final recording that ultimately is shared with music fans. Intrigued, I thought about how CMOs act as that "studio mixer," pulling all the components and team roles together to put out the best possible program, campaign, or event. How often do you ask someone to share their specific role with the rest of the team, provide feedback, then try it again and again? Manage and change the "volume" of each piece of a campaign on customer engagement program instead of all campaign vehicles on full volume?

4. Treat Brand Advocates Like Band Groupies: Give Them What They Want.

In an interesting conversation with one of the rock stars about groupies, he told me, "Sometimes you just need to give them what they want to keep them excited to be your groupies and help sell the band." Think of your brand advocates as groupies, and instead of taking them for granted, give them what they want: early views of new products, special services, and personalized feedback. And don't forget to simply thank them and tell them how much you love them.

5. Look to Other "Genres" for New Ideas and Inspiration.

I was surprised to hear how many hours a day many of the rock stars at the camp practiced other genres. Hearing the drummer from Guns N' Roses or lead guitarist from KISS talk about the hours they spend playing jazz, blues, and classical to improve as musicians and make their own music even better is also a great idea for marketers. Look at ideas from other industries and other marketing vehicles not commonly used in your industry to break through the clutter and engage your customers in new ways. Fresh ideas and big results can come from unexpected places and broaden your teams' perspective.

6. How Many Great "Studio Marketers" Do You Have?

Throughout the camp the rock stars spoke with admiration about a great studio drummer or bass player or keyboard player who performed with

Continues

Continued

their bands on records and tours. I was surprised to hear that and expanded my thinking to our marketing teams. Obviously we need our lead singers/storytellers, but there's also a role for "studio marketers"— the best in the industry—for specific areas across all brand programs, campaigns, and events. Have these seasoned "studio marketers" work closely with your lead storytellers.

7. Let Your Marketing Team Feel the Rush of a Great Show.

I asked a number of rock stars what they missed most from their biggest rock-star days, and almost everyone talked about the "tightness and feeling of family" during and right after a great performance. One star said, "Having a packed house of fans screaming and begging for more makes all the hard work worth it." As CMOs and marketing leaders, treat your programs and campaigns like live performances and allow your teams to celebrate and feel the "rush" of success. While it's easy in this day of "what did you do for me today" to lose sight of the group, don't underestimate the power and inspirational value of creating a band-worthy team environment.

8. Keep Playing the Hits, and Use Them to Introduce New "Songs."

One rock star told me right before our live performance at Whiskey a Go Go, "We get fans to concerts with our big hits, then introduce them to new songs once we get them there." This is an interesting approach for CMOs and brands to consider. Don't replace a successful program or message with the new version too quickly. Brand messaging consistency matters, and once brands have customers' attention and interest, they can begin a slow release of new "songs."

As I look back on my five days of rock-star glory and all that I learned from rock stars, I've not only come away as a better keyboard player but a better marketer and CMO. Now I can say, ". . . and then one time at band camp" with confidence, pride, and a new respect for brand advice from rock stars.

—Peter Krainik

Chapter Thirteen's Greatest Hits

- Every idea is different and deserves unique treatment.
- Early on, you need to begin thinking about your exit strategy.
- You have a responsibility to your business's stakeholders to sell smartly.
- So keep an eye on the timing.
- It's also important to know whom to sell to.
- One of the best parts about selling your business is the sense of accomplishment you get.
- Not every business needs to have an exit strategy; sometimes playing it to the end is the wisest move to make.
- You can get a lot of creative ideas by looking at start-up projects in other countries.
- If you spend your whole life chasing money, you're going to find yourself really miserable.

14

Takin' Care of Business:
RUN YOUR COMPANY LIKE YOU'RE A ROCK STAR

Throughout this book, I've shared with you the principles and formulas behind my success. I've defined the invisible touch that has to come from within to get your idea off the ground and help make it fly like an eagle. And in the process, I've invited you into my world to experience my journey of serendipitous failures and celebrated successes, including my dream that wouldn't die—Rock 'n' Roll Fantasy Camp.

My goal has been to inspire you to apply the principles of rock and roll to your business. These principles can be translated into success in more ways than one—promoting individual successes, the growth of team spirit, and the increasingly elusive corporate company pride. When you have all of that, your company can flourish in any economy.

Rock 'n' Roll Fantasy Camp has proven to be a great example of how rock and roll and corporate America can coexist in great harmony to mutual benefit. The camp is a business after all. But through it, I've been able to show big executives from corporate America how the principles of teamwork within a rock and roll band can apply to their companies as well. If music is a universal language, nowhere is it more evident than at rock camp. Campers have fun working together and succeeding together, as a team, but can also revel in their individual accomplishments as musicians or singers.

I've mentioned that people often don't think of rock stars as hard workers. They're more often associated with excess in a variety of vices. But when you look at the long-term success and popularity of rock and roll musicians like Mick Jagger and the Rolling Stones, Bon Jovi, Bono and U2, the Beatles, and countless others, you realize they wouldn't be where they are today without believing in their music, taking risks, pursuing their musical passion, and eventually making their creative endeavors a business.

For each of them it all started with an idea—an idea for a song, an idea for a band. What followed was the positive attitude and the commitment to follow through with making music. I mentioned in chapter 1 that a good idea has to produce a gut reaction. But you've also got to believe in your idea and live it to make it happen. In rock and roll, the musicians translate their ideas into music and they perform them, hoping to produce that gut reaction from their audience. That gut reaction is what sells singles, albums, and tours.

In rock and roll, the musicians translate their ideas into music and they perform them, hoping to produce that gut reaction from their audience.

Succeeding in the corporate world is no different. An idea becomes a product or a service, and if you pursue your idea with the same persistence and passion that a rock and roll musician or band pursues their craft, you, too, will succeed.

To succeed and survive in both rock and roll and corporate America, you've got to be consistent and persistent. In both worlds, obstacles and perceived failures will always present themselves. A rock and roll band may take a musical risk that results in a flop album. A company might take a risk on a new product line that's not well received, causing its stock price to drop. Sometimes a lesson in what not to do is a confirmation of what *to* do. Like the persistent rock and roll band who keeps churning out music to overcome the challenge that a perceived failure presents, you've got to answer that challenge in business by getting creative and continuing to find ways to make your client base happy.

Case Study: Hard Rock Cafe

A big part of being successful is knowing how to build and support your business once it's up and running—and knowing that the most important part of a business is the employees. They are the tools you need to create the magic and fulfill the vision that you started off with, so you are going to have to treat them like rock stars. If you truly want to treat your employees like rock stars, the best place to go for inspiration, of course, is the Hard Rock Cafe, where everyone from the server who sits down at your table with you to the busboy clearing your dishes is a rock star . . . or at least looks like one.

If you've ever looked closely at your server or host at a Hard Rock Cafe, you might notice the body piercings, tattoos, and spikey, colorful hair that certainly wouldn't pass muster at your neighborhood TGI Friday's or Olive Garden. The Hard Rock encourages such individualistic appearances because it wants creative, rock-music-loving employees who are maybe a little bit on the edge. But what's that on your server's wrist? A Rolex? That's right. The Hard Rock Cafe offers each of its 30,000 employees in fifty-three countries the opportunity to earn a real Rolex watch for ten years of service. If they stick around for twenty years, they get a diamond encrustation upgrade for their Rolex. If they stay five more years with the company, they earn a free, one-week trip to anywhere on the planet. And the trip is first-class.

The head of employee training is my friend Jim Knight, who's been with the company for twenty-one years, which means that he's one year past his Rolex diamond upgrade and four years away from his free trip. But Jim is no stranger to travel, as he has employees to visit everywhere from Cairo to Cape Town, from Oklahoma City to Kuwait City. With all this experience, and then some, Jim knows the secrets of turning employees into rock stars.

Although the watch giveaway may be the best-known aspect of Hard Rock's efforts to ensure employee loyalty, especially in a turnover-prone industry like hospitality, Jim asserts that the program is the least important in terms of employee retention and happiness. Instead, he talks about the daily motivation Hard Rockers experience, simply because they are allowed to think, act, and look differently from their cohorts at other companies. They simply couldn't look the way they do at Hard Rock anywhere else. Nor could they sit down at the customers' tables, rap about rock music, or even—gasp!— touch them. Hard Rock employees simply have more freedom to be themselves, although of course they adhere to the company's limits. Within Hard Rock's structure is plenty of freedom, which creates loyalty and fun on a daily basis.

Jim describes his approach to training as similar to that of Michelangelo, whose approach to sculpture involved chipping away from the block of marble to reveal the beautiful sculpture within. He seeks to create what he calls a "guest-obsessed" mentality in his workers—a sense of "never good enough, never fast enough urgency" that belies the outward rocker appearances. Hard Rock employees would have to tone down their appearances, cover up their ink, and remove their piercings to get jobs elsewhere, but why would they want to do that? Instead, they have found a happy home for themselves in what Jim calls his "island of misfit toys," where "individuality is instrumental." It's more fun when you can come to work and be your authentic, irreverent, unpredictable self, Jim says. He describes the role of server as "hanging out with your good friends. For our guests and our employees, not knowing what's going to happen next should be part of the deal. Unique people create unique experiences. It's not vanilla ice cream. We think people might like some chocolate, too. We're the chocolate."

"We pay more than industry average," says Jim. "We don't need to do that because so many people want to work for us, but we do it because it's the right thing to do." Hard Rock also offers outstanding bonuses and a solid 401(k) program. Perhaps more important is the fact that Hard Rock is, in Jim's words, "a massively forgiving organization." If an employee commits an unpardonable sin, such as fighting, theft, or disrespecting customers, he's gone. "If someone is wounding the brand," Jim says, "we'll vote them off the island immediately. But if they're messing up, we'll go to any lengths to help them get things right."

Jim says that the success of Hard Rock's employees comes from the hiring process, where, in addition to the usual waitstaff skills, the company also looks for "storytellers"—individuals with the gift of gab who are not afraid to talk about the rock star who was sitting at the same table the day before, the concert they saw last night, or the latest piece of headbanging music they saw on YouTube. The workers are indeed performers, whether they might jump up on stage and sing either *Y.M.C.A.* or something from Queen, depending on what the mood suggests. "We ask, 'What's your favorite band? What was the first concert you went to? What was the most recent concert you went to? What artist would you want to meet the most?'" explains Jim. "We're all about the music, so naturally we want to hire people who love music and aren't afraid to share their love of music with our guests."

As a result, Hard Rock Cafes more often than not change to fit the culture of the countries where they operate. "Everybody all over the world loves American rock and roll," Jim says. "We bring it to them. Of course, we adapt our practices to local customs. The Hard Rock Cafe in Kuwait City is the only one in the world where alcohol is not served, because it's against the law to consume alcohol publicly in Kuwait. And in Iraq, we have no tables for two—just tables for six, ten, and even more. When people go out to eat in Iraq, they'll bring ten or fifteen people—they'll bring their whole family or all of their friends. They'll order everything on the menu and eat for hours. We cater to their expectations."

Another essential aspect of Hard Rock corporate culture is its commitment to philanthropy. "We believe that business and society must be more connected than ever," Jim says. "People are making their decisions about what businesses to patronize, where to eat, things like that, on a more socially conscious basis than ever. We can't exactly have posters on the wall saying, 'Save the planet' or 'Love all, serve all,' and then not be recycling or practicing Fair Trade in our purchasing or not buying organic. The company's founders believe that business and spirituality can mix. Philanthropy is like oxygen for us. It's a vital part of who we are, and our employees grasp that fact and love that about us."

"Philanthropy is like oxygen for us. It's a vital part of who we are, and our employees grasp that fact and love that about us."

—Jim Knight, Hard Rock Cafe

Jim says that it's easy for companies to write big checks to major national organizations like the American Red Cross or the United Way, and the company certainly does so. It means even more to Hard Rock employees to be able to support smaller, music-related charities, often tied to performing artists and the causes they care most about.

"For example," Jim notes, "Shakira builds up schools in her native Colombia. So at our Rock Shops, we sell T-shirts she designed herself, and the proceeds help build schools and put shoes on children's feet in that country. Similarly, The Edge created a foundation to replace the instruments of New Orleans street musicians who lost their instruments in the wake of Hurricane Katrina. Edge's group, Music Rising, sells its products exclusively through Hard Rock, and thus we are able to help preserve New Orleans' musical culture."

Hard Rock's commitment to philanthropy extends to its massive music festivals, such as Hard Rock Calling, the London festival averaging 80,000 people a day. A typical beneficiary of philanthropy at Hard Rock Calling is Nordhoff/Robbins, which is deeply involved in music therapy. In fact, 50 percent of the charity dollars raised at Hard Rock events go to local, music-related charities. "It's all very well," says Jim, "to serve people and make good money for yourself in the process. But when you're able to lay your head on the pillow and know that you're able to help these significant charities because people went and bought T-shirts to memorialize the Hard Rock experience you created for them, that's something special. That creates a bond of loyalty between us and our employees."

So what's the Hard Rock Way?

"Your boss needs to be your friend," Jim says. "Managers need to be on a first-name basis with all of their employees, who are allowed to be unique and to be themselves. Our culture is all about asking for forgiveness instead of permission. We need different from our people. To get it, we put them on pedestals, and they respond to that.

"Secondly, we create a guest-obsessed service mentality, and third, we insist that philanthropy must be part of the business.

"As a result, even when that Rolex watch seems incredibly far in the future, our people get to be individuals instead of having to conform to corporate norms they may not relate to. They get to have fun. And they get to change the world."

Sounds like a great recipe to me!

The Discipline Behind the Music

No rock and roll musician or band is successful without practice and dedication. A successful concert tour is all about discipline, practice, and preparation. Make like a rock star and know your business, product, or service like they know their music. Be a rock star in your business by dedicating yourself to learning, practicing, and preparing. You wouldn't watch a concert if the band got up to perform and didn't know its music. Why would clients buy your product or service if you can't provide a benefit and educate them about it? In both arenas, knowledge is power.

I couldn't have created Rock 'n' Roll Fantasy Camp without implementing every piece of advice written in my book. I talked about the value of bartering and the establishment of key relationships. Through bartering, I created many relationships that expanded over the years, enabling me to get new ideas off the ground and continuing to breathe life into existing ones. In the music and entertainment businesses, there is a lot of thinking outside the box when it comes to marketing, advertising, and promotion. Rock 'n' Roll Fantasy Camp became a reality with the help of my relationships; without harnessing their power, I would never be where I am today.

I was able to leverage my business relationships to get Rock 'n' Roll Fantasy Camp off the ground, promote it, and keep it growing. I saw it not just as a vehicle to make money for myself and my partners but also as a vehicle whereby other businesses could grow their relationships—and consequently their revenue. That's how I created an extended value for our campers. You can do the same. Simply put: Like musicians who extend their value by continually putting out new music and touring, if you create an extended value in your business for your clients, they'll keep coming back for more.

Like musicians who extend their value by continually putting out new music and touring, if you create an extended value in your business for your clients, they'll keep coming back for more.

The sound of rock and roll of today has evolved from what it was decades ago. Music as a business has changed, and it continues to do so, but rock is a classic genre of music that continues to deliver, year after year. That's why Rock 'n' Roll Fantasy Camp continues to deliver pleasure to campers. They keep coming back for more.

Likewise, the corporate world of today is vastly different than it was decades ago. Technology has changed the

304 ROCK YOUR BUSINESS

landscape of the corporate world forever, and it continually shapes the way business is done. But one thing remains constant: To succeed in the changing climate, it's all about the people. Just like the success of a band depends on the collective members, for your business or company to thrive, your employees and your clients need to feel like part of a team working together.

I'm proud to say that I've been able to realize my dream of creating Rock 'n' Roll Fantasy Camp. I've had my share of obstacles, successes, and, yes, failures. But along the way, I learned so many valuable lessons from the business of rock and roll, and now I've had the opportunity to share them with you.

If I could do it, you can, too. Don't stop believin', keep the eye of the tiger, and rock your business. It's time for you to rock and roll!

THANK YOU'S

First I would like to thank:

my co-author, Michael Levin,
my editor, Debbie Harmsen at BenBella Books,
my publisher, Glenn Yeffeth,
and Liz Lomax for her cover art (www.lizlomax.com).

Thank you to the following people who worked hard in creating, editing, and reading this manuscript in advance:

Sara Straton
Rabbi Shlomo Einhorn
Courtney Clonch

Thank you to those who contributed to the book: Ed Oates, one of my partners at Rock 'n' Roll Fantasy Camp; Jim Knight from the Hard Rock Cafe; Bill Zanker of the Learning Annex; Brien Meagher, producer of *Shark Tank*; Barry Rosenbaum, owner of Empire Chicken; and Darren Feldman of Guitar Center.

Also I'd like to thank my business partners: Paul Caine, Bernt Bodel, Ricki and Debby Rudy, David Stone, and David Eilenberg of Mark Burnett Productions.

I've had the privilege to work with many famous rock stars, but one gentleman stands out as a friend and advisor, and has been there for me through it all, Roger Daltrey.

For fifteen years on tour with Ringo, I heard the lyrics nightly "With a little help from my friends," and so I would like to thank:

Billy Amendola from
  Modern Drummer
Dave Basner
Mordechai Ben David
Bruce Berkowitz
Mark Burnett
Jennifer Breithaupt from Citi
Andrew Chao
Ken Ciancimino
Dave Cudiner
Marlene and Gerrard
  Einhorn
Sandy Eisenstat
Lesia and Mark Farner
Hank Fawcett
Jim Felber
Miles Feldman
Vince Ferragamo
Al & Elle Finkel
Avram Fried
Debbie Gibson
Hank Gilman
Raz & Liza Ingarssi
Simon Kirke
Bruce Kullick
Morty Landowne
Joe Mara
Nick Mason

Perla and Herman Mulhstein
Myer Offman
Anthony Olheiser
Susan Parkes
Mark Prows
Patrick Reily
Tom Ross
Jeff Rowe
Harry Sapir
Rudy Sarzo
John Shaw
Eric Sherman
Scott Sibella
Honorable Sheldon Silver
Phil Simms
Gary Smith
Steven Spira
Michael Starr
Terry Stewart
George Travis
Larry Valen
Kip Winger
My pals from Sackett Lake
Lois & Tara at The Door PR
  Firm
My friends from VH1 Classic
"Mancow"
Max Roberts

My wonderful and dedicated staff: Erin Calhoun, Beth Porter, Jessi McMaster, J. Maseli, and Dugie.

I want to thank anyone who has ever attended a Rock 'n' Roll Fantasy Camp. Your continued support and constant array of e-mails have kept me going and have helped make Rock 'n' Roll Fantasy Camp what it is today.

To the additional folks at BenBella behind the scenes: Photo Editor Thuy Vo, Production Manager Leigh Camp, Marketing Manager Jennifer Canzoneri, and Strategic Positioning Manager Adrienne Lang.

The following is a list of rock stars whom I've been privileged to not only do business with, but also gotten to know either on my fifteen years on tour with Ringo Starr and His All-Starr Band, attending Rock 'n' Roll Fantasy Camp, or my early years producing The Monkees and the Happy Together and Dirty Dancing tours. It is important for me to thank these folks because each of them helped shape who I have become today:

Ace Frehley, *KISS*

Alan White, *Yes*

Alice Cooper

Artimus Pyle, *Lynyrd Skynyrd*

Barry Goudreau, *Boston*

Bill Medley, *The Righteous Brothers*

Bill Wyman, *Rolling Stones*

Billy Preston

Billy Sheehan, *Mr. Big*

Bret Michaels, *Poison*

Brian Wilson, *Beach Boys*

Bruce Kulick, *KISS*

Bruce Pictor, *The Association*

Burton Cummings, *The Guess Who*

Carl Giammarese, *The Buckinghams*

Charles Connor, *Little Richard*

Cheap Trick

Chris Slade, *AC/DC*

Chris Squire, *Yes*

Chubby Checker

Chuck Negron, *Three Dog Night*

Clarence Clemons, *E Street Band*

Clem Burke, *Blondie*

Cliff Williams, *AC/DC*

Colin Hay, *Men At Work*

Cory Wells, *Three Dog Night*

Danny Hutton, *Three Dog Night*

Danny Seraphine, *Chicago*

Darlene Love

Dave Davies, *The Kinks*

Dave Edmunds, *Rockpile & Love Sculpture*

Dave Ellefson, *Megadeth*

Dave Mason, *Traffic*

David Hodo, *The Village People*

David Ryan Harris, *John Mayer Band*

Davy Jones, *The Monkees*

Dee Snider, *Twisted Sister*

Del Ramos, *The Association*

Denny Doherty, *Mamas & the Papas*

Denny Laine, *The Wings*

Denny Seiwell, *The Wings*

Diana Ross

Dickey Betts, *The Allman Brothers*

Don Brewer, *Grand Funk*

Don McLean, *singer/ songwriter*

Dr. John

Eddie Kramer, *producer extraordinaire*

Elliot Easton, *The Cars*

Eric Bazilian, *Hooters*

Eric Berman, *The Animals*

Eric Carmen, *Rasberries*

Felipe Rose, *The Village People*

Felix Cavaliere, *The Rascals*

Gary Brooker, *Procol Harum*

Gary Burr, *Carole King*

Gary Hoey, *solo artist*

Gary Lewis & The Playboys

Gary Puckett, *Union Gap*

Gene Clark, *The Byrds*

Gene Simmons, *KISS*

George Lynch, *Dokken*

George Thorogood, *The Destroyers*

Gilby Clarke, *Guns N' Roses*

Glenn Hughes, *Deep Purple*

Greg Lake

Hal Blaine, *drummer extraordinaire*

Howard Jones

Howard Kaylan, *The Turtles*

Howard Leese, *Heart/Bad Company*

Ian Hunter

Jack Blades, *Night Ranger*

Jack Bruce, *Cream*

Jamie Moses, *Queen*

Jane Wiedlin, *The Go-Gos*

Jeff "Skunk" Baxter, *Doobie Brothers*

Jeff Foskett, *The Beach Boys*

Jeff Pilson, *Great White*

Jerry Shirley, *Humble Pie*

Jim Keltner, *Dylan/George Harrison*

Jim Yester, *The Association*

Joe Satriani, *guitarist extraordinaire*

Joe Stefko, *Turtles*

Joe Walsh, *The Eagles*

Joey Kramer, *Aerosmith*

Joey Molland, *Bad Finger*

John Anderson, *Yes*

John Moyer, *Disturbed*

John Phillips, *Mamas & the Papas*

John Waite, *Bad English*

Jon Lord, *Deep Purple*

Jules Gary Alexander, *The Association*

Juma Sultan, *Todd Rundgren*

Kane Roberts, *Alice Cooper*

Kelly Keagy, *Night Ranger*

Kenny Aronoff, *Chickenfoot*

Kevin Cronin, *REO Speedwagon*

Kip Winger, *Winger*

Larry Ramos, *The Association*

Lemmy Kilmister, *Motorhead*

Leslie Gore

Leslie West, *Mountain*

Levon Helm, *The Band*

Lita Ford, *The Runaways, solo artist*

Lou Christie

Mackenzie Phillips, *Mamas & the Papas*

Manny Charlton, *Nazareth*

Mark Farner, *formerly of Grand Funk Railroad*

Mark Hudson, *songwriter/ producer*

Mark Rivera

Mark Slaughter, *Slaughter*

Mark Volman, *The Turtles*

Marky Ramone, *The Ramones*

Matt Sorum, *Guns N' Roses*

Max Weinberg, *E Street Band*

Meat Loaf

Mel Schacher, *Grand Funk Railroad*

Michael Anthony, *Van Halen/ Chickenfoot*

Michael Lardie, *Great White*

Mick Ralphs, *Mott the Hoople/Bad Company*

Mickey Hart, *Grateful Dead*

Mickey Thomas, *Jefferson Starship*

Micky Dolenz, *The Monkees*

Mike Love, *The Beach Boys*

Mitch Ryder, *The Detroit Wheels*

Nancy Wilson, *Heart*

Neil Murray, *Whitesnake*

Nick Fortuna, *The Buckinghams*

Nick Mason, *Pink Floyd*

Nicko McBrain, *Iron Maiden*

Nigel Kennedy

Nils Lofgren, *E Street Band*

Paul Rodgers

Paul Stanley, *KISS*

Peter Frampton, *Humble Pie*

Peter Tork, *The Monkees*

Phil Ramone, *Billy Joel*

Phil Solem, *The Rembrandts*

Phil Soussan, *Ozzy*

Rami Jaffee, *The Foo Fighters*

Randy Bachman, *The Guess Who*

Randy Jones, *The Village People*

Ray Simpson, *The Village People*

Richie Kotzen, *Poison*

Rick Danko, *The Band*

Rick Derringer

Rob Grill, *The Grass Roots*

Robbie Krieger, *The Doors*

Robert Sarzo, *Hurricane*

Robin McAuley, *The Shenker Band*

Roger Daltrey, *The Who*

Roger Hodgson, *Supertramp*

Ron Nevison, *producer*

Rudy Sarzo, *Quiet Riot/Blue Oyster Cult*

Russ Giguere, *The Association*

Sam Moore

Sammy Hagar, *Van Halen/ Chickenfoot*

Sandy Gennaro, *The Pat Travers Band*

Scott Ian, *Anthrax*

Share Ross, *Vixen*

Sheila E.

Simon Kirke, *Bad Company*

Slash, *Guns N' Roses*

Slim Jim Phantom, *Stray Cats*

Spanky McFarlane, *Spanky and Our Gang*

Spencer Davis, *The Spencer Davis Band*

Spike Edney, *Queen*

Stephen Pearcy, *Ratt*

Steve Stevens, *Billy Idol*

Steve Vai, *guitarist extraordinaire*

Steven Adler, *Guns N' Roses*

Steven Tyler, *Aerosmith*

Sully Erna, *Godsmack*

Ted Bluechel Jr., *The Association*

Teddy Andreadis, *Guns N' Roses*

Terry Kirkman, *The Association*
The Contours
The Four Tops
The Rascals
The Spinners
Tim Bogert
Timmy Cappello
Timothy Schmit, *Poco/The Eagles*
Todd Rundgren, *solo artist*
Tom "Bones" Malone, *Letterman Show*

Tommy James, *Tommy James and the Shondells*
Tommy Lee, *Mötley Crüe*
Tommy Shaw, *Styx*
Ty Dennis, *The Doors*
Vince Neil, *Mötley Crüe*
Vinny Appice, *Black Sabbath*
Warren Haynes, *The Allman Brothers*
Zak Starkey
Zakk Wylde, *Ozzy*

I apologize if I left anyone out. It was not intentional.

. . . And to all the rock stars of the future.

ABOUT THE AUTHORS

David Fishof has brought the world some of the most original, successful, and exciting live shows in music over the past thirty years. He has earned a reputation as one of the most creative and innovative entertainment producers in the world.

Through his years of experience producing rock tours, Fishof got the idea for the one-of-a-kind Rock 'n' Roll Fantasy Camp. His goal was to give music fans the opportunity to see their rock dreams become reality by learning from some of the most influential artists in the industry. That dream came to fruition when Rock 'n' Roll Fantasy Camp became a reality in 1997. Since then, Fishof has been giving individuals a once-in-a-lifetime opportunity to live like a rock star and jam with their idols. Over the years, Fishof has brought the world's top rockers to Rock 'n' Roll Fantasy Camp.

Some of David's career highlights in the entertainment arena include:

- Reuniting The Monkees and introducing them to a new generation of MTV fans with a string of blow-out tours across the globe in 1986
- Going to Ringo Starr and together creating the All Starr Band that began touring in 1989 (David has

produced eight All Starr Band tours around the
world over the past fifteen years)

- Producing a variety of successful concert tours,
including Dirty Dancing: The Concert tour, Dick
Clark's American Bandstand tour, the Happy
Together tours, Classic Superfest, American Gladi-
ators Live tour, Mortal Kombat Live tour and the
British Rock Symphony with feature vocalists Peter
Frampton, Roger Daltrey, Alice Cooper, and Jon
Anderson

In the sports world David has represented legends such as
NFL greats Phil Simms, Mark Bavaro, Vince Ferragamo, and
Jack Reynolds, and baseball stars Lou Piniella, Dave Magadan,
and Randy Myers.

David is a charismatic lecturer. He is well-known to corporate America for his experience and the innovative ideas he
has contributed to the entertainment industry. He has spoken
for numerous corporations and colleges and was a featured
speaker at National Speakers Association (NSA). For more
information or to book David as a speaker for your next
event, visit: www.davidfishof.com.

Michael Levin, nationally renowned *New York Times* best-
selling author, has written, co-written, or ghostwritten more
than 100 books, of which eight are national bestsellers. He
was a featured speaker at T. Harv Eker's "Never Work Again"
event in Sydney, Australia, in July 2011 and appeared on
ABC's *Shark Tank* on January 20, 2012.

He has co-written with Baseball Hall of Famer Dave
Winfield, football broadcasting legend Pat Summerall, NBA
star Doug Christie, Hollywood publicist Howard Bragman,

three-time Super Bowl winner Chad Hennings of the Dallas Cowboys, and FBI undercover agent Joaquin Garcia. As a publishing consultant, Michael numbers among his many best-selling clients Zig Ziglar, Michael Gerber, and Jay Abraham.

He has published with Random House, St. Martin's Press, Beacon Press, Penguin, Wiley, BenBella, and many other houses, with his books receiving outstanding reviews in such leading publications as the *New York Times*. One of his own novels became *Model Behavior*, an ABC Sunday night Disney movie of the week.

Michael lives with his wife and four children in Orange County, California.

ABOUT ROCK 'N' ROLL FANTASY CAMP

Rock 'n' Roll Fantasy Camp is the ultimate music-making experience, giving people a once-in-a-lifetime opportunity to jam with legendary rock stars, write and record an original song, and play live in front of family and friends at a major concert venue. At Rock 'n' Roll Fantasy Camp, we nurture the inner rock star and bring that persona to life, welcoming musicians of all levels, as people share the limelight with rock and roll legends. Participants are placed in bands with a rock star counselor as they jam, rehearse, and record over the course of three to five days. They are immersed into the rock and roll lifestyle as they learn or perfect their knowledge of music.

Rock 'n' Roll Fantasy Camp's Corporate Program is a unique and cutting-edge team-building experience that engages your company as your employees rewrite and perform a popular classic rock song with lyrics that reflect the company's values, goals, and message. The Rock 'n' Roll Fantasy Camp method delivers lasting results every time and is guaranteed to impact your group in the most memorable, innovative, and creative way. It is the ideal fit for any company's next corporate retreat, training seminar, convention, sales meeting, or dinner.

David realized his dream came true when the MGM Grand Hotel & Casino in Las Vegas invited Rock 'n' Roll Fantasy Camp to make their hotel its permanent location. The MGM Grand will host camps, nightly jams with rock stars, and team-building events throughout the year and will be home to the first ever Rock 'n' Roll Fantasy Camp merchandise store. Las Vegas is the perfect location for all who love rock 'n' roll to come and experience what it's really like to be a rock star.

Rock 'n' Roll Fantasy Camp Team Building Program key benefits:

- Develops leadership skills—*every band needs a leader.*
- Ignites the inner rock stars of your company—our program features REAL ROCK STARS—*nothing is more motivating and inspiring than learning from the best in the business.*
- Improves communication skills and sharpened critical problem-solving skills through musical expression—it's about listening—*knowing when to come in, when to pull back, and when to assist.*
- Creates an environment to build trust—**get your team in tune through the universal language of music**—*The point of the band is to pick someone up when they fall and knowing that allows the artist to take creative risks*—same goes in business.
- Encourages collaboration—*whether it's by choosing a song, naming your band, or simply playing, there is **nothing more collaborative than making music**.*
- Challenges time management and strategic planning skills—*you only have so long before you have to take the stage.*
- Achieves peak performance—*because when the curtain opens, the lights come on, and your band takes the stage—you must deliver.*

INDEX

319